WELLESLEY ARON
REBEL WITH A CAUSE

WELLESLEY ARON

REBEL WITH A CAUSE

A MEMOIR

HELEN SILMAN-CHEONG

Forewords by
Ambassador Samuel W. Lewis
and
Lord Sieff of Brimpton

VALLENTINE MITCHELL

First published in 1992 in Great Britain by
VALLENTINE MITCHELL
Gainsborough House, Gainsborough Road,
London E11 1RS, England

and in the United States of America by
VALLENTINE MITCHELL
c/o International Specialized Book Services, Inc.
5602 N.E. Hassalo Street, Portland, Oregon 97213

British Library Cataloguing in Publication Data
Wellesley Aron : rebel with a cause.
I. Silman-Cheong, Helen

ISBN 0-85303-245-9

Library of Congress Cataloging-in-Publication Data
Aron, Wellesley, 1901–1988.
Wellesley Aron, rebel with a cause : a memoir / [edited by] Helen Silman-Cheong ; forewords by Samuel Lewis and Marcus Sieff.
p. cm.
Include index.
ISBN 0-85303-245-9
1. Aron, Wellesley, 1901–1988. 2. Jews, British—Israel–Biography. 3. Zionists—Great Britain—Biography. 4. World War, 1939–1945—Personal narratives, Palestinian. 5. Pacifists—Israel–Biography. I. Silman-Cheong, Helen. II. Title. III. Title: Rebel with a cause.
DS113.8.B7A76 1992
320.5'4'095694092—dc20 91-24774
CIP

Typeset by Regent Typesetting
Printed and bound in Great Britain by
BPCC Wheatons Ltd, Exeter

CONTENTS

LIST OF ILLUSTRATIONS

Grateful thanks are due to Rachel Hirsch of Ramat-Gan, Israel, for her expert assistance in providing photographs to illustrate this book. Other photographs are from the personal collections of the Aron family and friends.

FOREWORD

Historians and biographers recount the deeds of warriors, rulers, statesmen, politicians and artists. Only rarely does a biographer record the story of a man or woman who is unlikely to earn even a footnote in the annals of this turbulent century, yet whose life could teach future generations much about moral integrity, idealism, loyalty, discipline and tolerance. One such story is the life of Wellesley Aron. Among those whose lives have brushed against mine during a diplomatic career on three continents, Wellesley was truly unique.

I met him first at a Rotary Club luncheon in Tel Aviv not long after arriving as United States Ambassador to Israel in the late 1970s. Almost a caricature for an elderly, proper English gentleman, Wellesley's abrupt directness brooked no idle conversation. I soon understood that Major Aron's background as a founder of Rotary in Tel Aviv and as the legendary senior Jewish officer in the Palestine contingent of the British Army in the Second World War entitled him to special respect among club members. Yet they merely tolerated with bored familiarity his passionate speeches on the need for something called 'peace education'. I also felt, however, Wellesley's charisma: a combination of missionary zeal, undisguised anger at bureaucracy, shortsightedness and deceit, a boundless belief in the educability of the young, and incredible persistence. Moreover, he practiced what he preached. That is what drew me steadily into his orbit and led me to try to help advance his dream. Thus, during most of my eight years in Israel and continuing after my return to the United States and his passing, Wellesley's quest for a place to teach peace, tolerance and genuine coexistence among Arabs and Jews inspired me as it has so many others.

Neve Shalom/Wahat al-Salam – the 'oasis of peace', high above the Latrun Monastery between Tel Aviv and Jerusalem – became Wellesley and Coral Aron's home during his last years. He had finally found a place where 'peace education' could flourish. It seemed hardly a setting for an elderly, sophisticated, ex-British couple to start their second lives together; 'pioneering' is much too glamorous a term for that concrete box on a windswept, barren, rocky hill into which they moved. A comfortable old age was not for them. But as the 'patriarch' of the young Arab and Jewish couples struggling to create a cooperative existence there, Wellesley brought many of us curious pilgrims to appreciate the importance of his dream, and to lend whatever support we could. Nothing I did in Israel was more rewarding.

I knew Wellesley only in those last years. This splendid book encompasses an extraordinary life that went before. In its sheer variety, it has few equals. Raised in luxury as a proper English gentleman, a graduate of Jesus College, Cambridge, who excelled at all sports, barely Jewish, Wellesley came of a family that was sharply divided between German roots and English branches. The First World War cast him adrift in search of his core identity. He found it in Zionism, and in Palestine.

Throughout the years of war and upheaval, 1939–50, Wellesley's life intersected with momentous events: the British North African and Italian Campaigns, rescuing Jewish survivors in Europe, exhorting Zionist rallies in England and in the United States, and recruiting American volunteers to fight for the new, beleaguered Israeli state. He worked for Chaim Weizmann in London, knew several British High Commissioners and many leaders of the World Zionist Movement, and dealt episodically with Moshe Sharett, Golda Meir, and David Ben-Gurion.

Yet, despite subsequent success in various business ventures and public service endeavors, Wellesley never seems to have quite found his special niche until he and Coral moved to Neve Shalom. There his lifelong commitment to honesty, tolerance, reason, humanity, and the importance of educating young people to live together peacefully all finally came together. He was seeing his dream realized; it was teaching the next generation how to live together in peace. And this aptly named 'Rebel With A Cause' died in the knowledge that his cause would be carried on by young Jews and Arabs who share his dream.

This is a book, and a life, that nearly span the twentieth century. Wellesley Aron's long odyssey of self-discovery and Zionist commitment is the story of a highly unusual man. Anyone who reads it will envy me for having known him.

Samuel W. Lewis
President, United States Institute of Peace
U.S. Ambassador to Israel, 1977–85

McLean, Virginia
August 1991

FOREWORD

Until the last ten years of Wellesley Aron's life we met rarely. When I got to know Wellesley well he was the leading light in the development of the then recently created settlement of Neve Shalom/Wahat al-Salam, The Oasis of Peace, where he lived.

Neve Shalom/Wahat al-Salam is a settlement of 50 per cent Jews, 50 per cent Arabs, near the Monastery of Latrun a mile or so off the Jerusalem–Tel Aviv road. It was originally established by Father Bruno Hussar in an attempt to create an ecumenical community and improve Arab/Jewish relations. But Father Bruno, who still works at and for Neve Shalom/Wahat al-Salam, soon learned that what he wished to do required wider and different leadership. Wellesley, together with his wife Coral, became interested and involved in the leadership and development of the community. From then until his death three years ago he was Neve Shalom/Wahat al-Salam's leader and inspirer.

I have visited and visit Neve Shalom/Wahat al-Salam regularly when I am in Israel, generally twice a year, and follow its remarkable development with much admiration and respect. It is today the leading example of how Arab/Jewish co-operation in Israel can develop; this development was largely due to Wellesley's leadership and hard work.

There are now seventy-four members in the settlement consisting of sixteen families and six unmarried people, two Christians, two Jewish and two Arabs. A number of the families who live at Neve Shalom/Wahat al-Salam have had children born there in addition to those who came with them. There is a kindergarten and a school, originally for the members of Neve Shalom/Wahat al-Salam, but more recently a number of young Arabs from a small town nearby go daily to the school. The children are bilingual, and I have heard Arab children asking their parents why their Hebrew is so poor, and Jewish children asking theirs why their Arabic is poor.

In addition Neve Shalom/Wahat al-Salam set up the School for Peace, to which for a number of years Jewish and Arab youngsters between the ages of sixteen and twenty have been going for short joint courses; a number of these youngsters remain friends after they return home. Wellesley was again one of the leaders in developing the School for Peace.

Now there is a waiting list of Arab and Jewish families who wish to join Neve Shalom/Wahat al-Salam. The spirit there is inspiring and shows what can be achieved in getting Jews and Arabs to live and work peacefully together. What Wellesley achieved in the last years of his life is an example to all of how people of different faiths who have had little contact and often hostile relationships in the past can be brought together and live peacefully together for the benefit of all.

It was a privilege for me to see something of this development, which I believe without Wellesley Aron's leadership would not have taken place. I have great affection and respect for what Wellesley achieved, for which all who live in Israel are in his debt.

Marcus Sieff
London, July, 1991

A PERSONAL MEMOIR

When I read the splendid Forewords to this book it struck me that they concentrated solely on Wellesley's involvement with Neve Shalom/ Wahat al-Salam. Even Coral's relationship with Wellesley only begins there. It seemed to me that no-one who knew Wellesley in his early days had contributed to this story, which was a pity. It was suggested to me that as I am the only person still around who knew him well as a young man, some personal recollections of his earlier days would be appropriate to give more insight into the younger Wellesley.

One day back in 1929, when I was studying for my law finals, I was called to the telephone. A strong cultured voice announced: 'You don't know me. My name is Aron, Wellesley Aron. We haven't met, but we were at the same school, although not at the same time. I am up here in Leeds to try to recruit some leaders for a movement I am creating, it's called Habonim, and I would like to talk to you about it'. That's how we met.

I was immediately impressed by his enthusiasm, his sincerity, and his sense of mission. Although I eventually had to tell him that I was not the right person – I did not have his sense of dedication or the qualities he was looking for – we became firm friends from that first meeting. Indeed, he so much impressed me with the whole idea of the Yishuv, and that I must go to Palestine and see for myself, that I promised I would. So it came about that in 1932 I first arrived there. Wellesley himself was not there at the time, but he gave me an introduction to his brother-in-law (Rose's brother) and I went to work on his orange-grove in Rehovoth. Splendid days they were.

Wellesley returned, some time later, and took a teaching job at the Herzlia Gymnasium in Tel Aviv. He was pretty hard-up and for a time we shared a room on Hayarkon Street, for which we paid the princely sum of one pound per week. The room contained one single iron bedstead only, so we solved that problem by putting the straw-filled mattress on the floor and taking it in turns to sleep on it, while the other slept on the wire framework, waking up each morning with the criss-cross of the wires deeply impressed on our backs.

Wellesley gave me a hilarious explanation of why he had no money from his teacher's salary: he was paid in 'Shtarot', the promissory-note system by which so many existed in those money-scarce days. Wellesley was relaxed and enjoying life.

Rose came out shortly thereafter, with her baby Sharona. She and Wellesley took a flat in Bialik Street, and I moved in as paying guest. Rose was a wonderful home-maker and their flat became the centre for a cheerful young crowd. Although they had little financial resources, they somehow managed to entertain a lot, and the flat was full of music and gaiety.

Wellesley and Rose were a very popular couple, particularly with the English-speaking Tel Avivites, and regarded as the doyens of that society. I remember that to celebrate Wellesley's birthday a number of us organised a surprise party for them at a local night spot, the invitations being headed: 'The Friends of Rose and Wellesley invite ...'. I think that this was probably the happiest, although non-creative, period of his life in Palestine.

Wellesley was very much involved with organising the first Maccabiah which took place in the stadium on the north-side of the Yarkon River. He, of course, played a prominent part in the Anglo-Saxon team, with his outstanding prowess as a high-jumper and sprinter. He even tried to persuade me to join the English boxing team, but I ducked out, as I did not fancy becoming a punching-bag for some highly trained sabra.

To Wellesley's disgust, I returned to England in 1933, and although after that we did not see much of each other for years, our friendship remained firm. Whenever he came to England we would meet and he would recount his latest series of adventures. We shared the same light-hearted approach to problems. Wellesley could always see the funny side as he detailed the unfortunate situations which somehow always seemed to befall him. It was this capacity to laugh at misfortune that, in my view, was the bedrock that enabled him to surmount each obstacle that presented itself in his endless, restless striving after his objectives.

Wellesley used to confide in me, and I can never forget the underlying bitterness (though he told it as a joke), when after the world war in which he played such an outstanding and courageous role as the first Jewish Palestinian officer to be promoted to field-rank,[1] he obtained from Sir Harold MacMichael the grant of an area of land for a Shikun for ex-servicemen; yet upon his return from his mission to America for the Haganah, he found that in his absence it had been parcelled, but no plot reserved for him. Nor indeed when the Jubilee of Habonim was celebrated, the name of Wellesley Aron, the man who conceived it with his vision and worked tirelessly in its creation, was scarcely mentioned. All the kudos was heaped upon his successor who took over after he left England. Nor was he ever offered any sort of recognition from the Establishment in the Yishuv. What a first-class Ambassador to the Court of St. James he would have made, or even, with his fluent English, French and German, an Israeli representative at the United Nations!

But Wellesley was never an Establishment person, he could not fit in with the kowtowing required to find advancement in those circles. That is why this book is so aptly entitled: *Rebel with a Cause.*

Julius Silman

NOTE

1. The fascinating record of the feats of the Jewish-Palestinian contingent under Wellesley's command is contained in his book *Wheels in the Storm* (Canberra, 1974). In a Foreword Major-General Paul Cullen C.B.E., D.S.O., wrote: 'He put into his war effort, with its dual aim, the energy and fulfilment of at least two ordinary men .... Idealists were usually stimulating. Wellesley, as a practical and achieving idealist, was also inspiring'.

INTRODUCTION

I first met Wellesley in 1953 on the day his daughter Sharona married Arthur Broza, who was distantly related to my first husband. Twenty-seven years later Wellesley took me to visit the tiny community of Neve Shalom/Wahat al-Salam. This was the beginning of a totally unexpected 'fairy story' romance which was followed by eight years of togetherness and shared interests and endeavours such as only few can be privileged to enjoy in their senior years. I really didn't get to know Wellesley well until we began to live together and he regaled me with an endless stream of anecdotes which were not only fascinating and amusing, but which filled in my knowledge of Israel's history and many of its personalities.

During our years together I never ceased to wonder at the extraordinarily wide field of endeavour and experiences which Wellesley had crammed into his life, and at his enthusiasm and ever-youthful approach to everything. For all his intense and serious thinking, he had a lively sense of humour which we shared with tremendous pleasure. Even though I heard most of his 'stories' told many times to a variety of audiences, they never palled or became stale in their retelling. And just as often as I heard Wellesley recount these numerous episodes in his life, so did someone say to me: 'You must make sure that all this is recorded and not lost to history.' Thus it was that I persuaded him to record as much as possible and, after his death, I set about trying to get it published.

The fact that I have been successful is due entirely to the generosity of two wonderful friends: Julius Silman, whose friendship with Wellesley goes back 60 years to their student days and who was the best man at our wedding; and Robert Goodman, who came into our lives through his interest in and support for Neve Shalom/Wahat al-Salam and became one of our warmest friends. Julius took it upon himself to take care of the details of getting this book published. He entrusted all the materials I had gathered to

Helen Silman-Cheong. Although unable to include all his anecdotes (and I am sure that many people will be saying '... but what about that wonderful tale he told about ...'), Helen has portrayed the man as we knew him by using his own narratives. These sections she has linked by sensitive biographical work based on her own friendship with Wellesley over many years.

I do want to express my affection and gratitude to these special people who have enabled me to realise what would, otherwise, have been an unfulfilled ambition – that of keeping Wellesley's charismatic presence among us for as long as we are here to be warmed by remembering it, and of leaving in the annals of history a record of at least some of the contributions which he made to them.

I know that Wellesley would have wanted any record of his life to be associated with the members of Neve Shalom/Wahat al-Salam with whom he shared his last years. They helped him to give substance to his vision and, through them, he glimpsed the possibility of achieving his ultimate ambition – the creation of an international peace academy. In his inimitable way he bridged the generation gap and earned the respect and affection of young and old alike, who thus still remember him.

Most sincerely I record my deepest appreciation and thanks to Ambassador Samuel Lewis, Lord Sieff and to Julius Silman, who graciously agreed to add their personal words of introduction.

I think of this book as Wellesley's bequest to his grandchildren, David and Talia, who loved him deeply and whose love was returned in full measure and with much pride; to their children Moran, Ramon, Adam and Omri, the three eldest of whom may retain some memory of their great-grandfather; and to my own grandchildren Yael, Michal and Nir, who for those few years adopted Wellesley as their Grandpa and enjoyed with him a loving and delightful relationship.

Coral Aron
Neve Shalom/Wahat al-Salam, Israel
January 1991

PREFACE

Wellesley's autobiographical notes and the transcripts of his taped memoirs contain little about his life as a son, friend, husband and father. The few family anecdotes he recorded I have included; but he has left nothing about his close friendships; nor about his own feelings for family life. This is not a biography and I have not researched beyond Wellesley's own material and my knowledge of him. However, encouraged by his widow Coral's confirmation of a number of my speculations, and by checking a few facts with his lifelong friend Julius Silman, I can offer, in the final chapter, a sketchy portrait of the missing Wellesley. I knew him for seventeen years and often wondered what inspired him to recognise that the prevailing attitudes and beliefs would lead nowhere new, but rather served to preserve the status quo, however unpleasant that might be. He held steadfastly to a personal vision, however unpopular or unrealistic other people found it. I never asked him directly because he fended off probings into his personal feelings, but I would still like to know what fuelled Wellesley's overriding commitment to his own truth, what fired his irrepressible spirit. Each person who reads this book will have a unique response to it; nevertheless, for those who knew Wellesley there will be many shared memories of a larger-than-life figure who enchanted and inspired us for many hours with a stream of reminiscences spanning some eighty years.

I have included lengthy, edited extracts from Wellesley's own autobiographical material as no one can relate his stories better. His spelling of names was erratic, and I have had to choose from several versions in some cases – no disrespect is intended if I have selected the wrong one. Occasionally, his recollection of time and place seems unlikely, but the substance of his anecdotes is reliable.

I have some heartfelt 'thank yous' to express. First to Julius Silman and Coral Aron, who trusted me with this project; to Elizabeth Silman for the perfect title; to Carol and Hilmar Schonauer whose love restored my trust in myself; lastly to my husband Keith. We went together to visit Coral at Neve Shalom/ Wahat al-Salam in December 1989. He responded enthusiastically, just as I had done on my first visit, and on our return to England we watched a video tape of Wellesley relating a variety of his favourite stories. Keith too was drawn to this man whom he had never met. I sold my car and bought a lap-top computer and a printer, although unable to use either. Keith patiently mastered both machines and then taught me. He helped and encouraged me throughout, cooked for us and kept our home going when I was immersed in the manuscript – these words are an inadequate expression of my gratitude and love for him.

Margaret Goodare, Vallentine Mitchell's editor, was patient, sensitive and very helpful during the stages before publication. I am indebted to her for this.

My greatest hope is that this book will inspire young Israelis – especially my daughter Naomi Silman and Eyal Weizman, now doing their national service in the Israel Defence Forces – to take heart from Wellesley's life and to work for peaceful co-existence wherever they may find themselves.

Helen Silman-Cheong
London
February 1991

CHAPTER ONE

Childhood

Wellesley grew up in an outwardly ordered and calm atmosphere, but conflict and turmoil was just below the surface. He was the only child of his German Jewish mother, but the fifth child of his German Jewish father, a man who had spent most of his life far removed from his Jewish family and traditions. Maurice, his father, told him many hair-raising stories about his extraordinary years in Australia. These delighted Wellesley when he was a little boy. He heard them over and over again until they became a part of his own life.

Maurice's commercial enterprises in Australia culminated in his leaving the bush, where he had set up a general store and post office, to establish a home in Sydney. There he continued to prosper, soon to become a renowned, wealthy, eligible bachelor. He married a beautiful woman, Minnie McKail, whose Protestant origin overshadowed her Jewish descent. She and Maurice had four children, three sons and a daughter Violetta. The youngest son Eustace and Violetta's own son Berwick became Wellesley's closest childhood companions and mentors. Whether the children were baptised or not may have been unknown to Wellesley, but he does recall that they declared themselves to be Christians on official documents. They were buried in Christian cemeteries.

What prejudices Maurice Aron had to endure in Australia were either not told to his youngest, indubitably Jewish son, or have not been recorded. Wellesley himself speculates that, in the absence of an observant Jewish community in Sydney, his father had no choice but to set aside his own origins. Wellesley's early years echoed with the praises heaped on his half-brothers and -sister and his paternal uncles and German cousins, all of whom, he was constantly reminded, were exceptionally gifted.

Maurice and Minnie Aron lived in Sydney in great style, displaying their affluence to the full. One of Wellesley's own early memories is strikingly telling about his father's dependence on the social prestige which the wealth and trappings of aristocracy brought him. More poignant though is the motto Maurice adopted for himself. In Wellesley's own words

> Their style of life was set according to the social requirements and very soon they had a carriage and pair and I know that the colouring was chocolate, gold and black. There was a carriage cushion in my childhood home with a coat of arms embroidered on it, as was often affected by people who had attained a certain degree of prosperity and opulence. The coat of arms consisted of a hand surrounded by a heraldic girdle. The girdle carried a motto which said 'Perserverentia vincit' – 'Perseverance conquers'. I was always fascinated by this cushion because it was very thick with leather on one side with the coat of arms embossed in gold and deep velvet on the other side.

Wellesley's own retelling of his father's odyssey which took him from his birthplace in Doltzig-am-Mein, in Upper Silesia near the Polish border, via Berlin, Liverpool, Colombo in Ceylon and Australia to London displays his great admiration for his heroic adventuring father. A father who had triumphed over snakes, infamous highway robbers, a fearsome sea journey and the abject poverty of his own childhood. Only later did Wellesley realise that in so doing Maurice had abandoned his childhood faith and practices. These he had learned from his own father, who was rabbi to a remote handful of Jews struggling to support themselves in an inhospitable forest region of Upper Silesia. Maurice impressed his youngest son deeply with accounts of his own mother's valiant efforts to support five children, whose father was more often than not offering support and succour to Jews elsewhere while his own family hungered. That two of these children became millionaires was a source of pride to Maurice, but the loss of their Jewish identity and their inability to attach themselves deeply to any other religious or national identity was for many years an untold source of confusion and distress for Wellesley and his siblings.

Doubtless to a child's eyes, Wellesley's mother had a much less glamorous history than his father. She was descended from a family who had lived in the same poor Jewish community as Maurice Aron. It was common belief that her grandmother had been a benefactress to Wellesley's father and family in Doltzig-am-Mein.

She met Wellesley's father at a family wedding in Berlin where they were seated side by side. Their only child describes their meeting as love at first sight. Maurice had been a widower for ten years, living with his only daughter Violetta in a luxurious but totally non-Jewish environment in Albert Bridge Road in London. She was

> . . . Agnes Gerechter a buxom lady of about 35 years old, 25 years younger than my father, who had been brought up in Breslau in a typically straitlaced and provincial way.

Although Wellesley left no details of their courtship, he notes that Agnes was promptly assembled, together with her extensive trousseau – every piece of linen emblazoned with her initials – and shipped across the Channel via Hook of Holland to be married in the New West End Synagogue in St Petersburg Place London. Wellesley was born one year later and now takes up his own story.

> My life began in London on the 18th of June 1901, the anniversary of the Battle of Waterloo, which was won by Arthur Wellesley, the Duke of Wellington, so Wellesley I was named. I have very clear recollections of my early youth, but I learned very little about my ancestry prior to my grandparents. My mother's bedroom had a stained glass coloured window above a wash basin with running water connected, an unusual convenience, and hers was the only bedroom in the house to have it. I remember asking how I'd come to live here in the first place. I can remember the reply too. A stork had tapped on the window which was opened to let me in. Until I was six or seven I didn't doubt that this explained my existence, but then someone disillusioned me with the brutal statement that that 'was a lot of nonsense'.
>
> I had a day and night nursery. There was a succession of nurses who looked after me and I can remember asking one to leave a light on so that I shouldn't be left in the dark and I know that there were coal fires in my nurseries in winter. There were fires all over the house and a scullery maid heaved scuttles of coal from cellar to attic several times a day. I witnessed with wonder coal plunging through a hole in the pavement making a black Niagara, which in turn created a black mountain in our cellar. My evident fascination with the constant movement of coal and maid was curbed of course

with gates and other devices placed strategically across corridors and staircases.

I had more freedom in my daily trip to the park with nurse, who trundled me across Albert Bridge Road alongside the Thames and into Battersea Park. My nurse introduced me to the warden, who wore brown, kept the park clean, and stopped children going near the flower beds, whose crops were being nurtured for the Battersea Flower Show, which I soon gathered was a very important event. A policeman chatted to my pretty nurse as she pushed me round and about for several hours a day. Eventually I graduated to my own legs. Now I could run by myself, sometimes with a hoop. I loved this very exciting activity.

I have vague memories of talk about the Boer War and Edward VII, not much from the people who lived upstairs however, but rather from the cook and maids downstairs and mostly from the butcher's boy who befriended me a little. As soon as I was able I escaped from nurse, governess and parents to be with this cheerful, whistling joking youngster who talked to me about his work and how many deliveries he had to make before he could go home and be free. We used to meet in our small back garden whenever he delivered meat to our kitchen. Upstairs I learned to recognise the strata in society, and what was done or not done within each one. Downstairs I could be myself and relax in a way not possible upstairs with my parents.

In due course, on my mother's initiative, I was provided with a German governess. My mother, unlike my father who had sent his third son and first grandson to Rugby school, believed strongly in German educational methods. She had no time for games or sports or anything except serious study. She abhorred the English emphasis on games, whereas I was being nurtured by Eustace and Berwick to become an English sportsman. My first gifts, the things that I wanted and liked, came from this younger generation rather than from my parents, who really did not seem to understand the interests of a child being brought up in England. My mother was particularly Teutonic in her attitude, rather severe, and, while utterly devoted to what she considered to be my welfare, she failed to establish any deep rapport with me. Her greatest concern was to see that I ate properly and dressed warmly. My father on the other hand, who was already over sixty, would return from the office to spend a few minutes with me. Generally he'd bring me little toys and things that he'd picked up from street pedlars on his way home from the City.

My youth was punctuated with an annual upheaval which I came to detest. It was the health pilgrimage to a 'Kurort'. This was always in the summer and the first one I experienced when I was only a few weeks old. Well swaddled, I was stowed away in a horsedrawn cab with all the basket trunks crammed with linen and other essentials which accompanied us to the Continent. My nurse came too of course to take care of me on the trans-Channel voyage, which for me meant being woken up in very damp surroundings at midnight and carried from the boat train to the ship. The crossings to Vliessingen in Holland were often very rough. The journey continued by train again right across Holland to the German frontier and finally up the Rhine. Eventually we and our baggage were unloaded at that season's resort – Bad Kissingen, Oberhof or Wiesbaden – or whatever other place the protracted correspondence between my mother and maternal grandmother had designated.

As I grew older, these annual journeys were nothing to look forward to. Like most children, I disliked intensely being carried or pushed around, being deposited on uncomfortable railway seats, in fuggy compartments, or being made to go below deck where every adult seemed either to be engaged in being seasick or preventing themselves from succumbing to seasickness – all very uncomfortable and for me thoroughly traumatic in many respects. From time to time the ship's engines raced dramatically, the bows rose almost perpendicularly and every now and then I'd think it was my last moment. Surrounded by women, as I usually was, a good deal of hysteria and fear was likely to be transmitted to any sensitive youngster.

Nothing improved on arrival. The excessive emotion when meeting my German relations; their very strange habits; their assumption that because I was of the same blood we had to be deeply affectionate; that they had claims on me, had the right to discuss and direct my way of life, the clothes I should wear, the food I should eat, especially the foreign Continental food, all this I gradually found to be obnoxious; a view generally shared by my nurse and any other English members of the retinue who accompanied us. I soon discovered that there was no love lost between me and all the Germans I came into contact with, irrespective of whether or not they were relatives. It was assumed that I would be glad to play with relations of my own age in the Kurpark, for instance, where the German band played strenuously while the visitors marched up and down sucking glass tubes through which they absorbed abominable liquids which apparently had curative powers. This happened each morning and afternoon. Furthermore I had to lie down immediately after lunch whether or not I felt like it.

I was embroiled in constant arguments and even physical violence with the German youngsters who ganged up against me when I was playing in the park or rowing on the lake or whatever I was doing, whether I was alone or not. Sometimes we'd all pile into a convoy of landaus each drawn by two horses, who would drag us over the hills and dales of Germany to see the views. These my parents and other relatives expatiated over, but they didn't interest me much. To crown my distress there was my maternal grandmother to whom my mother was completely devoted. On my every arrival she clutched me to her prickly bosom near smothering me in her feather boa, then she'd sit by me and force me to drink hot milk with skin on it, a liquid which I abhorred in any case, to the accompaniment of exhortations that it was good for me!

Although I could not escape the annual pilgrimages to Germany, I did succeed in disposing of the German governess who took up residence in Battersea. I was only four years old when she stood me up in my pinafore in the garden, gave me two wooden dumb-bells and proceeded to explain to me that I was supposed to go through a series of exercises which to me looked meaningless and certainly undesirable, especially when I could see the cook and housemaid grinning through the windows at us. This was a crisis. Somehow I scored a direct hit on my governess's forehead with one of my dumb-bells. To my amazement she collapsed on the spot and had to be carried upstairs. Shortly afterwards she left, but not before my father had been summoned to return home from a board meeting to deal with my mother who first had hysterics and then had to lie down all the afternoon with a tremendous headache. The atmosphere surrounding this whole incident affected me quite deeply, although in the end of course I discovered that I had won and was no longer going to be disciplined by any German governesses, much to the delight of the English staff at 65 Albert Bridge Road, who were solidly on my side including of course Eustace and Berwick!

Other scattered memories of this period of my childhood are the visits Berwick made to our house on his way from Rugby to Majorca where my half-sister Violetta lived with her second husband. It was he who introduced me to that horrible game of Bogeyman which he used to make me play by hiding in the dark corners, and there were many of them on the staircase and in the hall. We had no electricity of course and the gas lamps were not always well placed. Such a house can be fearsome to a young child, and I got many shocks when proceeding up or down stairs from a blood-curdling shriek as Berwick jumped out at me with raised hands and a distorted face, shouting: 'The Bogeyman is coming.'

Berwick initiated me into activities other than cricket and the Bogeyman game. One of these was the fascinating pastime of pouring water from a jug out of a window onto any passing top-hatted gentlemen. We felt very proud of ourselves if we managed to heave the hefty china jug from the washstand, lift it over the window sill and score a direct hit on a passer-by. The consequences were serious indeed. The gentleman in question would stop, turn back, walk up the front steps and ring the bell. Then he'd complain fiercely. Berwick and I would by this time have fled to a distant part of the house realising full well what awaited us. We were soon dragged out to stand before the injured party and were made to apologise humbly under threat of serious punishment.

I used to play a form of cricket up and down the long corridor to my nursery. My father or Berwick would bowl to me and I was considered pretty good – I could always hit a ball straight and hard and although I was very small, I was able to give a good account of myself.

* * *

Sometimes we would have an invasion of family from the Continent, including my eminent uncle Professor Doctor Herman Aron – the inventor of the first electricity meter. He was immensely wealthy and lived very lavishly in Berlin. My father managed Herman's business affairs in London. He had a reputation for absent-mindedness which he lived up to and he had no idea where he was at any one time. As far as I was concerned he was famous for his generosity in handing me golden twenty mark coins every time he came across me. Whenever he and his wife came to London there was a heightened social atmosphere at home. They naturally stayed at the Savoy in grand style, but we did a lot of entertaining at home and everybody was mobilised to that end.

Other flashbacks to my German childhood include seeing one of my mother's relatives in a German military uniform with a spiked helmet and a very upturned moustache in the style affected by Kaiser Wilhelm II. This was the period leading to the first world war and I remember a great many troops goose-stepping around, with much saluting and ostentatious displays of military rank. I have a vague memory too of being carried shoulder-high by my maternal grandfather to view a parade of German soldiers accompanied by a military band marching past his Berlin home. Even the Berlin police sported spiked helmets, swords and a swaggering military posture.

Now and again there was a full-scale gathering to celebrate some family occasion such as a wedding. I was dragged along to these events which I found elaborate, vulgar and tiring. I was introduced to my German cousins – the ones who were always top in their classes. Of course they played no games and looked and behaved accordingly. When I was alone with them I found them nasty with no sense of decency or sportsmanship. What damned them in my eyes were their pale pimply faces and their below-knee-length trousers and buttoned boots. They repelled me. Yet all these boys were held up to me as paragons of virtue and the epitome of boyhood, whereas I, it seemed, had achieved nothing with which my parents could show off, except perhaps a medal or cup that I'd won for some athletic feat. But Germans derided that kind of thing and regarded such pursuits as completely useless to man or beast. It didn't take long for me to know deep in my heart that I would never feel at home in Germany or be able to enjoy my visits there, even though I had learned to speak fluent German from my mother and her relatives in Germany.

* * *

My sister Violetta used to regale me with stories about my mother, who was obviously a figure of fun to her and the household staff. Violetta evidently enjoyed being the centre of attention, and she would entertain her audience with mocking accounts of other people's shortcomings. It was she who described my mother's arrival in England to me. Apparently horrified to discover that there were no 'Bügel' available for her use, my mother is alleged to have gone rushing up and down the shopping streets trying to make herself understood. Finally, she succeeded and came home laden with coat-hangers! This, Violetta emphasised, caused a good deal of amusement, especially amongst the staff, who were all agog to find out what she had wanted.

My mother had two quirks, which I was told provoked both mirth and resentment. Every day after dinner she would sit down at her writing desk to pen a lengthy letter to her own mother. These epistles were completed every two or three days and mailed to Germany. My father, meanwhile, feeling rather weary and looking forward to some conversation and relaxation in the evening, would wait reading the *Financial Times* or some other newspaper, commenting audibly that he got very little of my mother's company as a result of all this letter-writing.

The second of my mother's peculiarities was her addiction to accounting down to the last farthing for every day's expenditure. This she had apparently been trained to do at her home in Breslau. My father waited daily while she analysed expenses involving the purchase of vegetables and other foods and household commodities all of which were apparently very cheap in those days. The complication involved in the breakdown of the pennies into halfpennies and farthings sometimes had her struggling for hours trying to square the cash left in her purse with the amount spent.

Initially somewhat amused with all this, my father soon

became bored and said to her, 'Look here, my dear, don't worry about a few pennies, shillings or even pounds. I'll give you a five pound note whenever you feel like it to cover the difference.' 'No', said she, 'this is a matter of principle. I must find out. Maybe I was charged more than it says here in the account from the green grocer, or the butcher or whoever it is.'

I overheard some of these exchanges when my nurse brought me in to the drawing room to be fondled and kissed goodnight by my parents. I found the room snug and comforting with its heavy silk or damask curtains, softly shining gas lamps and glowing fire. Here I felt secure. My mother, who was a fairly proficient pianist, would sit down at the piano and accompany herself as she sang a fairly extended repertoire of German songs by Schubert, Schumann and even some more popular tunes by the fashionable Strauss. My father was very sentimental I noticed, and whenever she sang certain songs known to him as a young man, he wiped away the odd tear with a large bandana handkerchief which he carried for such purposes.

In keeping with my parents' concern to maintain the very best of appearances, their youngest offspring, accompanied by his mother, was taken off to a fashionable Chelsea hairdresser where she closely supervised the clipping of my blond curls. She also introduced me at a very early age to the buyer in a celebrated emporium which catered for young men who were just beginning to wear suits and trousers. This morning-coated personage saw to it in years to come that I was always properly attended to.

So my first few years passed rapidly by, marked chiefly by some painful experiences when I was stopped in my tracks by some parental or fraternal disciplinary action; there was pain too from unavoidable contact with material things such as walls, carts, or stoves; sometimes even from a ball which had been hit directly at me.

The most colossal upheaval in my life so far, which outdid even the annual trips to Germany in its enormity, happened sometime around my fifth year. My mother finally succeeded in persuading my father to sell the house in Battersea and to move to a more Jewish area of London. We landed up in a place called Priory Road in West Hampstead. My life changed in more ways than one. Shortly after our arrival I found myself being taken off to kindergarten. The compensation for this was that I ceased to be subjected to someone whose *raison d'être* was to supervise me.

Sometime before my eighth birthday Eustace went off to Brazil to seek his fortune. He wrote often and well but this did not console me. I missed his benign and understanding presence and was later told that I became so obstreperous after his departure that I had to be sent away to boarding school. This was yet another upheaval, which strangely enough suited me in unexpected ways. My parents took me to Cambridge to deposit me in the Jewish house of an English boarding school called the Perse. They hovered around for some time, expecting perhaps some show of affection or fear from me. They got neither as I couldn't wait to join in the games and other boisterous activities with boys of my own age. My parents finally departed with scarcely a kiss goodbye, and I was left to begin life anew with twenty other Jewish boys ranging in age from eight to eighteen.

It did not take me long to find out that athletics and sports of all kinds were my forte. Within my first year I distinguished myself by an obvious inborn ability to sprint fast. I was very quick off the mark, well coordinated and obviously destined for considerable distinction in this field. Since the school system involved inter-house competitions, I became a popular and useful member of the little society within which I now existed. I was at Perse for five years during which time I accumulated a collection of medals and trophies in the form of cups and other silver shapes which gradually filled the house: for I brought all these proudly home to my parents at the end of every term. I was even in the running for the under-fifteen Victor Ludorum in spite of being just twelve years old. I captained the school under-fifteen rugby football team and the house under-fifteen cricket team. I could run cross country in rain and snow, or I could sprint the one hundred or two hundred and twenty yards with equal ease. Finally, I discovered that I was going to be an outstanding high jumper when I won the under-fifteen high jump event when I was still only twelve by clearing, to everyone's astonishment, four foot eight inches. The school record was then only about 5 foot 1 inch. There was Scouts too. I became a patrol leader and began to recognise my ability to influence others and to lead them, by example, to victory as a team or group.

During my school holidays, spent either at Priory Road or somewhere in Germany, I became fully aware of the family rift over Jewish belief and practice with which I was now becoming familiar because of the compulsory Jewish observance at school. Eustace and Berwick who had experienced no Jewish upbringing worthy of note were vocal in their refusal to have anything to do with it and I sided with them instinctively. My parents seemed incapable of putting up any persuasive argument against them. The only sign of our being a Jewish family was my mother's lighting of candles on a Friday evening and the eating of a chollah loaf at the meal that followed. I remember no blessings.

* * *

In the middle of the summer term, nineteen-fourteen, I had by far the worst shock so far in my life when the matron at school suddenly informed me that I was to pack up and leave the Perse the next day. She had no explanation, but I gathered later on that my father's business interests required him to move immediately. My London home was being sold and we were moving lock, stock and barrel to Germany. I was appalled. The whole house, juniors and seniors gathered round to commiserate. I was showered with gifts and mementoes of all sorts and everyone saw me off to London thence to Germany with my parents, who chose this moment to inform me that I would now be tutored to take the entrance examination to the Realschule in Dresden, Saxony. Why Dresden? My maternal grandmother had moved there from Berlin and she, it seemed, was dictating our new lives.

My mother of course was delighted. I could finally, as she put it, start my education in earnest instead of playing around at games of no use to man or beast! I detested the thought of going to a German school especially because I knew full well that all my most popular and natural propensities would be of little consequence. My days of glory on the games field were over. The entrance exam loomed large especially as I was ill-prepared for the science papers, but I felt that with hard work I could cope with Goethe and Schiller. I managed to join a tennis club though and often swam in the exceptionally modern swimming baths.

* * *

Wellesley overheard that the reason for their move was the sudden departure after eight years of Holt, their cook, and Florence, their housekeeper. His first few months in Germany were beset with difficulties, not the worst of which was his attempt to study for the Realschule entrance exam. What distressed him more were the constant arguments between his father, whom he supported, and his mother and her relatives, primarily his grandmother. These scenes predictably revolved around the irreproachable rightness of the German government's policy and England's indefensible resistance to Germany's legitimate expansion. England and Englishmen were vilified, with no regard for the feelings of Wellesley and his father. This was particularly cruel when the German relatives knew that two of Maurice's sons and his only grandson were all volunteers in the British Expeditionary Forces. Wellesley was impotent to protest. He could not stand up for his country, nor defend the two dearest people in his young life, Eustace and Berwick. Since his earliest years, he had had to endure the mocking of his mother and everything German by his half-brothers and -sister and the domestic servants in his London home; now the position was reversed and he had to suffer in silence while his mother's family took their revenge. He was taunted by strangers too. 'German kids waylaid me in the streets: "Gold gab ich für eisen Zeppelins off to bomb London." '[1] In an act of symbolic defiance he bought a bugle and unbeknown to anyone he used to walk out to a deserted hillside and play every scouting and British Army bugle call he remembered.

Dresden was seized with spy phobia, one ironic consequence of which was that Wellesley's father, then in his seventies, was interned. Wellesley, a youth of 13 or 14 years, had to report twice daily to the Dresden police which virtually ended his studies because the journeys, which he made on foot, occupied most of his day. These were weeks of the greatest anxiety for Wellesley. Soon his father was reported to have had a stroke, following which he was suddenly released. Perhaps this misfortune goaded Agnes into

[1] 'I've given money for the iron zeppelins off to bomb London.'

recognising the awful situation that her husband and son were having to endure. She arranged visas for the three of them to travel to Switzerland. At night they crossed over into Zurich where, Wellesley notes, he had his first good night's sleep for many months.

Yet another change of language and educational system awaited Wellesley, first in Geneva and finally in Lausanne. He had to learn French to gain admission to a Swiss cantonal school. No games were played. Wellesley, by dint of tremendous effort and personal discipline, passed the entrance exam to the Collège Scientifique and actually completed the college course.

> I suffered a good deal of mental anguish in the process, by having to learn facts which I knew were of little consequence and useless for anybody except a Swiss citizen who in time would become an officer in the Swiss army. Before I graduated I had learned to draw a map of the whole of Switzerland by heart and theoretically should have been able to mark on it every mountain peak and every pass and every village, city and river and every lake. I was supposed to know, and did in fact know, all the geographic and economic data of every canton in Switzerland. In the final test I drew a canton from memory putting in enough data to convince the examiners that I could have done likewise for the whole of Switzerland.

Wellesley's peers at this time were other displaced youngsters. He met young people from Latin American countries whose parents had sent them to Switzerland to be finished; and sons and daughters of refugees from the Balkans, Italy, Poland and other occupied territories. Once again Wellesley found himself in a minority, vulnerable this time to the barbed comments of his Swiss schoolmates who, taking their cue from their own masters, taunted Wellesley and others like him as exotic foreigners. As before Wellesley found consolation in sports. He learned to ski and to skate well. He did some simple alpineering and played first-class tennis. Mostly he loved bob-sleighing and tobogganing which he could enjoy in the company of others like himself.

Once the family had settled in Switzerland, Violetta, who had returned from Majorca with her husband and was living prosperously in Devon, kept them in touch with news of the English family. From her they knew that Berwick was commissioned in the Royal Fusiliers, while Eustace served in the Royal Navy. Maurice, who had never fully recovered from his incarceration in Germany, accompanied by Wellesley, his only son not in the front lines, would go down to the railway station to scan lines of prisoners-of-war passing through Switzerland on their way to being exchanged. Wellesley and his father were looking for Eustace who had been reported missing in action. News of Eustace's death reached them in November 1916. His homesickness for England did not diminish during the four years Wellesley lived in Switzerland. He was a young man when the war ended and he went back home with his mother. He had endured more than homesickness. His beloved father, two of his half-brothers and his nephew were dead.

> It was a terrible shock to us all and it certainly had an almost fatal impact on my father who simply could not stand the strain of the war news. He worried constantly about what was going to happen to the world in general. When in July 1917 we got news of Berwick's end in the mud of Ypres in Flanders, this was the final blow for my father. He died a few months later in spring 1918, believing that the war that he had thought would last at most a few weeks, would never end.

He was buried with Orthodox Jewish rites in a cemetery in Vevey.

CHAPTER TWO

Student Days – First Love – Zionism

When the First World War ended, Wellesley and his mother returned to London. Eustace, his brilliant half-brother with a double first in German and Spanish, continued to be Wellesley's idol. He strove to follow in this dead brother's footsteps and was accepted by Jesus College, Cambridge, for the Modern and Medieval Languages Tripos Part One. This mostly involved a study of ancient and modern French history and literature. He was then able to transform his wretched years in Switzerland to his advantage. For it was his enforced abandonment of organised sport and games that had channelled his abilities into disciplined academic study. He had gained self-confidence and could now enjoy his athletic prowess to the full while studying for his degree at the same time. Within a year his Cambridge life was halted by his mother's insistence that he return to London to keep her company. Torn no doubt between his own desires and hers, he decided to leave Jesus College and returned to London.

Unqualified for anything much, he sought advice from one of his father's executors, who at that time was managing director of the General Electric Company. Hugo Hirsch, later to become Lord Hirst of Witton, was also a Jew from Germany. He proposed that Wellesley be apprenticed for a year or two with the company to learn the business from top to bottom. Wellesley agreed. He passed swiftly from the Invoice Department which 'I found thoroughly boring' to the Share Department where he discovered 'something of the machinations of the capitalist system – not very prepossessing'. Then he went to the newly formed Radio Department which he found much more congenial. Here he had his first experiences in promotion and sales, which later in Palestine turned out to have been very useful. He travelled to exhibitions held in major provincial cities to demonstrate the wonders of the new invention.

We had crystal receivers and valve radio sets – some of them

> worked well and some not. No one knew then why some places had poor reception or none at all. I scrambled about over vicarage roofs in various parts of rural England, trying to discover why one of our sets was not living up to our advertising claims.

Working for the General Electric Company did not satisfy Wellesley's heart or mind, neither did it give scope for his natural talents. By an odd chance, created unwittingly by his mother, he found something to do in the evenings which became central in his life. Not for the first time, his mother insisted that he do what she judged was expected of a young assimilated English Jew of his generation. She persuaded him to go to a meeting organised to arouse support for a Jewish youth settlement in the East End of London. The idea was for Jews like Wellesley to spend an evening or two with their less fortunate co-religionists in the East End to inculcate standards of behaviour more befitting their future lives in England.

Up to that moment Wellesley had shown little interest in such 'good works', but he finally agreed to accompany his mother to the Portman Rooms where a programme of youth activities was to be introduced by Mr Basil Henriques and his wife Rose. This striking couple, both from wealthy Anglo-Jewish families, had actually moved into the heart of the slums not far from Limehouse in the docks area where they founded the Oxford and St George's Settlement for Boys and Girls. At the end of the show, the dinner-jacketed audience was asked to give practical support to the project. Basil Henriques' request for personal participation, coming as it did from a war hero and a truly English Gentleman, inspired Wellesley to rise to his feet and offer himself. Within a week he was invited to dine with the Henriques family.

> I must admit that I had never previously been further east than the Bank of England until that June night in 1921. The bus went along the densely packed Commercial Road area. I was appalled by the contrast between the conditions that I had left only an hour or so before in my mother's flat overlooking Hyde Park and what confronted me here. The obvious, outrageous injustice suffered by these masses of people who were spilling out of the massed tenement buildings onto the dirty pavements struck my heart painfully. In a state of heightened

awareness I navigated through the sights and smells which surrounded me until I found the Settlement where Basil and Rose greeted me. After a frugal meal with a few other guests, we went on to the Settlement's Boys' Club in Cannon Street Road, off Commercial Road. The clubhouse was rundown but packed with boys from eight to eighteen years old. Lots was going on, but the noisy disorganisation seemed chaotic to me. I was taken to a room where I saw some youngsters being drilled up and down by a red-faced fourteen-year-old. He was aping the traditional sergeant-major, freely using words and phrases which were coarse, brutal and highly unedifying to put it mildly. This was the Settlement's Boy Scout Troop. It was leaderless and I had been brought in to see whether I would take over responsibility for reorganising it.

I had always enjoyed scouting at Perse, where I had been well trained. I didn't feel unnatural standing before these young people. I looked them over and then quietly asked them to sit down on the floor with me while I explained something of the rudiments of the great movement they had joined. That first evening I outlined what I thought a boy scout could do in the rather depressing, and to my own mind hopeless, circumstances of life in the slums. Little did I think that within 18 months, the 36th Stepney Jewish Scout Troop would become known in London for its scouting prowess. Time and again our troop was chosen to give exhibitions in camping and woodcraft. We won many inter-scout competitions. It was a wonderful thing to see youngsters coming into the scouts' den after work or school had ended and transform themselves from scruffy-looking street kids into 'Scouts', eager and able to carry out very complicated activities and tests. By the time the second winter with them came round, we could go out to Epping Forest and keep ourselves warm and comfortable despite rain, frost and with the minimum of equipment. We could read maps; we knew our district intimately so we undertook all sorts of activities to help other people.

These scouts set an example for themselves as well as for others. They lived with high ethical standards which influenced other youngsters around them. All this they did despite being sneered at in the early days as so often happens when something new is tried. But they emerged strong-charactered, able people who did well in adult life. My mother was taken aback when I announced that I was going to live at the Settlement where I was already spending three evenings a week. The seriousness with which I had adopted Jewish 'good works' was not to her liking. It was certainly not what she had intended when she persuaded me to go to the Settlement's show months previously. She could not stop me from devoting myself to the challenge which I had found: trying to change the fate and character of an underprivileged group of youngsters. The two years I had with these responsive young scouts left a real and lasting satisfaction such as I have rarely experienced.

* * *

Wellesley decided to return to Cambridge after visiting Perse School to play in the Hillel House Old Boys' rugby football team. While he was there someone suggested to him that he might well become housemaster of Hillel House if he first completed his degree at Jesus College. This he determined to do again in the teeth of his mother's opposition. She would not support Wellesley financially if he went against her wishes, so he took the post of assistant housemaster at Hillel House to pay for his studies. Even so, he remembers getting into financial difficulties, but doesn't disclose how he resolved them.

His social development at this time was being fostered by his sister Vio, who was still living luxuriously in Devon. He spent several vacations there sailing, cricketing, riding and playing tennis. As he put it: 'I soon got to know all the young blood of the county and went to all the social occasions as they occurred each in its due season.' But his two years with the Settlement had changed Wellesley in ways which must have surprised him as well as his family. Something was stirred up in him when he discovered that his sister Vio had concealed from everyone that Wellesley, her half-brother, was a Jew. He felt that this put him in an invidious position, especially as he found himself greatly at ease with the local vicar, precisely because he liked to talk about things which were not normal social chitchat. The inevitable crisis came at Easter when Wellesley refused point blank to accompany his sister to church. She obstinately refused to respect his explanation that he would not make a demonstration of something that was not true. In particular he would not make a public gesture – for the occasion was more social than religious his sister reassured him – which would be misconstrued. Wellesley's commitment to his own truth, whether convenient or not for himself or others, had surfaced.

Wellesley's first romance happened during this time. He fell in love with a young woman who was one of the leading social lights in the Devon circles he moved in. His memoirs are reticent about their courtship, but Wellesley has movingly described their relationship from the time Allison said that he should speak to her father. Wellesley took up her suggestion.

> 'Well, Wellesley', Allison's father began, 'you have been almost a member of our family for some time now. We are all very fond of you but this idea of marriage between you and Allison is impossible.' 'Why?' I asked. He answered 'You are a Jew, aren't you?' 'Yes,' I responded, 'but I don't know what that means in the terms of this discussion.' Allison's father went on 'Well, I can't put it clearly into words except to say that it is something foreign and strange to us. We have never had our family associated with this sort of thing and we are not going to start now.' 'Can you tell me how we differ in our viewpoints, in our way of life or anything?' I asked. Back came his reply, 'No, I cannot, but I can only tell you that whether we say it or not we all feel that you are different and that makes it a fact.' I was staggered and paralysed by the brutal manner in which this thing had been brought to my attention. I had been living in a sort of never-never world of youth, beauty, excitement and social activities; and now I was deeply mortified for I had no reply within me. I came away from that conversation aghast and shattered. My mind was numb. I could see neither to right nor to left. I was at the edge of a deep, dark abyss. My world had foundered.

Allison and her mother were shocked when Wellesley emerged from the study in such a state. A family rift quickly developed which Allison's father contrived to close by proposing 'a dignified and decent finish' to their friendship. Wellesley, deeply in love and emotionally quite out of his depth, agreed first to dine with the family and then to go to the theatre in Exeter to see *The Mikado*.

> I held Allison's hand during the performance and it was all very pathetic and horribly depressing. Finally we were brought

> back to her house in the Rolls Royce. We were told to kiss for the last time, after which I was promptly driven back to my sister's home. I had been asked 'as a gentleman and a friend' never to see Allison again.

For days Wellesley went around feeling like a beaten dog: lonely, morose and above all deeply perplexed. His sister neatly deflected the signs of anti-semitism in her social world by dismissing the family into which Wellesley had hoped to marry as boorish and unworthy of further consideration. She was blind and deaf to the wounding betrayal which Wellesley had experienced and turned her back on his wretched impotence in the face of Allison's father's prejudices. Vio had no capacity for introspection and deep feeling, like most of the adults who influenced Wellesley's early life. Taking her father as her model, acceptance into the English Christian upper classes seemed to be the peak of her ambition, no matter the cost. As he had learned to do in earlier crises, Wellesley sought resources deep within himself to make sense of what had happened, for no one around him could help him.

Allison sought him out and tried to persuade him to marry her at once. Eventually, she reassured him, it would work out all right. Wellesley, already sensing the future implications for such a marriage, pointed out that he still had another year at Cambridge and no idea what he really wanted to do afterwards. The severe emotional blow he had taken left him uncertain and incapable of decisive action. So they parted and he returned to Cambridge where his closest companions saw at once that something was wrong. But Wellesley was not yet ready to disclose his inner wrestling with what, if anything, it meant to him to be a Jew. Allison's refusal to give up prompted her to write to Wellesley about a profound experience she'd had while kneeling in Eton College Chapel where she'd gone to visit one of her brothers. In her letter, she expressed a longing to have Wellesley kneeling beside her and it was this which awoke his first inklings that there were fundamental elements in English society which were alien to him and which he could not honestly accept. She had unwittingly weakened the emotional bond between them; she severed it completely some weeks later when she came across him in Cambridge where she and her parents were visiting another of her brothers, who was studying at Trinity College. Wellesley greeted her, she cut him dead. Wellesley, still vulnerable, was deeply humiliated and hurt, so much so that he wrote a final letter to end this painful first love affair.

As Christmas 1925 approached Wellesley decided not to spend it with his sister in Devon. Displaying exceptional insensitivity, she wrote back complaining that he had to come down because she had contrived to have him invited to the County Hunt Ball, an honour he could not spurn. She was not boasting, for soon enough the highly embellished invitation arrived made out to Mr Wellesley ARNE. Wellesley had reached another milestone. He returned it to the honorary hunt secretary indicating that it had perhaps been intended for someone else.

> My sister was furious. I knew that some people in our family had changed their name from Aron to Arne to camouflage their Jewishness and I naturally presumed that this was my sister up to the same sort of thing. Because I wouldn't go down to Devon, my sister and her husband went off to Biarritz instead. I was sad in view of my very strong affection for them both. However, I was not prepared to go down to Devonshire even for their sake, to wander around like a lost soul. By now I knew I would never expose myself to the sort of situation I had just left behind forever.

Wellesley's intense preoccupation with the uproar in his heart and mind abruptly halted his normal sociability. His friends were concerned enough to ask him what was wrong, but he confided in no one. He found solace and finally revelation through strenuous physical exercise. Most afternoons he spent alone running or walking through the Fens. His innate physical strength and coordination doubtless carried him through to resolve his crisis. Sometime in November 1925, after months of introspection while he sustained disciplined academic and athletic pursuits, Wellesley had an experience which permanently changed the direction of his life.

> I remember exactly where it happened – it was on the Hills Road, going out from town to the Magog Hills. I was running by myself and the sky was dark, overcast and there was winter rain in the air. As I reached the corner of a side road to await a passing car, I suddenly experienced a sensation which I find near impossible to describe. It was instantaneous, it was

> overwhelming, it was unbelievable and it was final. As I stood transfixed at the corner of this road, the sky lit up in a blaze of light and in my mind's eye I saw, much to my surprise, the word PALESTINE written right across it and it was gone! I felt deep, utter and complete release. I felt shattered, but at the same time I felt as though I had been through an experience which had shifted a great deal of the burden which had weighed me down for weeks and months – shifted it and dropped it.

Never content to accept fashions and trends in thought or deed, Wellesley delved as deeply as his own qualities allowed to discover truths for himself. Like all profoundly spiritual people, he had more courage to confront reality than most self-styled realists. The moment of revelation on the Cambridge road followed months of serious, silent thought. It was followed by many more months of enquiry through books and with people, both Jewish and Christian. He turned to anyone who he thought might help him bring into being his new life which would be lived in Palestine. With no support of any kind from his mother or other relative, and rejected totally and inexplicably by Basil and Rose Henriques, who had inspired him to become involved with Jewish youngsters in the first place, he began to equip himself to move to Palestine as soon as he had got his degree.

CHAPTER THREE

Zionist in the Making

His direction in life discovered, Wellesley burst back into the student world, assailing his Christian friends with questions about Palestine. They, not less curious than he, directed him to an economics professor who was a prominent Zionist. The professor, when ambushed by Wellesley after lectures one day, gave him a random fact or two and redirected him to the Cambridge University Zionist Society. Wellesley's enquiries revealed that the Zionists met every Friday night at Hawkins' Café. So he soon found himself amongst ten to twenty fellow-undergraduates listening to a lecture on the recently founded Hebrew University in Jerusalem. That was his formal introduction to his new world. Soon afterwards, he began to learn a fourth language – Hebrew. Private lessons were expensive at ten shillings an hour, but his teacher Shlomo Bardenstein, who, via Palestine and Russia, was studying at the London School of Economics, influenced his life from then on. Wellesley's only recorded comment on his new endeavour is that 'two or three girls from Newnham and Girton who showed up were quite attractive and amusing and brightened the lessons to some extent'.

What astonished Wellesley, after his traumatic clash with Allison's father, was his Gentile friends' enthusiasm for his transformation. They began to ask him about Jewish things. He couldn't answer their questions, but admitted that he was going to Palestine to find out about a new kind of Jewish existence. They apparently found that natural enough. Some even expressed their relief to Wellesley because they could talk to a Jew who was willing to discuss what that meant, without the shame and secrecy they said they had experienced with the few other Jews they had met during their public school days. They wanted to know why Jews tried to conceal their identities. Wellesley could not help them.

> I told them that I could not explain the whys to them and I didn't even understand what they were after. I myself was

> looking for answers to a variety of questions: Where do I belong? I agreed with them – in Palestine – but I didn't know why I belonged there.

One wholly unpredictable consequence of Wellesley's astounding candour was his election to one of the three elite societies at Jesus College, Cambridge. He had never sought membership although his athletic prowess made him a likely candidate. Out of the blue he received a handsomely embossed invitation – his surname correctly spelled – to present himself for the initiation ceremony to Rhadeguends Club. He accepted. The ceremony was uproarious: Wellesley, having gulped the obligatory three brimming goblets of port, led the other fifteen members of the Club on a steeplechase around the college grounds until he was finally captured to be doused in a freezing midnight bath. Had certain members of his family known the social significance of Wellesley's election to the Rhadeguends Club they might have jumped for joy; but would it ever have occurred to any of them that he had been adopted into that unique society not only for his athletic accomplishments, which they had thought little of, but also because of his courage when prejudice forced him to confront first who he was in Christian eyes, and then who he would choose to be for himself?

So the Gentiles courted Wellesley while his eyes were turned towards his fellow-Jews. His fervour provoked an invitation to debate for the Zionists against the Moslems as to whether the Mandate for Palestine was good or bad. He was honest enough to decline through ignorance of the topic, but he had no inclination for public speaking because he thought it was a typical Jewish propensity 'to get up on one's hind legs at the slightest opportunity and make a speech'. It was not long before he was introduced to Dr Chaim Weizmann.[1] Weizmann came to Trinity College to talk to some fifty people about the parlous state of Zionism in Palestine. The dominant message imbibed by Wellesley was that the move-

[1] 1874–1952, Orthodox Jewish upbringing in a poor family living in a small town on Russian–Polish border; excelled at chemistry and was an outstanding all-rounder; took a post at Manchester University in 1904. Prominent active Zionist and the inventor of a process to produce acetone – a substance vital to the British in the First World War – which gave him access to leading British politicians; primarily instrumental in persuading the British government to issue a statement known as the Balfour Declaration (after the then Foreign Secretary) in which the British government agreed to use its best endeavours to facilitate the establishment in Palestine of a national home for the Jewish people; in 1921 became President of the World Zionist Organisation and in 1949 took the oath as Israel's first President.

ment suffered from 'a tremendous shortage of money and a tremendous shortage of Jews'. His impression of Palestine itself was of 'an empty country waiting to be redeemed, a country full of sunshine, a country lying along the Mediterranean'. Wellesley, already famed for his declared intent to move to Palestine, was introduced to Weizmann who promptly asked him to lunch. There he explained to Wellesley and his other guests that Zionism was inimical to most wealthy Anglo-Jews. Wellesley began to sense the strength of the Jewish opposition, but was somewhat reassured because it seemed that there had been a breakthrough which Weizmann said would be announced at the forthcoming annual Balfour Dinner. Wellesley scanned the press for a report of the anticipated gift of one million pounds from Sir Bernard Baron, the owner of the Carreras tobacco company, to the English Zionist Organisation. Nothing materialised because, it was rumoured, a prominent Anglo-Jew, who certainly carried more social weight than the Russian immigrant scientist Weizmann, persuaded Sir Bernard to donate his money elsewhere.

As his last year at Cambridge rushed by, Wellesley began to face up to the practical aspects of his decision. Weizmann had already offered him a job in London with the British Zionist Organisation. When he declined, reminding Weizmann that he was too ignorant to contribute anything worthwhile to the movement's organisation, he added that he had been left without any real roots or feelings about anything and that it was now time for him to go and develop himself through practical experience. Weizmann offered to introduce him to people in Palestine who might be able to assist him there. Wellesley's Hebrew teacher was more perceptive and suggested that he wrote to Dr Biram, the headmaster of the private school in Haifa where he had been secretary, to ask for a post teaching English. This Wellesley did, no doubt expecting a swift, enthusiastic response. He was disappointed when after many weeks' anticipation he received a reply informing him that nothing could be discussed until he presented himself in Haifa.

It was not long before Wellesley's eyes were opened wide to the baffling inconsistencies displayed by English Jews in their reactions to the movement to reestablish a sovereign Jewish community in Palestine. Perhaps he knew that his mother and sister would be horrifed at his conversion to Zionism, if for different reasons, but he could not have anticipated the outraged response to his good news when he told Basil Henriques. Wellesley looked forward to approval and encouragement from this couple who had first inspired him to get involved with a Jewish project. What he actually got was at first disbelief, and then, from Basil: 'Rose, the impossible has happened – a tragedy, a tragedy – Wellesley Aron is going to settle in Palestine. Can you believe it, he has become a Zionist!' It was Basil who had often charged him with being un-Jewish for omitting all Jewish overtones from his Scouting activities. Once more turmoil engulfed Wellesley, pushing him ever deeper into examining the interaction between himself, other Jews and the Gentile world. He felt that his Christian friends understood, respected and applauded his decision; that Zionist Jews were eager to use his talents and to encourage him up to a point; but that the most significant Jews in his life and his family lacked all understanding of his passionate search for an authentic Jewish expression. He began tentatively to unravel the intricacies and contradictions inherent in his own upbringing which had, without his being conscious of it, confused him totally, and left him yearning for something clear-cut and unyielding to commit himself to.

> At the back of all this of course was the pressure which had induced my strange experience, and, as I fumbled to formulate a basic answer, I knew that I was involved here in a choice between orthodoxies. When somebody is left caught up with insufficient spiritual or traditional roots and when he is a member of a minority and is not equipped by his surroundings to live fully and independently, as a minority member he loses his way. I knew in my heart that I would have to find my way back to some orthodoxy in Jewish life – one alternative was the religious orthodoxy which I knew about vaguely and had seen on various occasions. When my father was buried in Switzerland, rabbis – bearded men – descended on us and trained me to say a few words at the graveside. I had had some prayer instruction and tuition in the aleph bet at school, but all this was frivolous in the face of the strains to which I had been subjected in my social contacts. I knew that there was an orthodoxy that would have to claim me; I would have to be attached to something – something deep, clear and lasting with roots which went far back into time and would give me a footing from which I could grow. It would either have to be a

> religious orthodoxy yet I could not for a moment envisage myself going back to the ghetto, growing a beard and side curls and getting down to a serious religious education associating myself with the sort of people whom I knew to be orthodox Jews, whom I largely regarded as archaic types, out of date, out of context, alien and completely exotic. I had therefore no alternative but to look to the non-Jewish traditions around me until I was propelled or guided towards the renaissance of the Jewish People as a political entity in its own homeland. Even so I had just the vaguest indications of what was involved – it was more instinct than anything else.

Years later Wellesley hinted that an explanation for his mysterious attraction to Palestine might have been a story told him by his father about Wellesley's grandfather, the rabbi

> . . . who carried with him a little sack of earth wherever he went. On enquiring what and why my father told me that my grandfather had one great fear – that he might die and be buried and that his head might not be lying on holy soil. He had purchased the little sack of Jerusalem earth so that when he was buried it would be placed beneath his head. So he was sure that his head would rest on holy soil. Even to this day when I think of Yerushalayim, or Jerusalem, there is an association so deeply embedded in me as to give me a feeling of complete and utter quiet and certainty as to the rightness of where I am.

Wellesley's headlong rush into Zionism did not in any way turn his heart against England. His final adventure before his departure for Palestine was his appearance as a special constable in the London docks during the general strike of 1926.

He completed his travel arrangements as cheaply as possible, because his mother influenced the trustees of the settlement arranged by his father for Wellesley, not to let him have a penny if he persisted in his move to Palestine. He threatened to take the trustees to court when his mother refused to authorise them to give him money to pay the debts he had incurred at Cambridge. They capitulated and his mother went to see him – in full academic regalia – receive his degree at Senate House. He paid off his tailor, college buttery and tuition fees and was left with £15 for his journey to Palestine. He has left a detailed account of his last night in England, but omits to say whether or not his mother was with him, whether he saw Vio before leaving, or whether anyone saw him off or wished him well.

> Having booked my passage and seen whatever was to be seen at the Zionist Offices in London, I returned to spend my last evening in England with my mother. It was not to be an intimate one, for she had decided to send me to the local Jewish Literary Society to hear a lecture on anti-semitism given by Rabbi Gollop. There was a handful of disparate Jews ready to be enlightened. As for me, I hadn't had any clear realisation that there was in fact a concept of anti-semitism. I learned that it was sociological in character, developed largely as a result of research and metaphysical and pseudo-scientific interest on the part of people who were violently possessed of a dislike for Jews per se. Afterwards there was a discussion. Suddenly the rabbi looked in my direction and said that there was someone here who he happened to know was leaving for the Holy Land and that perhaps he would contribute something.
>
> I stood up to applause. I was surprised and embarrassed. But I quickly collected my few thoughts on the matter and said that I was really unconcerned with anti-semitism; that I had no theoretical knowledge of it and that I even suspected that a lot of things regarded as anti-semitic were just the normal relations of a negative and prejudicial character arising between human beings in competitive fields of work and social activities and that I thought on the whole, Jews were inclined to make too much fuss about these things and will have to learn to live with them if they wish to. For my part, I did not wish to and I was in search of a basic solution to the tensions and misunderstandings that seem to surround the Jewish question, and that in my experience, there was really no alternative to either becoming an orthodox Jew and wrapping oneself up in a cocoon of Jewish tradition and religious activity, and isolating oneself from the Christian world as far as possible and continue in some sort of compromise arrangement with the majority, or going to settle in Eretz Israel – whereupon a burst of enthusiastic applause was engendered

by the bowler-hatted gentleman in the front row, who looked thoroughly alien to me.

The meeting almost broke up in disorder at this point, the Chairman just expressing a quick vote of thanks to Rabbi Gollop, and thereupon I was inundated by almost the whole audience with questions and handshakes and congratulations – an experience of warmth and excitement such as I certainly did not expect and as far as I knew did not deserve.

CHAPTER FOUR

Palestine – Beginnings

Equipped with a good second-class honours degree, a third-class ticket, luggage containing the most expensive, elegant and comprehensive Cambridge gentleman's wardrobe, and powerful hopes and dreams, Wellesley set off for Palestine. It was August 1926. In disturbing contrast to the courageous, unconventional, truth-seeking young man who had defied family and friends to venture into unknown spiritual and physical domains were Wellesley's ultra-conventional dress and manners. His own description of his travelling appearance is almost a caricature of the noble Englishman. Wearing Harris tweed plus-fours, seated on a wooden railway bench in the rear carriage of a Palestine Railways train crossing the Sinai desert during the hottest months of the year was Wellesley. The heat was intense, but Wellesley would forgo neither Cambridge tie nor jacket. In desperation though, he discarded his underwear, thereby bringing his skin and the Harris tweed into direct contact for many hours in what became a jolting, juddering rite of passage into the Holy Land.

Wellesley surely found the disparity between his prosperous appearance and his impecuniosity difficult to reconcile. He displayed to his social and material advantage the emblems of his Cambridge social successes. He wore his immaculately tailored, exclusive athletics clubs' blazers and ties throughout his journey. On the boat from Marseilles to Port Said this secured recognition from a first-class passenger who had known his brother Eustace at Jesus College. This in turn brought about an arrangement with the purser which elevated Wellesley from third-class steerage accommodation to the first-class bars and dining areas. There he was plied with drinks and advice on how to keep the 'bloody natives and wogs in their right place' by a group of young Royal Air Force officers on their way to Egypt. Wellesley hinted that he did not share their outlook, but neither did he withdraw from their company. No doubt he needed to feel included and accepted by those he considered his social equals, but had he had more money from his mother or trust fund he would not have been in the somewhat humiliating situation of being dependent on the goodwill of purser and passengers to free him from the discomforts of a four-berth cabin far below decks. There is a suspicion of contempt in Wellesley's description of the encounter with this group, perhaps to compensate for what he felt was a shameful situation.

> The conversation was about games and sports, the usual type of subjects, and was very cheerful, childish and immature. However, I enjoyed their company and they were very good to me. Since I was short of funds, I was unable to reciprocate their hospitality and it seemed unnecessary in the circumstances since they were very well provided for.

After a number of minor adventures on the way, Wellesley boarded the train which would take him from Egypt to Palestine. He took the cheapest ticket and travelled in considerable discomfort alleviated only by his ever keen observation of his surroundings both inside and outside the compartment. Lydda was the central railway junction in Palestine where one track went off to Jerusalem and the other northwards via Jaffa–Tel Aviv to Haifa. There Wellesley alighted to wait for his connection to Haifa. He saw his brother's Cambridge friend, who had recognised his college tie on the boat, so he went across to shake hands and to enquire what kind of a night he'd had. His fellow traveller described a comfortable night in a sleeping compartment. On hearing Wellesley's account of his torments in third class, he offered him some money so that he could travel in less discomfort during his journey's final stages. As he referred to the gift as a loan Wellesley's initial refusal turned into acceptance and he duly arrived in Haifa, where there was no one to meet him or to celebrate his triumph.

Before leaving Cambridge, Wellesley had been for an interview at the Colonial Office organised by the University's appointments board. He had asked for opportunities in education or administration and had been offered a post in the Sudan. His delicate enquiries about a British post in Palestine were fruitless; but the enquiry is perhaps not as curious as it first appears, although it was certainly naive. On the threshold between his student life in Cambridge and an unknown independent life in England or Palestine, Wellesley reflected on his feelings about the world he had striven to make his own and the world which he hoped would become a welcoming home. He could not escape his loneliness during May Week, but neither would he absent himself from the social events which heightened his feelings of being an outsider. He had found it a depressing experience although 'I was of course sad at the prospect of leaving behind familiar things. I was torn between two worlds and it was a painful state which I hoped I would eventually resolve.'

Had Wellesley been offered the opportunity of exploring Palestine as an employee of the British Mandatary Government, would he have accepted and resolved this conflict differently? As things were, the only contact Wellesley had made prior to arriving in Palestine was with the Beit Sefer Reali, a private secondary school in Haifa. He took a taxi from the port to Hadar Hacarmel, whose ordered European-style streets and buildings were a relief after the hot, noisy, oriental chaos which had greeted him on arrival. It was late on a Friday afternoon towards the end of Succot, and Wellesley was fortunate to find, first the caretaker, who had not a word of English, and then Dr Cohen, a teacher who happened to call in at the school. Dr Cohen explained that the whole school was camping higher up the Carmel mountain and that no one would be at the school until Sunday. He allowed Wellesley to leave his luggage in a classroom, where he took the opportunity to change into his brand new Scout uniform.

> Within a matter of minutes, I was transformed into a Rover Scout. I had with me the most modern scouting and camping equipment: rucksack, hatchet, axe, compass, map, groundsheet, blankets, cooking utensils – in fact I was ready for anything. I emerged in my shirt, shorts, scarf, Wood Badge, Scoutmaster's hat and plume.

Thus he appeared before 'two extremely pretty young ladies, dressed in white who greeted me with Shalom', when he emerged from Doctor Cohen's car. Wellesley never entirely escaped the spell of his first night amongst Jews in Palestine. Here, his dreams came true.

> From my tent I could hear plenty of noise and shouting, laughter and the usual expressions of exuberance that youngsters exhibit in freedom and at play. I saw groups of young people between eight and eighteen years old con-

gregated around a large marquee. I wended my way across as the sun was beginning to set and looked with great curiosity at this young generation of free Jews who, for me, were a completely new experience. They were all similarly dressed – the boys in khaki shorts and a white shirt, some of them wearing yarmulkes, most of them stockingless and all of them seemed to be wearing sandals. The girls wore blouses or singlets and skirts. Dr Biram was not tall, but he was very powerful and through his thick glasses his eyes flashed authority and his voice indicated that he was a man of clear and specific ideas and was accustomed to being obeyed. His wife was tall and dark and she too emitted a strong personality. She lit the sabbath candles and made the usual blessings. Dr Biram recited kiddush in a Hebrew which I was able to detect had a thick German accent. I was put not far from Dr Biram who told me that the question of my future employment would be decided after the weekend.

The tent flaps had been rolled up all round the marquee and from where I sat I could see the shimmering reflections of a full moon on the Mediterranean Sea hundreds of feet below, on the foot of Mount Carmel. As we finished our meal and the traditional and more modern chanting of psalm and song gradually spread across this large marquee filling it with the sweet, pure voices of the youngsters surrounding me on all sides, and as I watched their bright eyes and clear expressions and their lack of self-consciousness, their humour and something else too, which perhaps I imagined, like an innate dignity derived from the natural process of living in freedom; and as a harmony spread among this group I had a premonition, a certainty that I was home forever, that this was my place and that this is where my years would find fulfilment and perhaps my contribution might find its opportunity. I had no doubt at that point, nor have I at any period throughout the more than forty years which followed, doubted or questioned the validity or correctness or perhaps even the inevitability of my presence and association with the Land of Israel and its people. I was truly home and that was the night that confirmed my instinctive feelings. For pure beauty, for deep innate satisfaction, for all the wealth of emotion and spiritual values embedded by generations of consistent and persistent yearnings for an even-

> tual homecoming, this was the sum total, the quintessence, the pristine formulation which swept over me to the point where I was moved to prayer in the deepest sense of the word – an expression of thanksgiving, of spiritual peace and inner ease such as perhaps many others have felt at their time and place as they returned to Zion.

Such rare experiences may not survive daily contact with life's complexities. In Wellesley's case, the essence of these moments was forever his, but it was only a month or two before he was disenchanted with Haifa and the Reali school. The precipitating incident for choosing to go to Tel Aviv, where he accepted a teaching post in the Herzliya Gymnasium, was a pupils' strike at the school in protest against a master who had in anger struck a pupil on the head. Both the master's and pupils' behaviour shocked Wellelsey into re-examining his place as unpaid housemaster in the school's boarding house. His English public school years had convinced him that, whereas the ritualised beating of a child was acceptable to both master and child, a slap in anger was a disgraceful lapse of self-control. He tried to explain his views to Dr Biram who was unimpressed by the distinction between lawful caning and the behaviour of one of his masters. About the pupils' defiance Wellesley is silent, but comments about his own fiercely disciplined youth suggest that he had mixed feelings of admiration and dismay. Perhaps the Birams' Germanic zeal was too reminiscent of his parents' conflict between English and German culture and too unpleasant to confront again? Haifa had a significant number of German residents, Jews and Christians, which influenced his decision to move south to Tel Aviv, where, he speculated, he would find the somewhat anarchic Russian influence more to his taste.

While Wellesley was finding his bearings, he explored the Yishuv[1] in northern Palestine with his former Cambridge Hebrew teacher who was visiting his family in Haifa. Thus he began his practical Zionist education in earnest. It was not long before he ran into the underlying hostilities between the Jewish and Arab populations. He has reported one such incident.

> The relationship between the Jews and Arabs in Haifa when I arrived in the autumn of 1926, was on the whole friendly and

[1]The Jewish community settled in Palestine.

> there was a great deal of contact on the business level and to some extent, especially among the wealthier and well-established Arab families, there was some social activity too. However, shortly after I arrived in Haifa, a murder took place along the road in open country to the south of Haifa town. A Jew was killed and horribly mutilated, whereupon within twenty four hours, two Arabs were found killed in exactly the same spot – obviously an act of retribution by an organisation which I later discovered was the Haganah[1] or its offshoot. I was completely unfamiliar with this sort of political stress and strain and wondered what the outcome would be. I was told that it was essential to retaliate immediately and in kind, otherwise the majority which surrounded the Jewish population (mostly overwhelmingly Moslem but with a certain percentage of Christians) would overrun the Jews who were forbidden by British Mandate law to carry arms.

The seeds of Wellesley's determination to contribute something towards reconciling the different communities in Palestine were perhaps sown in these first few months. The conflicts he witnessed there reflected those which had beset him in childhood and youth and which he could not defuse. The clearest indication of his desire to bring people together harmoniously can be seen in his account of his first Scout jamboree in Palestine. He was asked to head a representation of Jewish Boy Scouts to a local jamboree to include all the Scout organisations in the area.

> To me this was unfamiliar since I always assumed that Boy Scouts were non-political and that they all belonged to the Baden-Powell Organization with its headquarters in England. Since I had been to world jamborees at various times and found scouts from all over the world of course participating without question, here I discovered there were Greek Orthodox Scouts, belonging to the Greek Orthodox Arab community, Catholic Scouts affiliated with Catholic missions, or schools and convents in the area, there were Protestant Scouts associated with some other organisation and then the Jewish Scouts who were co-educational, again to me a surprise, since

[1]Haganah, the Hebrew word denoting defence, was a semi-underground Jewish defence force in Palestine controlled by the official Jewish authorities before Israel's establishment.

in my experience there had always been Boy Scouts and Girl Guides. I expressed amazement but was told that this is how things were, so would I take the Jewish scouts to the jamboree which the new High Commissioner Lord Plumer[1] might attend.

I led them down to the foot of Mount Carmel to a sports field where we found a small and rather primitive grandstand filled with notables – Arabs in tarbush or the traditional kafiya of the Palestinian villager, as well as most of the English community of officials whether from the railways or the District Commissioner's Office or the Health and Public Works and other services, police – all in uniform. Everyone stood as 'God Save the King' was played by the police band and in came His Excellency Lord Plumer, then in his seventieth year. A distinguished soldier, although nobody in Palestine, certainly not the Jews, knew what he was really like and assumed that since he was old, he would probably be senile and useless regarding colonisation or development, rehabilitation of agricultural areas, draining of marshes and reconstruction of a rundown country, which is what Zionism implied and which was implicit in the terms of the Balfour Declaration according to the Jews' interpretation. Several people had told me that Lord Plumer was a deplorable choice to succeed Sir Herbert Samuel.

The scouts were all seated on the ground of this football field waiting to take part in various competitions and games. I was delighted and honoured to be introduced to the High Commissioner who predictably asked me a number of questions about how long I'd been in the country, what was I doing, where had I come from. I told him briefly. Then he asked me what I would really like to do here. I told him that I would like to spend my time, if possible, trying to bridge the obvious rift between the communities as exemplified here by these groups of children all in scout uniform but belonging to different sects and creeds as far as I could understand and divided to the point where they can hardly converse or have even sport or other intercourse.

To my great surprise, Lord Plumer looked me over and said,

[1]First Viscount Plumer, Herbert Charles Onslow, Field Marshal (1857–1932); Governor of Malta 1919–24; High Commissioner in Palestine 1925–28.

> 'Young man, if you can do any of that you will be contributing greatly to the happiness and future of this country.' Frankly I was taken aback by his directness and understanding of what I had implied. Then I knew that Palestine was in good hands and I was able to speak with personal knowledge of his intelligent and wise grasp of the fundamental problems which beset this much-promised land. I never had reason to change my views and in fact just so long as Lord Plumer was High Commissioner, all Palestinians, Jews and Arabs, began to lick their wounds and heal them and move forward, if not rapidly at least steadily.

Wellesley's desire to reconcile diverse sects and creeds did not extend to the integration of classes within a society. He had learned early on that 'downstairs' and 'upstairs' do not mix. His brief period of infant innocence when he could move happily between the two had ended long ago. However, Wellesley was disarmingly frank about his prejudices, perhaps because he wished no harm to those not in his class – he just did not want to mix with them socially. Imagine then his initial outrage when a dusty, overalled labourer sat down at his table in an outdoor Haifa café without so much as a 'May I?'

> He didn't even acknowledge my existence; since I was dressed in plusfours, tie and jacket I presumably ranked as a bourgeois hardly worthy of recognition. He perused his Hebrew newspaper, ordered his meal, began to eat while carrying on reading. I was amazed that anybody of this type should sit at my table uninvited, or not at least introduce himself or apologise or explain his presence. Suddenly, without a by-your-leave, he looked up and said: 'You speak English?' I nodded. 'What do you think of Bernard Shaw's *Pygmalion*?' It is difficult for me to describe my reaction to this extraordinary question. Neither the human species as exemplified by this dusty building worker who had come straight from the site opposite the café nor the surroundings, would have led me to expect a literary or grammatic question of the values or the quality of England's leading playwright's drama at midday. My jaw must have dropped and certainly I was put out of countenance by my innate snobbery. I admitted that I had seen the play in London. 'So then,' he continued, 'please tell me what you

think of it.' I realised then that he was not just making conversation. I asked him why he was interested and he replied that he'd just been reading *Davar's*[1] drama critic on the construction and social significance of the play. I knew that I was in the presence of a very educated man, in fact a man better educated than I, although I had just come from the source and inspiration of British culture, Cambridge University. I didn't dare ask this fellow where he came from but I assumed Central Europe. I did not ask him whether he had had a university education or whether he had been unable to obtain one due to the fact that he was obviously a Jew. I could only assume that here I was, faced with something new in my experience – a trade unionist, a manual worker, perhaps a skilled tradesman who was concerned with drama, literature and was up-to-date with what was going on and who was in step with progressive elements. For a quarter of an hour we exchanged views which I could hardly have conceived possible and could certainly never have duplicated in an average eating place. Then he returned to his building site and I went back to school to set forth on a camping weekend.

One of Wellesley's recreations during his time in Haifa was to play football for the Maccabi Haifa team against El Carmel, an Arab team captained by Caferati, an Irishman who was head of the Palestine police in Haifa. Many of the Maccabi team were professional Hungarian footballers, whose professionalism Wellesley as an English gentleman found distasteful. As it turned out, within minutes of the starting whistle, fouls resulted in fist fights on the field and then a full-scale riot between spectators. Caferati's inexperienced policemen, all Arabs, could not contain the situation. Wellesley stepped in and was instrumental in segregating Arabs and Jews; but the match was called off and subsequently the Maccabi Club was ordered to close its ground. Wellesley makes no comment on the unfairness of this decision which penalised only the Jews, whereas the brawl had engaged Arab and Jew alike. When asked by the Maccabi manager, he did agree to talk to Caferati to try to persuade him to change the decision. Caferati was unresponsive. He had been ordered by the District Commissioner to close the ground, because he could never again expose his policemen to the ignominy

[1] *Davar* was the Jewish trade union movement's newspaper.

of being trampled underfoot by rioting spectators. Wellesley appealed to Caferati's sportsmanship pointing out that sport developed character and that without a ground the Jews would have less opportunity to do this. Caferati's only concession was to let the ground stay open for inter-Jewish matches. Wellesley's reaction was predictable.

> The whole experience was for me fantastic since I had been brought up to play games in the traditional British sporting spirit to the effect that the game is the thing and that whoever won, won and it was not a subject for tremendous heat or passion and that the rules would be observed through the use of decorum and decency at all costs, otherwise the game was not worth playing – and here I was already embroiled in a major political riot which took place on the sports field. My education was certainly proceeding fast!

Football was also Wellesley's introduction to Tel Aviv, which was to be his home town, apart from the war years and for short periods in England, until 1981 when he moved to Neve Shalom/Wahat al-Salam, a settlement in the no-man's-land between Jordan and Israel. He was immediately attracted to the town which then had a population of not more than 40,000. Its sandy flatness found favour with Wellesley who was wearied by Haifa's rocky mountainside. He liked the Rothschild Boulevard area and Allenby Road – a lot of it not then built up – and he liked the city's atmosphere which was energetic yet casual. It had none of the 'oriental complications' which were troublesome to Wellesley in the non-European parts of Haifa; and none of the Germanic ethos which he kept bumping into in the European parts of that city. After a few days exploring Tel Aviv and long discussions with a number of residents, including a happily settled Anglo-Jewish family, he approached the two joint headmasters of the Gymnasia Herzliya, who were renowned Yishuv personalities from Russia. They agreed to take him on as soon as he was free; he accepted and returned to Haifa to say farewell.

Towards the end of February 1927 Wellesley arrived in Tel Aviv to receive his teacher's timetable from Drs Mossenson and Bograshov. He was as unaccustomed to a six-day week as he was to having boy and girl pupils who ranged in age from eleven to eighteen years. He taught them English. He did this with such fervour that English scout songs were soon heard echoing round the turreted and battlemented building at the end of Herzl Street. The experience of teaching outside England made him acutely conscious of his heartfelt commitment to the values he had imbibed through his earliest years from his half-siblings and schoolmasters. These had been reinforced at Cambridge. He attributed his exceptionally good relationships with his students to his sincerity. He taught young Palestinian Jews English through the songs, games and topics which most interested him and which he knew most about. He favoured no one, had a common approach to boys and girls, expected absolute honesty from his pupils and offered them his own integrity and sense of fairness. On his arrival he had been told that cheating was endemic amongst pupils. Horrified, he confronted this at once by setting out his rules unequivocally. The first time he found pupils breaking them he quietly confiscated their work, put nought against their names and confidently banished them from the class. Only rarely did he have to repeat that punishment.

> I experienced affection and respect at the hands of the literally scores of pupils of both sexes. Incidentally, this coeducational principle was for me a completely new one and at first, more than somewhat potentially embarrassing for me; I had never had any contact before with young girls as students or in any other manner, since I was brought up in a male environment from my earliest days at kindergarten. However, such was the freedom and naturalness of these young people, that no real embarrassment ensued to me.

He learned later that a number of the girls had crushes on him – about which he had been oblivious.

Wellesley recalls his eighteen months at the Herzliya Gymnasium as a period of fulfilment and deep pleasure, in spite of the arduous work as teacher and form-master to the fifth-year class of fourteen- and fifteen-year-olds. In his spare time he taught willing pupils his beloved games and sports and also prepared his lessons for pre-university pupils around topics chosen by them for their future use in their working lives. He has given two accounts of his decision to leave the school. Neither can be verified and it seems likely that his decision to leave resulted from a combination of two experiences that preceded his departure. Something happened at school which forced him to examine his own place as a Zionist Jew in Palestine.

Some of his fellow-teachers, dedicated Hebraists, accused him of assimilating the youngsters to English values rather than to their own intrinsic Hebrew values.

> I took these criticisms to heart to the point when I soon realised that I had really no future of any great value for the teaching profession. I realised that I would be dissatisfied in teaching English as a sort of technical adjunct to the general education. I recognised that as unfit as I was to teach Christians in England since I was not a Christian myself, I was also ill-equipped to become a teacher of any standing who could make a real contribution in the Land of Israel, since my Hebraic and Jewish education was so lacking.

Many decades later Wellesley realised that at the time he was not fully conscious of the tragic aspect of his own harsh assessment. He understood too late that his self-evaluation was distorted by his powerful need to be accepted in his full complexity as a Jew who had shown exceptional courage in moving to the embryo Jewish homeland, but who brought with him those experiences of an English upbringing which were of universal value. The prejudiced outlook he had sought to leave behind him in England had resurfaced in Palestine. Unable to trust his own judgements and those of his pupils or to continue his work, he fled from the community which had opened up his deeply hidden anguish about his divided, troubled youth. This experience coincided with an invitation from Chaim Weizmann to leave Palestine to work in London as Weizmann's assistant political secretary.

When he was not at school, Wellesley was usually spending time with other recently arrived Jews, who kept an 'open house' policy on Friday nights and Sabbaths. The brother of one of his Cambridge colleagues was one of his hosts and it was he who introduced Wellesley to the lady whom he married three weeks after their first meeting. Rose, like Wellesley, had broken away from her family traditions and was living alone in Tel Aviv where she worked as secretary and interpreter of Hebrew, Arabic and English to a Judge Copland. Like Wellesley, she was a very attractive and popular young person, who had shown rare independence by leaving her mother's orthodox home in Rehovoth to establish a life of her own. They married first in the District Commissioner's office in Jaffa with Dr Mossenson as witness. When Rose's mother was told she ordered them to have a religious ceremony at once and they complied on 21 March 1927. As soon as Wellesley's own mother received the news of their engagement, she cabled that she was on her way and that he should delay a final decision until her arrival. Greatly alarmed, her only son cabled in reply that he was already married. Bride and groom decided to live in their own separate accommodation until the school holidays, when they would honeymoon in the Galilee and then move into a small rented cottage in Bilu Street.

> We bought most of our limited amount of furniture from Arab carpenters in Jaffa and the whole collection could have been easily – and was in fact – transported by hand on a cart by an Arab who brought the chairs, table and other items to our place. Hardly had we moved in than we experienced something very frightening – an earthquake. Tel Aviv didn't suffer too much because it was built on sand, with reinforced concrete foundations – all we saw was the Balfour Street water tower sway from side to side and afterwards we saw that there was a crack in it.
>
> We settled down to our jobs. I bicycled to and from school where I had many interesting experiences. Once the three English teachers were in the masters' room discussing existing problems when to our surprise, we found we were suddenly left alone – there was nobody else about – we suspected that something was afoot. We went outside and saw the school treasurer. He looked up at us and said
>
> 'Oh, are there any more of you there?'
>
> 'Yes, the three English masters.'
>
> 'Well,' he announced, 'Unfortunately I have no more.'
>
> 'What do you mean no more?'
>
> He continued, 'I had some money and have been giving it out to those who haven't been paid for some time, like yourselves, and I have one five pound note left – and that's all I have.'
>
> 'Well at least let us have the five pounds.'
>
> We took the five pounds and walked out into the street in front of the Gymnasia because it was time to go home on a Friday midday and we looked at each other and one of us said, 'Well now, what happens to the five pounds?' Someone sug-

gested going down to Herzl Street to try to change it. We were unable to find any business or shop able to do this; and even the people sitting in the cafés discussing land transactions of some substance, were unable to produce five single pound notes to change our note. We looked at the five pound note and considered who had the priority.

The teacher from Brooklyn, New York said 'I have a family with four children and really we haven't had any money for quite a long time.' Then I said 'Well, we've just got married and haven't even got the wherewithal to buy the hooks to hang our things on the wall and settle in properly.' Then the third one – Levine from Bulawayo, Rhodesia – spoke up, 'I have a cow to feed out at Ramat Gan and I bring the milk in every day to give to the school, and the cow must have her fodder.' On hearing that we agreed that he had priority and we gave him the five pound note.

In those days we were often not paid in cash. We were paid in promissory notes. If we wanted cash for them, we had to go to the bank and have them discounted, assuming the responsibility – if there was any default at a later date – (of course not having any money at all there was a danger that we might end up in jail) and certainly we had to pay the discount rate at the bank for the privilege of having the cash that we'd earned in the course of our work.

When Rose and I were moving to a larger apartment, the landlord produced a lease for me to sign. I told him that I couldn't do that. He asked me why not and I told him where I worked. Then he said, 'Oh, you're the new English master, are you? Well, I understand; how can you possibly get paid when I owe the school fees for my two children? I've never paid them, so they can't pay you.' He added that his children spoke very highly of me and were getting on very well. I replied that I was delighted, but I was still faced with a problem; I didn't know if to sign or not. He said, 'Please sign; commit yourself and I will understand if you don't pay me because unless I pay the school fees, you won't of course be getting any money.'

The same situation existed with the woman who ran the grocery just around the corner. My wife went into her shop and said that we'd just moved into the house nearby. The shopkeeper responded, 'Oh yes, and don't worry about payment, you can have as much credit as you like and you'll pay me in due course.'

Soon after their marriage Rose became pregnant. Wellesley, very concerned for his wife and child, arranged for her to attend a gynaecologist who had a private clinic nearby. One day this doctor came to Wellesley for help. He showed him a letter from the British Mandatary authorities ordering him to close his clinic down. Very upset and not the least in awe of the authorities Wellesley arranged to see Dr Smith, the British chief medical officer for the southern district of Palestine. His office was in King George Street above the main post office. Their conversation was as follows:

'Excuse me, are you Doctor Smith?'

'Yes, what can I do for you?'

'Did you write this letter?'

'Yes I did.'

'Why?'

'Oh, we can't have people opening clinics wherever they like.'

'Do you know the man who opened this clinic?'

'No, I've no idea.'

'Do you know his credentials?'

'No.'

'Then why have you closed the clinic? Do you want to close the clinic?'

'It does not conform to London County Council rules and regulations.'

'What sort of regulations?'

'Well, every corridor must be at least three metres [*sic*] wide.'

'Have you been to see it?'

'No, but one of my supervisors has and he said it looks like a villa and not like a clinic at all.'

'It is a villa in a garden, it has been converted to a clinic and that is where my wife will have our baby. You had better not close it or I will take action in high quarters to find out what goes on here.'

The clinic stayed open and Sharona was born there in December 1927.

CHAPTER FIVE

Zionist Official – Founder of Habonim

In spring 1927, Wellesley heard that Weizmann was to visit Palestine and would like to see him. They met, and Weizmann invited Wellesley to go to London as his assistant political secretary in the political department of the World Zionist Organisation at 77 Great Russell Street. Wellesley explained that he was happy in Tel Aviv, that he was making a family life for himself and could not leave his teaching post on such short notice. It was at this time that Wellesley had his unpleasant encounter with some of his fellow-teachers who accused him of trying to assimilate his pupils to English rather than Jewish/Hebrew values. Weizmann solved his difficulty for him when he visited the school and spoke to the headmasters, who agreed to release Wellesley immediately. The expense of moving to England with Rose and Sharona, then a babe in arms, was an obvious anxiety. Yet, without explaining how, they managed it.

Their arrival in London was extremely unpleasant for Wellesley and indicates something very insensitive about Weizmann, who had apparently informed no one of his decision to appoint Wellesley to be his assistant political secretary. Weizmann was not in London for the first six months, but did invite Wellesley to join him in Berlin to meet the World Zionist leaders with whom Wellesley would have to work. He set off for Germany leaving Rose and Sharona in London.

> We had a very nicely appointed little flat in Hampstead. ... I met and came face to face, for the first time, with all the leaders of the Zionist movement – and a very mixed bag they appeared to me, they were shrieking and shouting and making a lot of noise at the conference and in the Aktions committee meetings – mostly in Yiddish, which I didn't understand, and a certain amount of Hebrew – but a tremendous amount of passion and excitement and hysteria seemed to be the order of the day.

After a couple of sessions he had had enough and asked Weizmann to excuse him as he wanted to see if any of his German family was alive, he hadn't been to Germany since the First World War. He found an Aron through the phone book and was invited to a family party where his youthful experience of being the odd one out repeated itself. They mocked his commitment to Zionism and Hebrew and scoffed at his warnings that it might not be long before they too might need to earn their livelihood in Hebrew. There were two youngsters who befriended him because they had joined a Zionist youth movement and already knew a little Hebrew.

The following day Wellesley contacted the son of the late Dr Herman Aron, the uncle who had slipped him gold pieces in his childhood. This first cousin conducted Wellesley round his industrial empire, which brought back some of Wellesley's youthful memories of being 'handed and bandied around the factory to be shown all the machines'. Manfred Aron had resolved his 'Jewish problem' by marrying a Christian and was bringing up his children as Christians. He utterly disagreed with Wellesley's predictions that the only answer to the survival of the Jews was to emigrate to Palestine and build a sovereign Jewish community there. Wellesley left, deeply disappointed in his father's relatives. Years later, he still spoke with anguish about their refusal to listen to his warnings. Nearly all were murdered in one way or another during the Hitler years.

On his return to London he took up his post as assistant to Leonard Stein,[1] an Oxford graduate and lawyer. He was given virtually nothing to do. He did have a few exciting days in August 1929, when he was left more or less in charge of the London Zionist office because the World Zionist Congress and Jewish Agency were meeting in Zurich. He received the first telegrams from Palestine reporting the murders of Jews by Arabs at the Western Wall in Jerusalem and the subsequent massacre of dozens of unarmed yeshiva students in Hebron. In neither case did the British authorities effectively protect the Jews or control the Arab leaders' incitements to violence. Wellesley cabled Zurich for advice and was told in reply to get in touch with Lord Melchett[2] for his suggestions.

[1]Leonard Stein (1887–1973); British barrister, political secretary World Zionist Organisation 1920–29; Legal Adviser to the Jewish Agency 1929–39.
[2]Sir Alfred Mond, later First Baron Melchett (1868–1930);, British Jewish industrialist and liberal politician; supported Zionist work in Palestine.

Before doing that, Wellesley telephoned the Prime Minister Ramsay Macdonald to register the Jewish Agency's concern about events in Palestine, but the Prime Minister would not engage in discussion over the telephone.

Then he spoke to Lord Melchett who was holidaying in Scotland. Having listened to Wellesley's report, he advised him to speak at once to the Prime Minister. Wellesley reported his lack of success in that direction. At Lord Melchett's insistence he spoke again to the Prime Minister informing him that unless His Majesty's Government put an end to what was going on in Palestine at once then the Jewish Agency could not be responsible for any further cooperation with HMG. Ramsay Macdonald pointed out that he had seen very little cooperation from the Jewish Agency so far. He told Wellesley that troops were moving into Palestine from Egypt and that a warship was sailing from Malta. He added that the British government was doing its best in a very difficult situation. Wellesley was very relieved when Zionist and Jewish Agency officials started returning from Zurich and he no longer had to deal with the press and others wanting to know what was happening in Palestine. As soon as he could, he returned to his other, much more absorbing work which he had taken up when his enforced idleness led him by chance to find a way to combine his twin passions for education and sport. In summer 1928 Wellesley bumped into Alec Reubens, a former Cambridge colleague who invited him to visit a Jewish youth club which he and some other Jewish Cambridge graduates had established in Bethnal Green. He went along one evening and watched the youngsters playing chess and table tennis, doing gymnastics, folk dancing and other activities. On the top floor of the converted house he found two boys reading. One said that he was studying Talmud, the other Jewish history.

When he was asked for his reactions, Wellesley's instant retort was, 'Why do you call it Jewish?' Asked what he would suggest to make it a Jewish youth club instead of a youth club for Jews, Wellesley was at a loss, but he was pressed to propose a scheme to add a Jewish dimension to the club's activities. His friend added that he could guarantee its acceptance if Wellesley took up the challenge successfully. With his usual honesty, Wellesley admitted that he did not know the answer, but he went away and attacked the problem with characteristic intensity and thoroughness.

I knew that there must be an answer, because this was no way

> to deal with a whole generation of youngsters who grew up as Jews yet who were ignorant of who they were and what they were, except for the occasional Bar Mitzvah celebration and some peripheral community work. After mulling it over for a time I suddenly had an idea and asked someone in the office if I could ask a typist to do some work for me. A certain Miss Silver then took down the outline of what was to be called HABONIM. Many years later when her daughter was a member of Habonim, I met the former Miss Silver who asked me if her daughter's Habonim club was descended from the scheme she had typed out. I told her it was. She replied how proud she felt to have been involved in typing the four or five pages of closely argued material outlining my ideas to the effect that there must be some method of interesting Jewish young people in their cultural background. Out of that paper the whole thing developed, in point of fact when it was ready, it was announced in the *Jewish Chronicle* that I would give a lecture on 'How to bring young English-speaking Jews to a better knowledge of their culture and heritage'.

On a November evening in 1928, in spite of his wife's protests he set forth in very foggy weather to 77 Great Russell Street, where his audience was assembled in the executive room. There were six people present though these few were scarcely visible through the yellow fog which oozed into the room through every cranny.

> My heart sank and I thought for a moment that it was hardly worth giving a lecture on a night like this to an audience of this size. I decided to carry on and talked for some 45 minutes. I was feeling rather depressed and tired by it all when a young man jumped up and said, 'My name is Norman Lurie, I am a student at the London School of Economics and I was born in Johannesburg and I'm over here to take my degree, and I want to say that this is one of the most exciting, important moments of my life. I've never heard anything so inspiring as what we have just heard. I would like to ask you a question, Mr Aron – Will you repeat your lecture on Sunday night at this place if I guarantee to fill it with students from Oxford, Cambridge and London universities?' I said, 'Yes, I'll repeat it ad nauseam wherever anybody is prepared to listen to it.' That is what happened. My scheme was not called Habonim at this time.

David Goiten suggested the name a week or two after the first meeting. At the end of the meeting, which he had arranged and chaired, Norman Lurie proposed the resolution 'that Mr Aron should proceed with the elaboration of his scheme and that we will find means of applying it when it's ready'. I agreed and we dispersed.

For the next few weeks I was completely occupied working out this proposal. I was looking for something symbolic which conveyed action and inspiration to young people between the ages of about ten and fifteen. My knowledge of Jewish history and Jewish culture was still pretty scant, although I had by now read Graetz and Margolis and a few other Jewish histories. I never regarded myself as knowledgeable in Jewish matters, so I had to look around for the flesh to put on the bones of this concept of Habonim. Now Habonim was really a new departure in Jewish education. It was not entirely original in that it was in some ways derived from Baden-Powell's extraordinarily farsighted and inspired methods. There was something in his Boys' Scout movement which appealed to and attracted me. I was convinced that there was a secret of great value in it from an educational point of view. The whole framework of Habonim was built in the same pattern as the Boys' Scout movement. But instead of woodcraft, camping, path-finding and a lot of other subjects which had no particular Jewish interest, I looked for ways to replace those elements with whatever I could find in the way of Jewish subjects. My own approach was to excite Jewish youngsters to take an interest in the project.

I decided that they should know something about Jewish history and then relate the past to the present. I knew also from my own experience that most Jewish children in the western world had only a vague idea about biblical times, the tribes of Israel and their lives in the Holy Land. They gathered that there was a period during the Diaspora when things got worse and worse until the period of the Catholic Inquisition in Spain, which culminated in the expulsion of all Jews from the Iberian peninsular. They were chased from pillar to post and then passed backwards and forwards across the frontiers of Europe, frequently massacred en route and always persecuted beyond measure. And this without mentioning the Crusader period. Generally the situation of the Jews was unfortunate and best forgotten. That would take history up to the time of the pogroms in Russia, whereupon we would then be dealing with the personal history of the parents of many of the youngsters I was concerned with. They had emigrated from eastern Europe to the land of the free – England – and knew no more of the sort of horrors and atrocities that they had heard about in their youth.

Now at that point the connection between the biblical and modern days was extremely vague and I felt that the continuity of two thousand years or more of Jewish history should be a strong thread in the minds of the youngsters. It should therefore make sense to them when they proceeded to flesh out all the plans and projects that I was going to give them to acquire Jewish knowledge and interest. I needed a version of Jewish history compressed into the smallest possible space for the youngsters who joined the movement to learn – not by heart – but by reciting the story and understanding exactly what they were involved with. I called it 'The story of My People'. I didn't know enough of it nor did I judge myself competent enough to write Jewish history in such a concentrated form, so I turned to a young lawyer named David Goiten and asked him to write the story of the Jewish people in one thousand words. He was fascinated by this and within a couple of weeks produced his version. It was written mostly like a fairy tale, he had always had a delight in legends and folk lore. I read it and found it too childish to be suitable.

Then I turned to Leon Simon, a senior Post Office official, philosopher, Oxford graduate and the translator of Ahad Haam from Hebrew into English. He wrote me a philosophical treatise of the Jewish people which I thought was so dry that no child would be able to read it. My third attempt was to talk to Cecil Roth, a historian, who was a friend of mine also from Oxford. He too was fascinated by the idea and agreed to try. He gave me a treatise on Jewish history with dates and names and practically nothing else. He said he couldn't include anything else with a limit of a thousand words. I was in the toils of this problem when someone suggested that I should go to a certain rabbi who was very interested in youth. He produced a religious treatise in which everything was transformed into a religious experience. I told him that I didn't want it to be like that, they can get this from their Hebrew lessons in the Jewish community, I want something educational and secular. It didn't do.

I then began to realise I would have to write this thing myself. I must admit that although I was extremely secularly inclined in those days and having come back from Palestine and having found my Jewish life in Zionism, I was rather inclined not to invoke the Almighty in the ordinary story of man. So I sat down and tried to write this history on the basis of all the versions I had in front of me, but with my own concept at the core. I went right through my material and found two elements that had to be included – one was the Land of Israel – which I was all for of course, and the other was the Almighty because you cannot account for the Jewish people's survival, nor for their ethical concepts and traditions without the intervention of some power outside which we recognise is the source of everything. I wrote one thousand words and had something that a child could read and absorb easily. It was one milestone.

Using knowledge picked up here and there, I then had to work out all the tests and promises and other things that the project required from the child. At one point I asked David Goiten whether he could provide a name for this project and he said, 'Yes, Habonim, the builders.' I said that is exactly what I want. 'Have you got a slogan too?' 'Yes,' he replied, 'Al tikra banaiv ella bonaich – don't call them your children, call them your builders.' I told him it was a lovely slogan and that we could build a whole movement around it. I proceeded to do so. One of the ideas was to let every child make a brick – levena – and decorate it with the symbols of his ancestral tribe, his own Habonim group, the Habonim movement itself and anything else he could find in the *Encyclopaedia Judaica*. This became a central feature of Habonim and helped the children to develop a certain interest in art and in research too, because the Jewish tribes of Israel began to emerge as the names of the local groups known by the Hebrew word 'gedud'.

Suddenly the children had a tremendous interest in Jewish knowledge. The movement spread very quickly, in fact faster than I could really produce the plan. It was first taken up by

Chaim Lifschitz who ran a Talmud Torah plumb opposite to the Basil Henriques club in Cannon Street Road in the East End. Norman Lurie was staying in my house for weeks, hovering near me waiting to tear the sheets off the typewriter as they came available and rushing down to the East End to put them into practice. I remember one item connected with a promise that a Habonim member had to make. I showed the wording to Neville Lasky, then a KC and a prominent Manchester Jew. In those days he was very pro-British and rather cool about Zionism. He insisted that I include a declaration of loyalty to the Crown and the British Empire. Accordingly the promise adopted by the movement contained appropriate words.

The movement took shape, but could not develop unless there was some instruction as to how it was to be applied. I called upon my students such as they were. Norman Lurie led them, but I remember few other names. I asked about twenty of them to meet me in the communal room at St John's Wood synagogue, where I would run a training course. I knew exactly how to do this, I don't know how, but I did and I worked out the whole scheme based on the premise that each one should go through exactly what a boy (boneh) or girl (bonah) would undergo when joining the movement. In doing that they would become familiarised with the whole process. They trained with me for about a month or so. Then they emerged as highly qualified instructors and leaders. This was fine and they went their various ways to set up gedudim, but this was not as straightforward as I had expected.

We were obstructed from the beginning. First a Miss Nellie Adler who was on the L.C.C. saw to it that all the L.C.C. schools were closed to us. I had hoped that we could rent school rooms after hours. Suddenly we were expelled and the reason given was that we were an anti-British movement – believe it or not. This and a lot of other difficulties including opposition from the Association of Jewish Youth, which was anti-Zionist in those days, meant we could get no proper recognition. It seemed to me that the most important thing was to produce a handbook or pamphlet which contained everything that was planned as well as what was already being done by the youth leaders (rashim) in various places.

I settled down to produce the complete handbook of Habonim. I was very moved when James Rothschild, then Member of Parliament for Ely, and a devoted Zionist, sent me a cheque for £150 towards the printing costs. His was the only donation I received from any source to support what I was trying to do. When the material was ready we could not afford to have it professionally reproduced, whereupon Norman Lurie offered to go to the Zionist Organisation offices at night and reproduce it on the Gestetner. So I gave him the stencils for the 20 to 30 pages which Miss Silver had prepared. The next morning I found stacked up on my desk 100 to 150 copies bound rather superficially in the well-known type of blotting paper used with Gestetner printers. It was light blue with purple printing. At the top was printed 'Habonim', beneath were the words 'A Jewish Cultural Youth Movement' and the date. It was then 1929. I looked through it and was satisfied that here was something that could be handled by any young person who wanted to take on the project.

It happened to be a Friday when the World Zionist Executive was meeting. Usually I took the minutes, but on that particular day Israel Cohen, who was the senior secretary, decided to do so. Consequently I was free. I returned to my own desk to look at my handiwork again. I was very impressed with it and wondered what I should do with it. Then I had a very bright idea. I took a copy for every member of the Executive, some of whom were in London from Palestine and the United States for this meeting. I placed a copy in the middle of Dr Weizmann's immaculate desk. I left a copy each for Brodetzky, Kaplan, Locker, Rosenruth, Kaplansky and so on and so forth. I went back to my office to wait for reactions. At 12 o'clock sure enough the meeting broke up and I heard them all come out of the executive room and disperse to their various offices. They put on their coats and I heard them chitter chattering on their way downstairs. When they had all gone I thought I'd have a look in their rooms. I went down to Dr Weizmann's room. My 'Habonim, A Jewish Cultural Movement' was no longer on the centre of the desk and I thought for a moment that he might have taken it home to read over the weekend. Then I had a second thought and looked in the waste paper basket. There it was. I redeemed it. I was very shocked. I went round to all the offices redeeming the unread handbook of Habonim. Now we had eight or nine more copies for use. Beyond every other consideration, it was a terrible moment for me because I realised they were not interested in what I was doing.

I happened to go into Dr Sokolov's office where I found one of the American Zionist leaders, Louis Lipsky. I asked him where he was going and he replied that he was off to catch the boat train to Liverpool, thence to New York. I said, 'Look here Louis, I have what I think might be a key to the problem of Jewish education for Jewish youth in my hand here, and I would like you to take it back to America and show it to someone.' He turned on me and said 'Education!' 'Yes,' I replied. He went on, 'We've no time for education, we're only interested in politics.' I was staggered. But he had told me the truth. Nevertheless I persuaded him to let me put my Habonim handbook in the top of his Gladstone bag which he closed up and then departed. We never heard any more about it and that is why Habonim became an entirely different thing in America.

Now I knew where we stood. I was engaged in work which I thought essential and vital. When I offered the scheme to Alec Reubens he said that his club would not accept it and that it could not be implemented – this in spite of the fact that he had originally challenged me to find a Jewish element for his Jewish boys' club. He had even promised to adopt any scheme which I came up with. He did something else to help me though by obtaining permission from a moribund Jewish club in Notting Hill Gate where hardly a soul could ever be found. There Paul Moscovitz and young Backstansky, both university students, asked me to train them as Habonim leaders and this I did. They established a successful gedud there, I think it was called Bar Kochba.

By this time there were demands from all over England for the handbook. Morris Zions in Manchester was already well away, starting one, two, three, four and five gedudim. There were clubs by now in Liverpool, Hull, Swansea and so on. Different communities were rushing to adopt the Habonim project. Suddenly there was an upsurge in the desire for Jewish information. Children would go up to their parents saying,

'We've been through the library Dad and there is not a single book on Jewish history there. We've no books in the house on Jews and I have to get some information for my gedud or my kvutza. I have to pass a test next week and I want to get all the information I can.' All at once Jews wanted to know about their own culture. Having got as far as this we were doing pretty well.

Then we were presented with a special opportunity. Each year the Association of Jewish Youth held a Gala concert or show at the Scala theatre. All their clubs and other organisations connected with the AJY, as it was known, had a chance to show what they did. At Notting Hill we were asked what we were up to. We replied that the only thing going on was Habonim. They asked what that was and we replied that we could put on a display at the AJY evening. To many people's surprise that's what we did. The Scala theatre was packed. Most women wore furs and jewels and men were wearing dinner jackets. After dining elsewhere they had come to spend an evening watching the Jewish youngsters whose activities they took an interest in. Item four on the programme was Habonim, A Jewish Cultural Youth Movement. The curtain rose up and there was a gedud in formation, each child wearing a blue and white tie and carrying a brick highly decorated with tribal and other ornamentations. They started the programme. The first Hebrew words of the evening were spoken. The audience shuddered. They had never heard a word of Hebrew before except in synagogue. The Jews in the audience were startled and did not know how to react. The gedud went right through its enrolment ceremony and all the other ceremonies we had developed to enable these children to participate actively in exploring their own cultural history. The curtain came down. There was silence. Nobody knew what to do.

I didn't know how much ill-will would develop from then on, but I did know that we had made history that night. I don't think we did very much more in the Jewish club area, but the movement itself grew and I was very pleased to be able to call together a small committee composed of Leon Simon, Arthur Block (then in the Patents Office, but previously a head of the Technion in Haifa), and Cyril Henriques who was the treasurer. There wasn't very much in the kitty, we never had any money really, and the thing was more or less self-supporting. I thought it was high time that we got a little help from the B'nai B'rith[1] and Arthur Block volunteered to approach them. It was all very small stuff and we didn't really know where to go from there. I saw that the dearth of leadership was going to hold the movement back, yet I had no idea how to find young Jews who had the gift of leadership and who would be interested in Jewish affairs.

I talked this over with a Cambridge friend of mine, Lionel Shalit, who was a very keen Maccabi man. We decided to form the Bar Kochba Association of England which was in fact a Maccabi movement. Through this I thought that we would come across men and women who had the character and ability to act as leaders for the youngsters. In the autumn of 1929, I recognised that with Palestine in the news daily, because of the Arab attacks on Jews in Jerusalem, Hebron and elsewhere, it might be the ideal moment to launch the Bar Kochba Association. Lionel Shalit and I advertised the first meeting in the *Jewish Chronicle* and a couple of other papers. It took place on a Sunday at Harrow on the Hill starting at 2 o'clock. In spite of the rain, about a hundred young Jews of all descriptions arrived by train to take part in football, hockey, lacrosse and other team games. The club's official colours were blue and white, the Zionist movement's colours. This meeting certainly launched something. Shortly afterwards a benefactor made available an office in Fleet Street and membership applications and donations from all sorts of sources began to pour in. It seems that English Jews, like their Gentile counterparts, had little interest in culture, but a great interest in sports. Eventually we hired a ground in Streatham and began to arrange fixtures for association and rugby football as well as for other sports. This was the founding of the English Maccabi movement. I was nominated to the Maccabi world union executive and soon met some of my counterparts from other countries in Antwerp. Although exhilarated by my success in this endeavour, I could not disguise my deep disappointment. I quickly realised that this was no way to enrol

[1] B'nai B'rith, a world-wide Jewish cultural and charitable organisation founded in 1843 in the USA by Jews mostly of German cultural origin.

> intellectual, educated, literary or cultured Jews who would take an interest in young Jews and become their leaders.

In the midst of his success with Bar Kochba and Habonim, Wellesley was summoned by Dr Selig Brodetsky.[1] Brodetsky told him what he already knew – that there was no budget for all his educational activities, which were uncalled for anyway. Brodetsky reminded Wellesley that he was assistant political secretary, ignoring the fact that Wellesley was persistently denied real involvement with the work in the political department. He then announced that Wellesley was to leave the services of the Jewish people, the World Zionist Organisation and Jewish Agency at the end of the month. Wellesley was too astounded to plead his own cause. Before picking up his salary cheque at the end of the month, he saw Weizmann and told him what had happened. Weizmann merely regretted his departure. In later years Wellesley had no doubts of the consequences of the short-sighted, blinkered, smug attitudes of these Zionist leaders.

> There was no budget for education in those days and of course we know perfectly well what the result of that has been. The tremendous dearth of Jews immigrating to Palestine from the English-speaking countries resulted very largely because no money, no facilities and no methods, apart from what we had done, were available for Jewish youngsters, who were offered very little of interest and who were rarely set an example by adult Jews who talked Zionism but remained where they were. Their sins of commission and omission have been paid for dearly by the modern state of Israel.

Unemployed, hurt and disillusioned with the WZO and its leaders, Wellesley decided to go back to Palestine. Rose was unwilling to go with him to cope with the material vicissitudes of re-establishing a home there, so she stayed in London with two-year-old Sharona.

[1]Professor Selig Brodetsky (1888–1954); mathematics professor at Leeds University; member of World Zionist Organisation's and Jewish Agency's Executives 1928–49; President of Board of Deputies of British Jews 1939–49; appointed President of Hebrew University of Jerusalem 1949.

1. Wellesley Aron with his mother, Agnes

2. Cambridge University Athletic Club, October 1919. Wellesley is in the centre of the back row with Harold Abrahams, the future Olympic gold medallist, seated in front of him (in singlet)

3. Wellesley the Scoutmaster, 1926

4. Wellesley with his first wife, Rose, on their wedding day, 21 March 1927

5. Major Wellesley Aron (centre) at the Consecration Service of the Unit Colours – British and Jewish – at Tahag in the Canal Zone, August 1941

6. With Moshe Sharett in Egypt, December 1941

7. Christmas Day in the desert, 1942. The officer with the Christmas tree, sitting on Major Aron's left, was the only Christian left in the Unit at the time

CHAPTER SIX

In Advertising

Wellesley had no idea what to do when he returned to Palestine. He wanted no more to do with the Zionist Organisation and had no confidence in himself as far as teaching was concerned. A chance meeting with an American who manufactured and exported porcelain false teeth gave him the idea of setting up on his own as an advertising PR consultant. The American acquaintance asked Wellesley to check through the English of a catalogue of his products which he had prepared for a dental exhibition in London. The American manufacturer was so pleased that he retained Wellesley as his advertising consultant. This gave him the idea of approaching other businesses and offering his services in the same field. He soon had enough retaining fees to tell Rose that she should return now because he could set up home again for her and their daughter. She returned to settle in at 13 Bialik Street. From then on Wellesley was virtually wholly occupied with surviving.

> My chief object was to do the work, get the money, pay my bills and get on to the next month. It was a great race against time and a great struggle and it certainly took it out of me. Life developed, I should add, with some difficulty because, for instance, although this seems incredible, I had to organise and run an advertising agency without a telephone. I had no telephone in my office, which was opposite the Post Office in Tel Aviv near the railway lines. I requested a telephone of course with many hundreds of other people who needed one urgently. Not knowing what to do and although most of my clients said they wanted to give me the business that they had, but couldn't do so because they couldn't get in touch with me and I couldn't be expected to go running to six or ten customers every day to find out if there was anything to do; apart from checking with the printers for urgent materials and scanning the newspapers to check advertisements and so on, it was almost impossible to carry on. Realising this I started a

one-man campaign in what was then the *Palestine Post*,[1] writing letters signed with different names from various parts of the country recording and recounting the difficulties these correspondents had everywhere in running and managing their businesses. I even suggested that 'we' form a club of applicants for telephones and that correspondence should be read at the public telephone booths, with excerpts from the government's replies to our applications as to why there was a shortage of telephones and so on. In other words, quite a campaign had developed.

Suddenly I had an invitation to go and see the chief postmaster in Jerusalem, a Mr Webster. In those days I rode a Norton, and I dashed up there and was wondering what on earth he wanted to see me about. As I went into his office, I saw a rather pleasant elderly looking man. He asked me to sit down and I saw on his desk a number of newspaper cuttings. I couldn't see them closely, but could recognise them as coming from the *Palestine Post*. He turned to me and asked me if I had any idea how these letters were reaching the *Post*. I asked him what letters. He handed them to me and I read them through with apparent interest and asked him what he wanted to know. 'Well,' he replied 'I'll tell you frankly, I wanted to thank whoever it is who is running that campaign.' I was flabbergasted. I said 'You really want to thank him?' and he went on 'I'll tell you why. The reason we have no phones to instal is that we cannot get a budget out of the chief secretary who sits on any money that the Palestine government has and puts it into the pension fund for his old age and the retirement of all the senior officials here. That is why nothing else is happening. I put in for one thousand telephones or five hundred urgently and I can get nothing out of him. But to my surprise, when I sent across these cuttings to him, he phoned me to say a further sum of money had been allocated for the Palestine Post Office to instal telephones because of the public uproar. He added that the public wouldn't stand for any more nonsense about the lack of telephones. So I want to thank you, because the man or woman who did this helped me in my job.' I admitted

[1] Palestine's English-language newspaper, renamed the *Jerusalem Post* after the state's establishment and still published today.

> that I was the author. He asked me what he could do for me. I said 'Well, of course, you can give me a telephone.' 'Right you've got that, any particular number?' he asked me. 'Yes,' I replied 'something suitable for an advertising agency, easy to remember.' I got my number and had it for many years in my office.
>
> I went out of my way to see that my customers were properly served and I soon acquired quite a growing clientèle among the leading companies, such as Shell Oil and the orange exporting company. I was appointed to be the Jaffa Orange advertising agency up to and right through the Second World War. I even did an advertising campaign for Ceylon tea throughout the rural areas of Egypt.

Wellesley came to understand that the Jews in Palestine had little scope to initiate political change. Rather, they became accustomed to react to the situations initiated by the Arabs. For example, only the strike by the Arabs stimulated the development of the north Tel Aviv port near the Yarkon river. The first cargo off-loaded at Tel Aviv came from a Greek ship whose captain had been bribed to take his cargo of cement first to Jaffa, where of course the striking Arabs refused to unload it. Eventually, they committed an act of recognised piracy by trying to cut the line between the ship and the lighter which it was towing to unload the cement cargo. This action gave the captain the legal right to unload elsewhere, which he duly did at the makeshift, primitive dock near Nachlat Binjamin. Wellesley heard the triumphant roars as the cement was landed and transported away.

After the 1936 White Paper,[1] riots and disturbances became increasingly frequent. The Paper recommended further restrictions on Jewish land purchases and immigration just at the time when Jews in Germany were becoming desperate for somewhere to go to escape Hitler's persecution.

> There were moments of unrest when Arab gangs organised assaults on Jewish settlements. We had to protect these communities, very often in the face of British opposition. An

[1]There were three British Government Commissions of Inquiry in pre-war Palestine; in 1922, 1930 and 1939. Each White Paper which followed diluted further the scope of the Balfour Declaration which had itself been incorporated into the League of Nations Palestine Mandate, given to Great Britain after the First World War.

example is the case in Rehovot. Rose's family had farmed there since the turn of the century when thirty or forty Russian Jews belonging to the Bilu movement[1] had settled there. It was called Duran then and was just an open area with two or three hillocks. My wife's father built the first stone house, and it was in there that all the women and children sheltered when the Arabs attacked. On another occasion, Arabs from Ramle tried to liquidate a new Jewish settlement and thousands of them started to march or run across the plain between Ramle and Rehovot. The amount of dust and noise and so on was enough to alert the farmers in Rehovot. The Haganah men, a couple of dozen able-bodied young Jews, armed with rifles, took up their positions on the hillside overlooking the plain and waited. One of them served in my unit during the war. He told me how they held their fire – there were only two of them in their position – until they could see the faces of the advancing Arabs clearly. When they opened fire the Arabs rushed away shrieking to high heaven, dropping the tins and sacks they carried to put their loot in. Arabs tried to infiltrate the edges of the Jewish settlement, but they were met with pitchforks wielded by the Jewish farmers to protect their families and homes. The Jews stopped the attack and the Arabs dispersed, whereupon the British police arrived. They looked around and said, 'Who's been firing rifles here?' Then they arrested the Jews concerned. It was with some difficulty that we got them released.

I heard another story when British policemen had arrested members of the Haganah who had been protecting the police from a crowd of hostile Arabs. The Haganah boys had a machine gun of sorts and when the Arabs finally ran off, the police turned on the Jews who had protected them and arrested them for being in possession of a machine gun. It was then illegal for Jews to have weapons, in spite of the dangers to which they were exposed. The incriminating evidence was, of course, the gun so they had to take it to pieces and drop the bits out of the window of the police vehicle which was carting them off to prison. When they arrived at police headquarters,

[1]Acrostic of 'Beit Ya'acov l'khu v'nelkha' – 'House of Jacob, come, let us go' (Isaiah, 2:5). A student and youth organisation founded in Russia in 1882 for immigration and settlement as farm workers in Palestine.

the evidence was not there. But that is the sort of cat and mouse game that was played with the British.

The situation deteriorated and I thought the time had come for me to say something. I got up at a Rotary Club meeting and made a plea for the establishment of a Home Guard. The chief of police, the district commissioner, judges and so on as well as leading Jewish citizens were all Rotarians. When I was finished I was asked by the police chief whether I would come and see him in his office as he was very much impressed. He thought the Jews ought to do something to protect themselves somehow. I said, 'It isn't only the Arab threat, I'm thinking about the possibility of another world war when our cities will be bombed from the skies and we have no civil defence of any sort.' He replied that if I would go and talk to the mayor, he would back us up and would somehow get equipment for us. I took up his suggestion and was elected to be one of the three men charged to run the organisation. Hundreds of Tel Aviv citizens enrolled. We had some training and were issued with batons, and arm bands, but I saw myself being tied down to being commander of the Home Guard and I didn't feel that it was my job.

As time went on, the political situation in the world deteriorated. Hitler had come to power in 1933 and the first indication I had of what he was doing was when there was a knock at my office door and I was told that there was a Mr Aron outside to see me. In came a rather stout young man with fair hair who announced that he was a second or third cousin of mine from Berlin and that he remembered my visit there. He recalled my prognostication at the time that he might learn some Hebrew and this he had done. I asked him what I could do for him. He told me that he had only arrived the night before, and that his wife, a Christian, had died in the early hours of the morning. He wanted to arrange her burial first and foremost. I did all that through the District Commissioner's office and then took him home. He said that he was one of the young men who had laughed at me some years ago in nineteen twenty eight or twenty nine when I was in Berlin with Weizmann because it sounded ludicrous that he should ever consider leaving Germany. 'My father was a jeweller', he went on, 'and I inherited the business and the Nazis came along and took everything from us, took my father away and have killed him probably in a camp. In fact the family has almost ceased to exist. I managed to get away and I have come to Palestine.' I asked him what he could do. He replied, 'The only thing I know how to do well is to blow the brass trombone. It was a hobby of mine in Berlin. I used to join bands occasionally and blow the trombone.' I thought to myself that it wouldn't be easy to find a place for a trombone player in Palestine at this particular time. There was no Israel Philharmonic Orchestra as yet and I didn't know what to do. Suddenly a bright idea came to me. I rang up the police band. The bandmaster was from Manchester, an English Jew and a very nice fellow. I asked him if he could do with a trombone player. He enquired why I asked this question. 'Well,' I said, 'a cousin of mine has just arrived from Germany and the only thing he says he can do is play the trombone.' He asked me if he was any good and of course I didn't know. So he told me to send my cousin up to Jerusalem with a chit from me and they would try him out.

My cousin went for his audition and Mr Silver, the bandmaster phoned me to say that he was a very good trombone player, but the trouble was he was an illegal immigrant and therefore the police band could not employ him. I assured him that we could soon deal with that if he would send him back to me. I explained, 'I'll get him to Beirut and you will arrange to get him an entry certificate and we'll bring him in as a trombone player.' That was what happened and my cousin's first job in Palestine was trombone player with the British police band. He went on from there to become an expert in mixing cocktails and served at the King David bar. Then he ran a restaurant for a while and finally, of all things, he became a highly qualified photographer at the Hadassah hospital, where he dealt with all sorts of technical photographs that had to be kept in the records.

One other German cousin of mine escaped death and reached Palestine. He got himself a job in Jerusalem in the Companies Registry. He worked in Israel's Foreign Ministry after independence and even served in Germany for a time.

Sometime in 1937 I again felt that I had to do something about the ever worsening situation. Once more I took the opportunity when I was at a meeting of my Rotary Club to express my views. I said that we should prepare in Palestine for the forthcoming world war in which England would be facing Hitler and Mussolini. The Mediterranean would be cut and we would be isolated. The members took it very well, but nothing happened. I decided to take the bull by the horns and I rang up General Wavell at British Headquarters in Jerusalem. I made an appointment to see him. At our meeting I told him that I had a plan in connection with the forthcoming war, which I reckoned would be on us within a couple of years. He agreed with me. I asked him what preparations were being made for this eventuality. He said, 'Unfortunately, nothing.' Well, I made my proposal and he was so impressed that he asked me to put it down on one sheet of paper so that he could forward it to the War Office in London. As I went out I saw two officers, both captains. One was the operations officer I think and the other was the intelligence officer. The intelligence officer turned out to be Captain Orde Wingate.[1]

I went straight back to the Jewish Agency and told Sharett[2] about the interview. He agreed to lend me a stenographer so that I could dictate my proposal and get it typed at once. As I was doing this the door opened and Reuven Shiloah, whom we all knew as Ben Gurion's hatchet man, came in. He was the Haganah's intelligence chief and he had with him someone he wanted me to meet. Through the door behind him came Captain Wingate still wearing his British army uniform. I was staggered and told Reuven that I had just seen the man in Wavell's office. He replied that he already knew that, that Wingate was a great friend of ours and wanted to meet me. We shook hands and he asked if there was an empty office where we could talk. He said that General Wavell had mentioned my plan to him, that he thought I was absolutely right, that he hoped it would get full support. He supported it wholeheartedly. I told him that the industrial potential of Palestine,

[1]Captain Orde Wingate (1903–44) made the Zionist cause in Palestine his own. To help the untrained, inexperienced Jews defend themselves against Arab attacks, he trained some 3,000 Jewish auxiliary guards in 'active defence'. His Jewish 'soldiers' became known as the Night Squads, and he was known amongst Jews as Hayedid, the friend.

[2]Moshe Sharett (Shertok) (1894–1965), head of Jewish Agency Political Department 1933–48; Foreign Minister for Israel 1948–56; Prime Minister of Israel 1953–55.

such as it was, should be harnessed to the war effort in England. I included Arab industries as well as Jewish ones. 'For example,' I informed him, 'in Nablus there is a soap factory and soap is always required by armies and there may be other things too. The point being that I don't only want to interest His Majesty's Government in war supplies. I think it is essential that a stockpile of basic materials of all sorts could be established in the Middle East and possibly in Palestine, so that when and if war broke out, there should be places where one could get what was absolutely essential for the continuation of the war effort and of everyday life.'

I took my one sheet of paper to General Wavell, who read it through and approved it. He took my telephone number in Tel Aviv and said he would let me know what happened. I took my leave of Orde Wingate too, but not before we had arranged to meet in Tel Aviv at my home. He visited us with his beautiful wife and we soon became friends. I heard nothing about my proposal for many weeks. I was impatient because I could see the months slipping by and knew that in a couple of years we would confront the problem which would involve a tremendous amount of improvisation unless it was taken in hand at once. Finally I went back to General Wavell and said that I would go to London myself to fight for my proposal. He gave me a very charming letter to General Ponnal which I presented in due course at the War Office.

Ponnal was an elderly general, a nice fellow, but he had no idea where this document of mine was. He looked for it and sure enough it was discovered in the in-tray of one of the majors on his staff. I went through the proposal with him. He explained, 'You know my hands are absolutely tied here. I can do nothing about this, although I think you're right. You had better go to the Ministry of War Production, or something of the sort.' I made an appointment with the director responsible for supplies who received me very nicely. 'Yes,' he began, 'I've read your proposal. Theoretically, it is very good, but of course it's ridiculous.' I asked him what was ridiculous about it. 'You can't produce the goods that we are turning out at anything like the price we are doing it here and now in England.' I replied, 'You know price is irrelevant, because you either want to have the stuff where you want it, when you want it or you don't. It's no good having cheap stuff in England available and not distributed where it's needed.' 'Well, I'm very sorry, I can't do anything about it. I can't see the use of setting up factories or supplies or anything else in the Middle East, when we are only now getting some war production going in England at last.' In reply to my request for some advice as to what to do next, he suggested that I go to see Hore-Belisha.[1] I tried to, but Hore-Belisha had flown off to Rome to see Mussolini.

It was nearly five weeks that I'd been in London, getting nowhere and seeing everybody I could. It was most frustrating. I told the minister's secretary that I was returning to Palestine. I asked him to write to me after he had duly considered my proposal, which I considered to be urgent. I left. In due course I received a letter in Tel Aviv from Belisha saying that while he agreed with me on all counts, there was nothing he could do at the moment. The budget wasn't there and the planning wasn't done yet; I should go back to the High Commissioner in Jerusalem and talk it over with him. This I did. I met Sir Harold MacMichael in the official residence outside Jerusalem, because he dared not occupy his office near the Damascus Gate in the Old City of Jerusalem. He was a dark, tall man who had spent a lot of time in the Sudan. He was very pro-Arab and very anti-Zionist, and I should think probably anti-semitic too. He didn't receive me with any cordiality, he just looked at me very keenly and said, 'I've got this report here. I can't understand why you're so interested.' I replied, 'On two counts at least. I'm a Jew and I'm a Zionist and I'm also an Englishman. All this mounts up to a very serious concern for the future of the British Empire and our relationship to it out in this part of the world. If Hitler and Mussolini declare war on England or vice versa, which I'm sure will happen, we will be isolated out here without any of the facilities required for waging war and winning it.' He conceded that I might be right, but didn't see why I should be wasting my time thinking about it. He said, 'I suppose you want to do it for profit. What do you want out of it?' I replied, 'As a matter of fact I am not doing it for any profit at all, but I won't object if there is a profit

[1] Leslie Hore-Belisha, First Baron (1893–1957). First chairman of the National Liberal Party 1931; Minister of Transport 1934; Secretary of State for War 1937–40; received a peerage in 1954.

involved in establishing industries in this part of the world. The Jews are very able and can improvise. Money can be found and I am sure that basic things required by the War Department can be produced here.' He agreed to appoint someone to carry out an industrial survey of the country. About a year later a report was produced, but it was very inadequate and unsatisfactory and nothing, *nothing* was done.

In 1936 Ylona, our second daughter, was born and it was nice to have a baby in the family again. Sharona enjoyed playing with her, but I was very busy by this time trying to help the British military establishment in any way I could. It was clear that there was going to be a garrison in Palestine and demands for various kinds of help were directed to me because they all knew me personally. I might add that I established a limited company to cater to this demand. We soon began to make considerable headway in the field of supplying the armed forces and it was a very profitable occupation because the competition was not very great and they were so delighted to have someone who could speak their language and who understood their requirements that they gave us all the available business.

As the number of British troops in Palestine increased, the Mandatary government decided that more leisure and civilian facilities for British personnel and their families were needed. Wellesley's company was asked to build a commercial centre including a cinema, shops and a club for the British forces and families. It is not clear whether or not the project was completed or even started, for in September 1939 war was declared. Wellesley scarcely hesitated.

Rose, you will have to understand that I can't sit by and watch Hitler overrun Europe and treat the Jews as he has been doing and destroy democracy wherever he finds it and taking the whole of the western world as his playground. I've got to get into this thing as a Jew, as an Englishman and as a Zionist.

He discussed his enlistment with Wavell's replacement, General Barker, who advised the thirty-eight-year-old Wellesley to go for the Royal Army Service Corps because his age would obstruct his entry to an infantry unit. He was eventually commissioned as a subaltern in the RASC.

CHAPTER SEVEN

The War – Beginnings

Wellesley has written a detailed account of his years in the British Army published in Hebrew and English with the title *Wheels in the Storm*. During the years 1939 to 1945 he had the opportunity to draw on all the resources of his English and Palestinian backgrounds as well as on his personal experiences with youngsters in the scout movement and Habonim. In the army he had the authority to implement his deeply held views as to how to bring out the very best of an individual's qualities in situations which, more often than not, were likely to produce exactly the opposite result. He has explained his approach to the very difficult problems encountered by Palestinian Jews, serving as volunteers in the British Army in the Middle East. Wellesley had the rare ability to recognise an individual's needs and at the same time meet the requirements of a larger organisation. He understood that the larger unit was only effective if the individuals who comprised it had their self-respect fostered by those in authority. His innate respect for people, already displayed in his work with the scouts in England and Palestine, with his school pupils in Palestine and with the Habonim youngsters in England, did not change when he very proudly took a commission in the British Army.

After a year or so of service, first behind the front lines and then in the advance northwards through the hottest parts of the North African desert, Captain Wellesley Aron was trapped, with his unit – 5MT (Works Services) Company – in Tobruk where they remained under constant aerial and artillery bombardment for several months until they were evacuated by sea to Egypt. During the siege Wellesley was promoted to the rank of major, thus becoming the senior Jewish officer enlisted in Palestine and the first to command a unit. At that time he was the only Jewish officer in the company. None of the NCOs were then Jews.

The whole of my life style had to change and I had to adjust myself to circumstances that I never envisaged. My promotion came about in the following manner. Since whoever had been ordered to replace our commanding officer, failed to report, the Deputy Director of Supplies and Transport (Tobruk) Lt. Col. Frencham of the Royal Australian Army Service Corps, A.I.F. under whose command we were, called me over to the cave in which his headquarters was situated and asked me how we were managing without a major. I replied that we were doing alright. He then said that he had decided to recommend me for my majority, and had signalled G.H.Q., M.E.F., by wireless to that effect. I said that I doubted whether his suggestion would be acceptable as there were surely still a lot of regulars in the R.A.S.C., M.E.F., or senior officers to me who would be awaiting promotion. His reply was that he would take on a bet with me that he would have his way. I was to provide a bottle of gin to celebrate my promotion when it came through. I said that to find a bottle of gin in Tobruk at that time was about as unlikely as my being promoted – but I accepted. A few days later I was reporting to his Staff Captain when Colonel Frencham called across and said, 'Do you know that you are improperly dressed?' I looked down at my battle dress and saw nothing wrong and told him so. Whereupon he got up, extended his hand and said 'Congratulations on your promotion, Major Aron – now where's the bottle of gin you promised?' He then removed the black Australian 'crowns' from the shoulder tabs of a jacket that was hanging up and removing my six brass stars from mine, fixed his 'crowns' on my uniform. His staff came up and shook hands with me and we arranged to celebrate that evening in the H.Q. cave.

I dashed back to my lines still incredulous, only to find my officers awaiting me and behind them the Company H.Q. staff all grinning and lining up to proffer congratulations. The army grapevine had relayed the news ahead of my arrival. I got hold of the Adjutant, Lieutenant Haines, and asked what he could do about a bottle of gin so I could honour my debt. He said he'd get busy, but didn't hold out much hope. We all knew that the only liquor in Tobruk by this time was the Chianti – red wine left by Graziani's army when it capitulated. At 17.30 hrs I happened to crawl into my dugout to get something, when lo

> and behold on my camp bed there reposed an unopened bottle of Gordon's Gin and beside it a packet of Player's cigarettes. I never could find out where these came from despite an earnest effort to repay the donor. As I walked into the Colonel's cave with my bottle, he saw me, turned to his staff and said, 'I told you – there's nothing these Palestinians can't get – when they put their minds to it.' It was a very pleasant, though rather noisy party disturbed by 'frightfulness' on the part of our ever present fleet of shrieking Stuka dive bombers. Thereafter, throughout another three months in the siege there was always a packet of 20 Player's cigarettes on my camp bed each day. My sincere thanks go to the donor who remains anonymous to this day.

Wellesley evidently found his changed position somewhat lonely, because his new rank and commanding position required a subtle change in the familiar friendships which he had enjoyed with his fellow-officers and men.

> A commanding officer's job is something like an iceberg. Much of it is invisible and beneath the surface. Within the unit he functions daily as the final arbiter in respect to countless decisions big and small. When it comes to the unit's relations with superior authority he must secure fair treatment and proper consideration, thus acting as a bulwark behind which the unit can operate to the best of its ability. Since, to his men, his word is law, he must deal with all comers without fear or favour, and must ensure that everybody under his command knows that justice will be done and that 'rank' will not be abused or exploited for irrelevant purposes.

Wellesley did not focus his attention on the army's needs to the exclusion of his anxiety for the safety of the civilian Jews left in Palestine, unarmed and totally exposed to German forces if the British withdrew to India, as was intended if Egypt fell. Knowing that his pre-war proposal to stockpile civilian and military supplies in Palestine had been ignored, he was particularly aware of the dangers faced by civilians at home. Later in the war he met a senior British officer who acknowledged that had Wellesley Aron's plan – submitted to General Wavell himself – been adopted, hundreds of lives would have been saved, for it would not have been necessary to ship millions of tons of supplies, many of which were sunk by enemy action, via the Cape of Good Hope route to the Middle East.

With his mind directed to the future of the Jewish community in Palestine, Wellesley took the chance to study the Jewish soldiers he commanded during the siege of Tobruk. After a month or two, he asked his senior colonel if he would transmit a memorandum to GHQ Middle East with particular reference to the problems which had arisen between the British NCOs and the Jewish personnel. Colonel Frencham agreed.

> My object was to provide some guidance, on the basis of experience, for those interested in the formation of Jewish units and recruiting in Palestine. I particularly emphasised the importance of care in the selection of officers and NCOs and the desirability of providing English personnel posted to such units with some knowledge as to the type of man they would have to command. …
>
> The problem of status and prestige for Jewish officers and NCOs had to be dealt with on lines for which there was little feeling and practically no tradition among the rank and file. So far as the Jewish officer was concerned, it was obvious to me that his primary duty was to set the tone and raise the morale of the men under his command. This was by no means an easy task. The Jewish soldier, finding himself in a strange and unknown environment was at first, and in fact for quite a long time, inclined to be over-sensitive.
>
> Leadership was called for to give the Jewish recruit the moral backing required to enable him to find some security of status in the alien conditions of the British Army. What the idea of Palestine had done to straighten the back of the ghetto Jew and raise his eyes from the ground enabling him to look the world fearlessly in the face as a free man, had also to be achieved for the Jewish soldier who found himself surrounded by a strange tradition and dressed in British uniform.
>
> The recruit is, in any army, very much at the mercy of those in authority. He is dependent for every privilege and every bit of freedom and goodwill on the understanding shown to him by his NCOs and officers within the framework of King's Regulations and the Army Act. Take, then, a Jewish recruit newly-enlisted in Palestine, speaking little if any English and

having perhaps already tasted the tyranny of Nazi rule and even the rigours of a concentration camp. He is indeed a vulnerable individual and obviously requires special handling. It is easy to see how needless bitterness was created by misunderstandings arising between a typical English NCO and a recruit of the type referred to.

Time after time, in the early days, distrust and dislike arose between the Jewish recruits and their English instructors. Disciplinary action almost invariably failed to improve matters, and in many cases tended to turn potentially good soldiers into men who, because they were not understood, gradually lost interest and gave up the struggle because the situation in which they found themselves looked hopeless. This was the point at which the Jewish officer had such a vital role to play. Apart from his regimental duties, it was for him to stand as a bulwark between his men and the inevitable causes of friction which tend to arise as between sections in a unit or between units and various authorities with whom they are in contact. It was for him to assist in creating an atmosphere of efficiency and harmony within the limits of his authority. He must act as a go-between and a buffer where contact with other units and formations was concerned, and by his bearing convince his men that so long as they did their job they need fear no let or hindrance and would at all times receive the utmost support available. In running a Jewish company, the problem of the individual became a group problem. There had been several attempts at different interpretations as to the characteristics which should be aimed at in a Jewish Palestinian unit. To me the question had always been perfectly simple and clear, and I consistently followed a definite policy in an attempt to develop this concept as a living reality.

To my mind, the first pre-requisite of an O.C. is that he must have complete confidence in the men under his command. It is only on the basis of such confidence that he can hope to evoke the confidence of his men in himself. It is a very natural question of action and reaction, for confidence breeds confidence as proved in my experience in command of Jewish troops. This confidence must take forms easily understood and recognised, either consciously or unconsciously, by every man who displays an intention of contributing something to the common cause. Where Jewish personnel were concerned, Hebrew was of prime importance in the Palestinian unit.

Enlistment into the British Army by Palestinians was a purely voluntary act, and the Jewish recruit appeared in his squad with a status as yet undefined, his strength or weakness unproved, his characteristics unknown, but his idiosyncrasies largely disliked. He had no state to support him, enlisted in a country going through a process of reconstruction, had recently been a wanderer, probably persecuted in Europe, where he had been regarded as an everlasting problem in the body politic. By joining the British Army he freely offered his services and, if need be, his life for the common cause. What could he look forward to as a sustaining force from day to day in the difficulties and dangers and boredom which are the usual lot of every soldier serving in time of war? What forms and what tradition could he find to express his natural self-esteem and to remind him that he was not a mere hireling, giving his day's labour in return for very inadequate pay? It was necessary to find some suitable form through which he could express his particular ideals as an individual and as part of a group, as a man as well as a soldier.

A Palestinian Jewish unit in many ways constituted a microcosm of Jewry. It contained representatives from every country in the 'Galut'[1] and types of men from every walk of life and a large variety of backgrounds. In an average Jewish unit enlisted in Palestine, it was possible to find up to twenty different languages or more, and it was not uncommon that individual drivers could speak, read and write between three and four. It was thus essential to encourage and develop the use of Hebrew as the living language by which the Jew from Yemen (whose mother tongue was Arabic), and the man from Salonica (whose mother tongue was Spaniolit) or the Polish Jew, from the Yiddish-speaking areas, might converse freely and on equal terms. Hebrew became, in fact, the living symbol of unity around which the corporate life of the unit began to develop. It proved itself the rallying point for the best elements among the men, who with Hebrew as the symbol, took their stand and found the necessary inspiration for building up the fighting spirit and devotion to a common cause. Hebrew

[1] The Jewish communities living outside the state of Israel (then Palestine).

became the instrument by which the process of renaissance developing in many walks of life in Palestine itself would from then on also include the military sphere.

The English language, for obvious reasons, played and continued to play a substantial part in the daily life of the unit, but, on the other hand, for all cultural group and communal activities the currency was Hebrew. Secular and religious celebrations were invariably conducted in Hebrew with dignity and decorum in their due seasons. In all groups organised on a military basis, the influence of the officers, and particularly that of the officer commanding, will obviously always be preponderant, but in a Jewish unit there are often groups of intelligent and public-spirited men whose influence for good can prove of basic importance in maintaining the tone of the rank and file. These elements must, however, enjoy the confidence and have the constant support of the O.C. For this purpose a cultural committee, 'Vaadat Hatarbut', was formed which undertook all the arrangements in connection with the Friday evening concerts and other unit functions of a religious or secular character. These activities must necessarily be of a voluntary nature, so that the committee was allowed a practically free hand, and almost without exception proved equal to the very considerable responsibilities which rested on its members. Jews, rather more so than others, 'cannot live by bread alone'. It was thus essential to develop a full group life covering a large variety of activities from sport to music, discussion circles, dramatics, and social functions on all and every occasion within the limits set by varying conditions of service. The Jewish soldier, more than most people, was desirous of understanding the why and wherefore of his duties, and once he grasped that his life was being planned for him according to some rational programme, his doubts and criticisms tended to die away, and he settled down to routine peacefully and normally. That restlessness which is a heritage from generations of homeless wandering gradually gave way to quiet poise and a constructive attitude which enabled him not only to get on with the job in hand but also to build soundly for the future.

As far as the officers' mess was concerned, it was always my intention to develop specifically Jewish characteristics and an atmosphere of its own. Within six months of leaving Tobruk I was able to implement it. This meant that certain outward forms would have to be revived and it was not possible or desirable to institute these until a sufficient number of Jewish officers had been commissioned and posted to the unit. It became clearer, and especially so in the rigours of the siege of Tobruk, that outward forms are important whenever groups of men combine for a common purpose. By and large it can be asserted that the Jewish soldier possessed many of the characteristics of his English comrades in arms. He was adaptable, full of initiative, and cheerful. On the whole, however, he inclined to fluctuate rapidly between optimism and depression and often in a quite unwarranted manner on the basis of some rumour, since the Jew has been trained by generations of persecution to live with 'his ear to the ground'.

Army discipline though alien as a system to the Jew (whose history in the Diaspora had long since been cast into a communal democratic mould) was no real problem in a Jewish unit, provided that it was applied with care and respect for the fundamental principles of justice. It is true that a certain number of the men had previously been trained in the Haganah or Supernumerary Police in Palestine during the disturbances. But these were a small proportion of the total recruits and their previous experience in such organisations did not necessarily give them any status or authority within the unit. A number of them, however, soon found their level and became NCOs.

Experience showed that the Jewish NCO could develop a gift for leadership very rapidly, provided that his authority was strictly endorsed by his officers on whose support he had to rely, and, if properly trained, to apply his power of command in an intelligent and tactful manner. There was generally ample material among the men with sufficient power of leadership required for NCO rank, and by relatively rapid stages every post from L/Cpl. to Sergeant Major was soon to be filled by the Jewish personnel of the unit. In a well-run company, one which is contented and happy in itself, the incidence of 'crime' should be very low. As the unit developed into an autonomous Jewish organism this fact emerged more and more clearly.

5MT Company, RASC, was besieged in Tobruk for four months before evacuation by sea to Egypt. During that time the artillery and air bombardment was almost continuous. Wellesley's unit was one of the last to be evacuated and his own account movingly records the courage and endurance of the soldiers in his command. The experience strengthened Wellesley's conviction that his role was not just to act as a conduit for orders from above, but was primarily to serve as a representative for his men. This was the way, he had no doubt, to ensure that the men would give of their best qualities for the war effort. Whatever fears he may have had for the possible adverse consequences to his own army career and popularity, he never failed to stand up for what he believed to be just. A fine illustration of this is his account of his return to Tahag, the mobilisation centre in Egypt for the Royal Army Service Corps.

> It was almost seven months since we had seen civilians in anything but a battle area, and four months since we had seen any other human beings except soldiers armed to the teeth and clad in khaki and steel helmets. We suddenly realised how much we had missed feminine company and the sound of children's voices. It takes a siege in the desert to make one conscious of such things.
>
> . . . I naturally asked that the Company be given leave, and was told that the men could have seven days in Cairo before we started re-forming. I patiently explained that with the exception of a few English sergeants and officers, everybody in the Company naturally wished to go home on leave to Palestine. The reply I was given was that there was no hope of anything of the sort, since fourteen days' notice was required according to the regulations, and that only parties of ten at a time would be allowed to proceed to Palestine. I am afraid my reaction to this came as a surprise to the DAQMG who must have recognised the danger signal in my eye, for after I had expressed myself unmistakably about those who sat at the base in relative comfort and their attitude towards Desert Rats fresh from Tobruk, I was told that my views would be immediately transmitted to higher authority. The next day I received a most friendly and quite unorthodox letter stating that all the conditions I had asked for concerning leave had been agreed to, and that the Company was given permission to

proceed immediately to Palestine in two parties for ten days' home leave.

We arrived in Palestine to find, much to our surprise, that the name 5MT Company, RASC, was a household word, and that the Yishuv had been watching us at a distance with some pride and considerable anxiety. '5MT' was known to everybody, it appeared, and I personally found it quite embarrassing to walk down the streets of Tel Aviv and to be greeted by unknown people who would walk up and shake my hand in a most friendly manner. I have no doubt that the veterans of Tobruk soon adapted themselves happily to the new and unfamiliar role which they had to assume quite unexpectedly, for I could see them in cafés and at street corners surrounded by admiring circles of friends listening open-mouthed to the stories they had to tell.

. . . The change from life at Tobruk to the atmosphere of home and family was so sudden that to many of us it appeared quite unreal. And it certainly took me the best part of my ten days' leave to realise that I was actually back at home. Quite a considerable effort was needed to register the varied and colourful aspects of normal life from which we had been separated for so long. Only seven months had passed, and yet it felt far more. Most of one's friends continued a normal peace-time life and seemed to be doing well at their business or professions, quite untouched by the war. Between them and ourselves, there was, in fact, an unseen but nevertheless palpable gulf – we lived in two very different worlds and would continue to do so until the war was over. Try as one would to ignore it, there were moments, often in a pause in the conversation, when the feeling arose in one's mind that no civilian would ever truly understand the significance nor get the true flavour of the life we were living. The fact was that we were no longer civilians; we had become soldiers not only by virtue of the uniform we wore, nor by the particular framework in which we lived – it even went much deeper than that, for we had indeed passed through a period of personal revolution, which had given us new and peculiar standards, and an outlook on life in general which no civilian could ever entirely share.

When the men returned from leave, 5MT was posted to Qena in Upper Egypt, where conditions were somewhat more favourable than they had been in Tobruk for Wellesley to implement some of his ideas to create a specifically Jewish ethos. Visitors to the camp were usually impressed by what he managed to accomplish in a very short time.

> To many of our visitors a Palestinian Unit came as quite a surprise. They were very well impressed with the camp, and particularly with the officers' mess. There were still English officers in the unit, but gradually, as the months went by, they were posted away and replaced by Jewish officers. For the first time, Hebrew began to be used in conversation in the mess, and it was made plain to English officers that no discourtesy was meant thereby. Every Friday evening 'kiddush' was said before dinner, and the candles lit at sunset. Thus, bit by bit, an attempt was made to create a specifically Jewish atmosphere in the mess, and our various Christian members and friends who visited us often commented on the home-like and pleasant tone which pervaded the officers' lines.
>
> On one occasion we were inspected by a colonel from Cairo who spent five days with the unit and investigated every detail of our life and activity, checked our equipment, and personally spoke to most members of the unit. At the end of that time, he said to me, 'I had no knowledge of what I was going to see when I came down here, and I was not particularly looking forward to the experience. I am now going to draft a report on your Company and I may as well tell you at once that I have been most favourably impressed. I knew from the first moment I entered your mess tent for breakfast that you had a good unit here, because it is an infallible rule that when the tone of the officers' mess is good, the unit is alright.' By dint of determined attacks on the fly scourge we had literally managed to eliminate flies from our camplines. And when the GOC visited me he exclaimed, 'My A.D.M.S. who inspected you last week, told me how surprised he was that there were no flies in your camp – he must have brought that one down here himself!' It was soon possible to arrange for leave parties to Palestine at regular intervals, and this was greatly appreciated by all ranks.

Another element in the development of the Unit's *esprit de corps* was the Unit Magazine, which led in turn to the establishment of a Unit Benevolent Fund. The idea for such a fund was aired in the magazine, which was produced in Hebrew with a small English supplement, in December 1941. When the Unit's committee of NCOs and other ranks had formulated their proposal Wellesley visted GHQ, BTE to get official recognition for the fund to be treated on the same lines as those of Regimental Institutes. The Brigadier replied that the proposal was purely an internal one which the OC could supervise. The Unit's sister company 6MT (Works Services) had a similar proposal, but its commanding officer Major H. Joffe had widely different views about his role as commander of a Jewish Palestinian unit. He and Wellesley epitomised two fundamentally different perceptions of the potential in human beings.

> Major Joffe and I later had a long discussion as to the objects of the Fund, and an argument developed as to whether it was to be used for purely philanthropic purposes or, (as I maintained) if it grew sufficiently, it should be used for attempting permanent resettlement of Jewish ex-soldiers in Palestine, preferably on the land, as farmers.
>
> During the whole of our period at Qena, our sister company was based on the Canal Zone with detachments busy helping in the construction of what proved to be the vital El Alamein fortifications, 40 miles west of Alexandria. 6MT was run according to a policy which in many ways was diametrically opposed to the one I had tried to establish since taking over the command. A good deal of mutual criticism was generated by the adherents of the two differing schools of thought. I therefore find it difficult to give an entirely objective analysis of the policy followed at that time in 6MT, but as far as one could judge, the tendency was towards what might be described as an English 'Regular' RASC Company, with the emphasis on rigid disciplinary action for formal breaches of King's Regulations, the regarding of 'Regimentalism' as an end in itself, and the encouragement of the tough-minded elements in the Company and their promotion to positions of influence and rank. There was for a long time little question of any particularly Jewish characteristics being infused, in addition to the purely military attributes. In 5MT on the other hand, an

attempt was made to attune the life of the Company in every way to that of the Yishuv, since we were volunteers and not regular soldiers, and a constant appeal was made to the men, calling for devotion to the Cause for which they had enlisted.

It had always been my view that no unit can be really efficient unless the men composing it are at peace with themselves, have plenty of self-confidence, and a clear understanding of the role they are playing in the great epic of War. 5MT was accused by its detractors as having a good deal of the spirit of a co-operative society or kibbutz about its general make-up. The fact that there was relatively little or no 'crime' and that on average 'Orderly Rooms' took place only once or twice a week was taken as proof that the officers and NCOs either had no authority or were afraid to use it. The creation of a cultural committee with a great deal of autonomy seemed to our critics to indicate the presence of a form of 'soviet' which they thought dictated policy, promotions, and the life of the company in general. At a distance, and based, no doubt, on the rather over-enthusiastic reports from men of the company, the impression created was undoubtedly that of a paternalistic and rather sentimental regime, which might breed intellectuals and unpractical idealists, but would certainly not engender the fighting spirit inspiring a unit to stand up to danger and physical exhaustion in the field. Furthermore, the kind of 'honour discipline' (which our critics misguidedly considered was exclusively being applied in 5MT) was not likely, they thought, to survive any sort of crisis such as units frequently pass through due to boredom and impatience with the very unromantic work on which all soldiers spend the major portion of their lives.

In actual fact, the truth was very different from the picture painted. At no time was 5MT any less regimental when this quality was called for. The discipline was excellent and the prestige and authority of the officers and NCOs never at any time fell short of the requirements. What was a fact, however, was the application of a considered and stubbornly pursued policy designed to inspire each man with a feeling of satisfaction and pride in his own personal contribution to the spirit of the unit and the achievements and good name of the Company as a whole.

> This policy proved itself an unqualified success as demonstrated by the manner in which the unit faced and surmounted the varying tests encountered at different times and places. By endeavouring to ensure that every man capable of contributing to the life of the unit was given an opportunity to do so, by removing purely formalistic obstacles wherever these were a hindrance to the development of initiative in the men, a tremendous surplus of energy was gradually released and canalized into constructive channels which found an outlet in the cultural life of the unit and the development of the *esprit de corps*, enabling the unit to give of its best at all times and whenever called upon. In any group of men under whatever form of discipline, there is always a limit as to what can be achieved merely by issuing orders. Anything that lies beyond the limits of routine and ordinary day-to-day work must largely depend on the sense of responsibility and good will of the rank and file. If the men are not interested or personally concerned in developing the group life of their unit and creating the necessary institutions for its expression, all the orders issued in connection with such matters are valueless and produce no effect. If such matters were relevant to the average unit, how much more so in a Jewish unit, composed of soldiers from a dozen countries of differing backgrounds. Without emphasis on the Jewish common denominators to rally all elements, such a unit would eventually develop into a sort of 'foreign legion', with the spirit of a group of mercenaries.

Wellesley's stubborn pursuit of his deeply held convictions was revealed in many, many different ways. His integrity was unbreachable whatever conditions he encountered. He never became a cipher for his superior officers; he could not be manipulated by ranks beneath his; he never lost sight of his own motivations in volunteering for the British Army as a Jew, an Englishman and a Zionist. He was perhaps helped by having no Jewish background of his own to serve as an immutable model. He had to think everything out for himself from first principles, untrammelled with personal family 'rights and wrongs' about Jewish festivals and rituals. So as each year went by he developed ever fuller ways to celebrate ancient events. His description of Passover 1942 reveals his thoughtfulness and originality.

> Passover, 1942, was a very happy and peaceful affair. By special arrangement we managed to get the whole unit together at Qena and had the pleasure of several civilian visitors from Palestine and Cairo whose first, and, as they said, most inspiring experience this was of contact with a Jewish unit in the field. Out in the desert a large square was formed by all the Company's vehicles parked facing inward. The vehicles were bedecked with palm leaves and greenery and within the square stood the long tables, to seat 600, covered with white linen and decorated with flowers. In the centre, Workshops had erected three large electric lamps which floodlit the assembly and were arranged to resemble a palm tree, covered with foliage and an artificial flower bed at its base. An entrance to the square between the vehicles was built to resemble an archway and carried a large banner with blue lettering welcoming the visitors, and at either extremity, the Zionist colours. I found the whole company standing silently beside the tables as I led our guests in, and could not help recalling the contrast between the atmosphere pervading this Pesach and the one before, in Tobruk. Ruth Kluger who was in Egypt on behalf of the Jewish Agency in an attempt to raise funds to ransom Jews in eastern Europe, was our only lady visitor. She lit the candles and said the blessing, after which I welcomed the visitors and spoke to the company on the subject of 'Freedom'. Mr Chaim Zadikoff, who had done a great deal for the unit in Cairo in connection with obtaining amenities, replied for the guests, and portions of the Haggadah were read in turn by a representative of every different type of Jew in the company. The evening passed quickly, and looking around at the jolly faces of the men and listening to their songs, one could feel how much progress had been achieved in welding the personnel into a homogeneous group.

The low level of crime in the unit was viewed, not with approval but with suspicion in HQ Cairo. Copies of the daily charge sheets were sent to the Area DAQMG as a matter of routine. One day Wellesley was ordered to report to Cairo, several hundred miles away. A major in the Gordon Highlanders confronted him.

> He told me he had been examining the charges preferred against the men in my unit over several months and was highly

dissatisfied with the punishments I had given them. . . . He said they were far too lenient and completely out of line with established practice. If I continued in this way he would have to draw the attention of the deputy Director of Supplies & Transport to what he regarded as unwarranted leniency which would adversely affect the discipline of my men. In reply I asked him if he knew anything about them. I then proceeded to explain that my Company was not composed of British troops. 'Furthermore,' I said, 'do you know who I am?' He shook his head. 'I am a Jew and that is why I was put in command of this unit. I understand my men and their problems. They are different in many ways from other troops and if you will look at the charge sheets you will see that I am right.' 'In what way?' he asked. 'Take drunkenness – for instance. How many charges have I had?' 'No idea,' he replied. 'Well, I'll tell you,' I said. 'Since this company has been formed and since I've commanded it we've had exactly one case. Now compare that with any British unit and you'll see what I mean. Most of the charges you'll find are minor ones except for traffic offences of various kinds – particularly driving and exceeding the speed limit or causing damage to W.D. property through accidents. You'll notice an occasional case of insubordination brought by an NCO. Also you'll find charges for loss of W.D. property, equipment or being improperly dressed. Taking it all in all I should say we had a very good record, in fact as good, if not better, than most units.'

The DAQMG took up the file of charges again, 'You don't seem to dock their pay much do you?' 'No', I replied, 'that's one thing I try not to do especially where married men are concerned.' 'Why?' he asked. 'Do you know what rates of pay and allowances Palestinians get?' I asked in my turn. 'No.' 'Well, I'll tell you. Maltese rates. That means less than enough for a family to keep body and soul together. I will not deduct pay as a punishment. My wife is on the welfare committee in Jerusalem, I know what a problem it is for these families, for wives to give their children an education and so on. I hear regularly of the real suffering of these families if they live in the cities – and are not members of a kibbutz.' What was a kibbutz? Well life's a bit short to explain all this at one session. I simply said if there were no further comments I thought the subject was pretty well exhausted. The DAQMG appeared to agree – and I departed fairly certain in my mind that the matter was closed as far as Cairo Area was concerned. It was.

CHAPTER EIGHT

With the Eighth Army – Tobruk and Malta

CHANUKA AND CHRISTMAS 1942

5MT together with four other Jewish RASC units went with the Eighth Army advance into North Africa. In December 1942, Wellesley and his unit found themselves back in Tobruk. Rabbi Rabinowitz, the chaplain to the Jews serving in the British Army in North Africa, suggested a joint chanuka celebration. 5MT undertook to arrange it.

> There were four RASC Jewish units in Tobruk, and the normal number of detachments of other arms, all of whom got wind of what was taking place, so that on the night itself there were about 1500 Jewish Palestinian officers and men assembled in the improvised hall we had built. It was constructed out of the skeleton framework of some German huts to which we added our vehicles to form an area large enough to house everybody. The ceremony was particularly impressive, because of the associations of the place. Nearly two years before, within a few hundred yards of where the service was held, the first small group of inexperienced Jewish soldiers had met to discuss Passover arrangements for the Jewish personnel of 5MT (Works Services) Company. Looking round the packed place with the large electric menorah radiating brightness and hope, one realised how much had been achieved and how much easier life had become.
>
> ... We still had one non-Jewish officer in the Company, Lieutenant Ewen, who had repeatedly asked to remain with us, because he liked our life and got on very well with the men. A day or so before Christmas, I suggested that he contact his padre, who was on the staff of our particular group of units, in order to ascertain what Christmas services were going to be held in the field, in our vicinity. The padre (C of E) whose duty

(and obvious pleasure) it was to attend to the spiritual well-being of our group of RASC units, had already made our acquaintance in early December at Capuzzo. In point of fact, I personally met him as I was in the somewhat unmilitary act of bending down to pick a desert crocus which lay in my path, and whose unexpected beauty and appearance in the wastes of Cappuzo had shocked me out of the usual brooding mood associated with desert life. I looked up to find a cheery smile on the face of Padre M., who seemed equally surprised to see a rather stern-looking field officer engaged in this silent communion with nature, and we introduced ourselves.

It was during the most hectic days of the great advance, and the constant roar of mechanical man on the move amidst clouds of dust, gave an impression of the migration of a people – rather like the hordes of Asia moving across the Tibetan wastes – ever westward.

We lived like true nomads – a night here, a couple of days further on, picking up tents and structures of Italian or German designs, using them for a span and then jettisoning them as something more practical turned up. The atmosphere of roar and rush and strain was ever with us. Convoys would loom out of the dust storms, picking their way dexterously among our lines, guns and limbers, tanks and carriers, staff cars and motor cycles, all heading forward, would swerve and swirl around our mess, leaving great pockets of crumpled sand to blow into the temporary structures as each fresh gust of wind burst in under the tent flaps.

And one night Padre M. dined with us – it was the Eve of Sabbath – and the candles were somehow lit and the kiddush recited, and he beamed acknowledgment at this miraculous cleaving to tradition in the midst of alarums and excursions. We all liked him and he us. After dinner we played the Mendelssohn Violin Concerto on our portable gramophone, and thus discovered a fresh bond of friendship and common interest.

Christmas Day found us at Benghazi with seas of mud, vehicles axle deep in clay, and tents flooded and a tearing wind uprooting our temporary quarters. We decided to entertain Lieutenant Ewen ourselves, for he had evidently not made any arrangements to join in other Christmas celebrations. Thus, despite the appalling weather, our faithful mess corporal, Corporal Lucacz, a Hungarian Jew, produced a small Christmas tree decorated with cotton wool snow, silver paper, sweets and candles. There it stood that Christmas night 1942 and in front of it a picture postcard in colour of the Madonna and Child, and on either side the various gifts we had purchased and bartered in Benghazi, a silver cigarette case, fountain pen and odds and ends in the 'goody' line. Our Christian brother officer was, needless to say, as amazed and touched by the whole *mise-en-scène* as we were, that bleak and black night 'in the blue'. Toasts were drunk and compliments exchanged with due formality, shot through with real and lasting affection.

Next day Lieutenant Ewen, who at my insistence had attended the Christmas Day Church Parade at 8th Army HQ, told everybody that he reckoned that he'd had 'the finest Christmas party in the Eighth Army'. Padre M. came around with the Colonel to return in person the greetings we had sent all units in the column on behalf of their Jewish comrades. As we sat chatting to the accompaniment of squelching gum boots and the drip, drip, drip of rain on the sodden tablecloth, the Padre turned to me and unfolded his plan for the establishment of a road-side chapel nearby, where, as he said, soldiers might pause a moment in their toil and sweat and spend a little time in the presence of higher things.

'Would you', he asked, 'help me in this scheme? I know you are of a different faith, but I feel you will understand the need for which I am catering.' I was, of course, rather taken aback, but immediately assented and said how gratified we felt by this request, which evinced the spirit of co-operation which underlay our unity of effort. I asked for particulars – not being au fait with the appurtenances required for the chapel in question. Having obtained a list of what was wanted . . . I detailed our mess corporal, whose fame for acquiring all manner of things was already legendary in the unit. I warned the Padre that I could not vouch for the orthodoxy of style or type as far as the equipment for the proposed C of E chapel was concerned. In fact, I definitely implied that the corporal's tastes (coming as he did from Hungary with its close affiliation to Byzantium on matters spiritual) would veer towards the ornate and variegated Sanhedrin of the early Christian fathers, rather than the simplicity of the post-Reformation established Church of England.

With that casual warning, arrangements were completed, and in due course the corporal returned and reported to me. I must state that he was quite a unique character, versatile to a degree, and competent in everything he undertook (with the exception of learning Hebrew – which was absolutely beyond him – and I had to capitulate in this particular struggle, so we conversed in French and German).

'Well,' I enquired of Corporal Lucacz, 'Did you deliver to the Padre what he asked for?' Clicking his heels and without a glimmer of a smile, he replied, 'Oui, mon commandant, naturellement. Bei mir kann er Jesus en gros haben . . .'

And here is the epilogue:

Padre M. came around that evening and this is what he told us: 'As I was having a stand up bath in my tent, there was a knock on the tent pole and your corporal's head appeared around the flap. "Padre", he said, "I have all for you." And before I could even don a towel, a life-size figure of Our Lord was thrust into my arms. There followed in quick succession a whole galaxy of major and minor ecclesiastical celebrities, some large and some small, highly painted with flaming haloes, shepherds' crooks and pedestals. Candelabra and incense burners and I know not what accumulated around me.'

There he stood, nude and helpless in his canvas tub, receiving this theological treasure trove from the battered ruins of some bombed-out shrine in the area. And finally, with a magnificent gesture to complete a job carried out to the letter, if not strictly in accordance with the spirit, our corporal handed him the 'Sacred Heart' flashing scarlet in the flickering light of the hurricane lamp. Shivering with cold and clutching this emblem of eternal travail to his naked bosom, the Padre stood in what space was left to him in his now overcrowded tent. Corporal Lucacz saluted smartly and marched out.

Needless to say, most if not all of the appurtenances were duly returned and handed back to the Roman Catholic authorities in Benghazi for safe keeping, and the roadside chapel was apparisoned with the meagre regalia required by the traditions of the Church of England. For several weeks it provided opportunity for solace and spiritual sustenance to many soldiers then engaged in chasing Rommel out of Africa.

MALTA

Wellesley's unit left Tripoli on 3 May and became the first Eighth Army unit to appear in Malta. They formed part of the first convoy of troops to arrive in Malta since the blitz had started.

> By 10 o'clock we had moored alongside the quay and from our position could see the vast amount of damage caused by the incessant bombing. The quantity of shipping sunk was quite apparent from the wreckage, and the harbour installations were a mass of twisted metal among the debris of sheds and buildings that lined the harbour front.

The contrast between conditions in Malta and the North African desert could hardly have been more extreme. Vehicles had to be driven on the left-hand side of the road – English style – through very narrow lanes bordered with high stone walls. In spite of the danger posed by the continuing air raids, there was no space to disperse the Unit's lorries and other transports, which made the Unit's precious equipment vulnerable to destruction from one direct hit. The Army's dress regulations were strictly enforced and resulted in the Unit's soldiers being regularly held up by the Military Police. The troops were also subject to the civilian police authority and had to share their quarters with Maltese citizens, many of whom had become homeless as a result of the Luftwaffe's successful bombing campaign. Wellesley's men took a couple of weeks to adjust and were then fully occupied transporting ammunition, petrol and other supplies to the docks for transfer to the Eighth Army which was taking part in the invasion of Sicily. When this period of intense activity was over and it became clear that they were not going to be included in the invasion of Italy, boredom became the Unit's enemy.

> In order to counteract the boredom, an effort was made to reorganise the cultural work in the Company. We introduced into the Friday evening programme items like the 'Brains Trust', mock trials and general knowledge quizzes. These resulted in a slight recrudescence of interest, but there was a

> good deal of lethargy apparent on all sides, the men obviously preferring to get away in the evenings to their civilian friends, rather than participate in Unit activities. A weapon training wing was again organised and with the assistance of Command H.Q. realistic exercises were staged by the whole Company, as well as by platoons, with the use of blank ammunition, smoke, etc.

At the end of July Wellesley handed over to his second-in-command, Captain Sacharov, and left for 28 days' special leave in Palestine. His family had no advance warning and were surprised and highly delighted when he arrived in Haifa. He toured the Jewish communities again, relating the Unit's experiences in an effort to stimulate recruitment to the British Army as he had done two years earlier. He became more aware of the reasons for the reluctance of most Palestinian Jews to do this and on his return to Malta it was arranged for him to dine privately with Brigadier McCandlish of the General Staff to discuss the problem.

> The relative failure of a continuous recruiting movement in Palestine was discussed and I enumerated the many reasons for the lack of response. Among the points raised was the question which had in the past caused so much feeling, both in the units and among the general public – the matter of the right of Jewish units to carry and fly the Jewish national colours. It was at this particular time that a specific order had been given for the Jewish colours not to be flown. This was regarded as an affront by every Jewish soldier and resulted in numerous incidents affecting morale and discipline, and repercussions were naturally felt in Palestine and provided another excuse not to enlist . . . To the Brigadier's argument that permission to fly the colours would provide us with a status to which we were not politically entitled, I replied that it was a status of this sort for which we were striving and to which we felt we had every right.
>
> Another point discussed was the question of utilising Jewish Palestinian units in combatant roles. The fact that battalions of the Palestine regiment and units of the Technical Service were, apparently deliberately, to be retained in backward areas, resulted in considerable disgruntlement and disappointment among all ranks in such units. This was a constant source

of complaint among the Palestinians, who regarded themselves as equal in their combatant qualities to their comrades in whatever other arms or formations, and considered their continuous use on the L of Cs as a reflection on their military qualities and lack of appreciation of their desire to participate actively on the field of battle.

. . . For over a year there had been talk of endeavouring to group the Jewish RASC companies into some sort of independent formation. From the point of view of internal efficiency this was an obvious step to take and would, had it been carried out, undoubtedly have obviated many difficulties with personnel, promotions, and general policy connected with the life of the units. This matter I also discussed, and attempted to show that even this had repercussions on recruiting, since the conclusion drawn by the rank and file and the public at large was that the refusal to create an independent command was an unjustified frustration.

In Cairo I also visited the chief base censor, who, during my absence from the Unit, had informed us that the company magazine would no longer be passed for dispatch to relations and friends in Palestine. After a close examination of the position, and after my giving a personal guarantee regarding the policy and contents of this publication, he agreed to raise the ban on the basis of certain fixed 'Censorship Stops'. A day later I again took plane and passed over the desert to Benghazi, where we landed for twenty minutes at the aerodrome close to where we had camped some six months previously, and reached Malta the same afternoon.

Shortly after my return, Captain Sacharov was posted to 462, our sister company on the island, and took over command. This meant that every Jewish Palestinian RASC unit was under the command of a Jewish major, and in a way it was the end of the epoch which had begun in the autumn of 1940.

The forty Maltese Jews were overjoyed by the arrival of the Palestinian units. They provided generous hospitality to the desert weary soldiers. In turn the units organised services and celebrations for the New Year and Day of Atonement festivals in autumn 1943. Some 500 Jews, soldiers and civilians, dined together, including American Jewish troops and British Jewish soldiers, sailors and

RAF personnel from the many different units on Malta at that time. Ever mindful of his vision to educate Jewish children so as to awaken in them consciousness of their past and future in Palestine, Wellesley called a meeting of Maltese Jewish parents to talk to them about forming a Habonim movement there. The response was enthusiastic and a corporal in the Unit undertook to organise it.

> It proved unexpectedly successful due to the energy of certain members of both the units, and even after we left the island, the group continued actively according to the Habonim programme, instruction being given at a distance by members of the Unit. They carried on a lively and inspiring correspondence with the children, whose ages ranged between 8 and 16. The Habonim organisation in London was contacted and was delighted with the news of a branch of the movement, however small, being established at Malta. Handbooks, badges and other material duly arrived both from London and youth movements and settlements in Palestine, and the isolation in which the Jewish community had existed for so many years was overcome by the enthusiasm of this handful of children to the benefit of all concerned.

Wellesley exhorted the Unit's cultural committee to develop more systematic activities to relieve the boredom and frustration. They were still in Malta when autumn arrived and had no indication as to whether or not they would ever join the invasion troops in Italy. Thoughts were directed to the post-war situation by some of the men. One group formed the nucleus of a transport co-operative society, another formed an agricultural co-operative society called Yael, whose members intended to settle on the land in Palestine as smallholders. However, these groups could not act on their plans and the frustrations increased. Wellesley, ever mindful of his men's emotional needs, devised some training exercises to counteract the weeks of relative inactivity.

> We had vistas of unending frustration and routine duties of shifting supplies from harbour to stores or dumps. Hence, as on previous occasions, the decision was to try and employ the Unit's time to some purpose which might prove useful in the future – perhaps on our eventual return to Palestine.
>
> We therefore informed Fortress Command that we wished

to draw blank ammunition for small arms and Bren guns. The request caused some raising of eyebrows by the staff officers – especially when we drew some mortars. I had some difficulty in explaining that the exercise we planned was the ambushing of a convoy in hilly country and that road blocks we would set up to halt the convoy were just the sort of obstacles we might have to encounter in Central Italy particularly in the Abruzzi mountains or elsewhere where the Germans would certainly be using mortars to destroy the vehicles. I did not add that when we returned to Palestine after the war, such training might prove invaluable in keeping the roads in the Judean Hills or in Galilee open in the event of possible trouble from whatever quarter it might develop. The arms and ammunition we required were finally issued to the Unit and training began. The finale was a set piece carefully planned to test the efficiency and initiative of the participants. These exercises had caused some comment from the Fortress H.Q. staff, and the general who had previously promised to visit the Unit asked whether he could witness the set piece at the end. I therefore extended an invitation to him and to his staff to join me on the roof of a tower not far from the road along which one of our convoys would be passing, and within sight of the actual ambush and road block. He therefore was able to observe the whole operation clearly and it turned out to be a most instructive and quite impressive display of military competence.

Hardly had the convoy reached the road block, when fire was opened on it from the ambush whilst the drivers and personnel on the vehicles de-bussed at speed to take cover and hold off the attack, and dispatch riders roared off down the road for reinforcements. The Bren guns opened up and the rattle of small-arms fire made us keep our heads down, and soon the mortar fire added to the noise of what looked like a major engagement. Towards the end, a special display of mortar fire was staged to prove the accuracy of this weapon, and the staff officers were able to see for themselves that the training had been seriously and effectively carried out.

The general asked if he could address the men, who were rapidly assembling after the exercise had been completed. He congratulated all those who had participated and said it was a first-class demonstration of efficiency. He referred briefly to the situation in Palestine and said he hoped the men would now have no further cause to worry about the safety of their families.[1] He went on to say he knew how anxious we were to leave the island and to get into the war again. He said we would soon be leaving Malta behind – at which the Unit burst into cheers – but added perhaps we would yet look back nostalgically to the months we had spent on the Island, as there was still a lot of fighting to do in Europe before Hitler was finally crushed. Little did he realise, that as compared with many other troops, we had a special desire to get ashore on the continent of Europe for a purpose that was becoming clearer to us from day to day.

Chanukah was approaching and we prepared to celebrate the feast of lights together with our sister unit and the Jewish community on the island. The men's mess hall was decorated and a special programme prepared by the members of Habonim, boys and girls of 10 to 15 years of age, was rehearsed for the evening's celebrations. A day or two before the chanukah party I received a 'most secret' signal from Fortress H.Q. ordering the Unit to prepare for its departure. Then I was given a Movement Order setting the date of our embarkation – the first day of chanukah – destination not stated.

[1]While the Unit was in Malta, news of the notorious raid by the British on kibbutz Ramat Hakovesh arrived. The farmers were armed to defend themselves against frequent attacks by Arabs from the nearby village. The British, determined to ensure that the Jews had no weapons, raided the kibbutz, severely injuring some of the members and deliberately causing extensive damage to kibbutz property. The outrage felt by most Palestinians serving in the British Army almost provoked a mutiny. See *Wheels in the Storm*, pp. 127–8.

CHAPTER NINE

Rescue in Italy

Wellesley's unit was taken with its vehicles in two landing craft to Taranto in Italy. Once the preliminary military formalities were dealt with, Wellesley did something which he and his men did many times wherever they went during the advance northwards into Italy.

> . . . I got into my staff car and found the main street of the town. My car, like all the Unit's vehicles, bore signs on it, the light blue disc superimposed by a white Shield of David, one on the front wing, one on the driver's door and one on the rear of the car. I told my driver to go ahead slowly keeping close to the kerb and I would walk behind. My intention was to establish contact with any Jews who might be in the town and I felt that despite the signs on the car, the presence of an officer might be a deterrent. It was not long before I spotted an emaciated individual observing the staff car from a doorway. He soon moved to another entrance further along the street. He then crossed the pavement and walked a few paces by the side of the car and was soon in excited conversation with Corporal Kramer, who in accordance with my instructions stopped – whereupon I came up to hear their fluent conversation in Yiddish.
>
> Within a few moments I was being directed to an apartment house down a side street, the gentleman dashing ahead to announce the surprising fact that a Jewish Unit from Palestine had arrived. I mounted the stairs to a large flat and was ushered into a room with a crucifix over the bed. The Jewish occupants had deliberately left it there when they took over the place. Within a few minutes the room filled to overflowing with men, women and children all looking at us in disbelief as I tried to explain who we were. They were all Jewish refugees from Central Europe or the Balkan states who had somehow survived and managed to evade the German and Italian authorities in Italy, and were therefore still at large and not

herded into the concentration and refugee camps which were later found in various parts of the Italian peninsula. Everyone wanted to tell us his story and there was deep emotion, and tears, and exclamations of amazement, relief and joy at the incredible fact that we had landed. Sergeant-Major Bankover soon joined me and we had a hurried consultation after which I asked those assembled around me to be ready at 1400 hours as they and other Jews in Taranto were invited to visit us that afternoon.

Arrangements were made for some vehicles to pick them up and bring them out to us. I then left and arriving at the staging site along the roadside, I called the officers and men together and told them we were giving a tea party to some very important guests and despite the fact that we had all been up most of the previous night – I asked them to set up trestle tables and benches under the trees and bring whatever unofficial rations I knew they always managed to carry with them and make a real effort to receive our visitors hospitably. They knew of course by this time that we were in contact with our first refugees. Within an hour the scene was set and the Unit waited under the olive trees while the cooks were busy brewing up tea.

Three or four of our vehicles came down the road towards us and drew up. The civilian passengers got down, turned and faced their hosts. There was a long silence as these Jewish men, women and children, in whatever clothes they still possessed to look presentable, stood gazing across the road at the two hundred seasoned troops in British battle dress. An old man beside me put up his hand to my shoulder and touched the word 'Palestine' on my sleeve – and softly asked in Yiddish – looking at the soldiers 'Are they ours?' 'Yes,' I replied 'from now on that is exactly what they are' – for we became dedicated to the Jewish refugees and their welfare from that time on until war's end – and for some of us – beyond that too.

For many of the men this moment was to be the beginning of an odyssey which took them all over occupied Europe as it was liberated – in search of their families and friends, a hunt for clues and traces of those from whom they had been separated since Hitler came to power and began the systematic destruction of Jewish communities and individuals wherever the lengthening shadow of the Nazi conquest fell across the face of Europe.

Nobody present at this first meeting by the roadside can ever forget those moments of reunion. The whole gamut of emotion was run in a setting which was dramatic in its symbolism. On the one hand remnants of the decimated Diaspora, worn down by experiences which they described in harrowing detail accompanied by tears and sobbing; on the other, a group of Jewish soldiers armed, disciplined and hardened by service in the Western Desert – part of a great army of liberation.

Soon drivers were coming up to me in great excitement to tell me that they had found out that their relations had been in such and such a place. One informed me that his parents were situated in a refugee camp in southern Italy called Ferramonti and could he have leave to go and find them. And so the few hours passed until it was time for the party to break up as the Unit prepared to move on through Bari north to Foggia on the plain near the Adriatic Coast. Shortly after arriving in Foggia the platoons began to travel all over southern Italy transporting supplies, equipment and stores for the units based on the Adriatic Coast.

As soon as our presence in Foggia became known to some of the Jewish refugees in the area, a stream of men, women and children began to arrive at our platoon H.Q., either brought there by individual trucks or sometimes picked up by our convoys as they passed through the towns and villages in the hills. It was soon necessary to establish some sort of organisation to handle this influx of people who needed food, clothing, housing and general care and supervision. Every driver was given a form to carry with him at all times on which he reported the whereabouts, number and description of Jewish refugees that he might hear of or contact in the course of his journeys. ...

Bari became the central receiving point for all the people who passed through our hands, sometimes at the rate of over one hundred a night. Unofficially we drew extra rations for them from the supply depots. We gave them blankets and such warm clothing as we were able to obtain or purchase from various sources including civilian shops and stores which we found in corners of Foggia. Our Friday night concerts were always at that time – and for many months afterwards – attended by those Jewish refugees who happened to be passing through our lines on those occasions.

This was the beginning of what later developed into the organisation called 'The Net' or 'Reshet' which gradually as we advanced northwards spread across Italy and later into Austria and Germany. ... A few weeks later I went down south to visit Ferramonti, a large refugee camp, and persuaded the young American captain in charge to let me in to talk to the people . . . Having no official authority I had to argue my way in and was soon surrounded by inmates, who were of course surprised to see a Palestinian Jewish officer and promptly took me to their appointed camp leaders. In the afternoon I spoke to all the Jewish refugees, when I explained my presence and the intention we had of helping them on their way to Palestine to a new life – as soon as possible. This and similar meetings of refugees (or Displaced Persons as they were to be called in official English parlance) always became emotionally charged and ended as a rule with 'Hatikvah'[1] being sung while few could restrain their tears. For this was all part of the process of liberation from a background of suffering and physical danger in which for many, sheer survival was a miracle in itself. ...

Back in Foggia, I was informed one morning by a driver that he had witnessed the arrival of a small vessel at a fishing port called Manfredonia, a little way up the coast. The ship was filled with refugees from Yugoslavia and he had seen casualties lying on the deck. Apparently the ship had been machine-gunned by Germans as it crossed the Adriatic, and there were dead and wounded. He said that there were some Yiddish-speaking civilians on board, that first aid was urgently needed and that nobody seemed to know what to do.

I immediately requested Capt. I. Gobernick to take a vehicle with a field kitchen and food, stretchers and several men and proceed to Manfredonia and provide all assistance. By mid-day he was back and reported that there were some hundred refugees on the ship, that they had escaped from Yugoslavia,

[1]Hatikvah – 'the Hope' – the Zionist Movement's national anthem which became the State of Israel's anthem.

and that he had taken off the dead and transported some wounded to the hospital and had provided others with a hot meal. Among them were some thirty Jews, who had implored him to allow them to disembark as they had had unpleasant exchanges with the non-Jews on board during their escape. He said that he was considering doing something about them when the military police arrived and ordered the ship to proceed to Bari under escort.

As he was concluding his report an American major walked into the mess and asked to speak to me. This was Major Birt, welfare officer for the Foggia area. He asked me whether I had authorised the activities of my officer and men and when I replied in the affirmative, asked me why I had done it. His name was known to me from reports I had received about a welfare officer who was trying to stop us purchasing clothing from stores in the town, but I nevertheless asked him to join us for lunch and then explained who we were and that we were deeply concerned with the refugee problem. I added that when we learned that there were Jews on board the ship we had to take whatever steps we considered the situation required irrespective of the consequences. At this point he said, 'Now I understand – and will you please accept my personal thanks for doing a job that I should have done – had I the men and vehicles and equipment at my disposal.' From then on we became firm friends and co-operated on various projects, he calling on me for vehicles and manpower whenever he could not obtain adequate help from his official sources.

However, I was by no means finished with this ship, and decided to take C.S.M. Bankover with me to Bari. We travelled through the night and got to Bari docks at dawn in time to find the ship alongside and the first trucks being loaded with the displaced persons. We followed the trucks to the centre of Bari where they pulled up outside a large empty department store which occupied the whole street corner. A strong cordon of military police surrounded the approaches to these premises. My staff car was stopped and we were told to keep away from the area. Driving round the corner the sergeant-major and I got out and I told him to stay close to me as I approached the cordon of police. For a moment it looked as if I was going to be stopped and turned away, but I spotted a captain, hailed him and walked with the Sergeant-Major through the cordon and spoke to him. He asked me who I was and I told him I had come to give a hand with the people assembling in the store – and so I went inside to find a milling crowd of bedraggled civilians, many almost in rags. The dawn was cold and they were obviously worn out, hungry and at the end of their tether. Now the problem was how to sort the wheat from the chaff and establish contact with the Jewish refugees for whom we had specific plans.

The Sergeant-Major looked around, moved from group to group and soon returned. Piloting me through the crowd to a corner of the building, he introduced me in Yiddish to a few people huddled together. For a moment we looked at each other and I said 'Shalom' very quietly. At once one of them drew himself up to his full height – a small man and very thin, with stubble on his emaciated face. He was wearing short tattered trousers without socks, his feet in torn canvas shoes, a patched thin overcoat around his shoulders and spectacles attached with a string. Standing to attention he gave me his name and added with some pride the title 'Rechtsanwalt' – lawyer. I took him by the hand and told him how pleased I was to meet him, and asked if he was Jewish. 'Of course', he said, 'and there are other Jews with me.' I then told him who I was and asked him to assemble the Jews quickly but unobtrusively and I would tell them what to do. Within minutes they were together, young and old men and women, and I quickly explained that they should try and leave the building and that the Sergeant-Major would lead them to a truck waiting to take them to friends in the town.

Five minutes later they were gone and I was just about to follow them when I saw one of the women coming back through the door. I asked her what she was doing 'Oh,' she said, 'I forgot to take my bag with me.' I said, 'But you passed the police cordon once, why try it twice?' She shrugged her shoulders, smiled wanly and was gone. I wondered how many times she had risked her life and liberty during the past few years in passing through frontiers, cordons of Nazi storm-troopers and other obstacles, on her road to freedom. I met them all a few weeks later after they had recuperated some-what from their ordeal – they were in trouble with an unsympathetic commandant in charge of the displaced persons camp outside Bari.

Many children, mostly orphans, were found in southern Italy, often in convents, where they had been given refuge by Catholic nuns. For these youngsters, we established a farm school outside Bari, and found a large unoccupied estate with plenty of rooms in the villa and ample land for agricultural instruction. Men in the unit who were kibbutz members and teachers, volunteered to act as instructors for the children, if we could provide the necessities. Camp beds were assembled, blankets obtained, battle dress in small sizes were dyed blue and rations were found or scrounged, and all this had to be transported to the farm school – unofficially. The teaching staff were given leave passes by me to protect them in the event of the M.P.s and other military authorities questioning their presence away from their units. Our vehicles passed by from time to time and dropped off supplies of food and clothing for the children.

I went down to inspect the place while still in Foggia and was amazed at the speed with which the children learned Hebrew, and how changed they were from the time we had seen them first. Their appetite was such, however, as to cause a serious problem of supply and as the military authorities were gradually tightening up in order to combat the vast traffic in black market army rations and other supplies of which the Italian population was in dire need, movements of our vehicles were subject to question as to what they carried and why. This problem was fast becoming a battle of wits between our drivers and the M.P.s and field security services. ...

As Passover was approaching we were again visited by the U.S. chaplain, Rabbi Honig, regarding the Seder arrangements. The pattern was established (which seemed symbolic of the relationship between the Diaspora and the Yishuv) that he, representing the U.S. Army and its Jewish personnel, would supply some of the special rations required for the Seder service, and we would organise the programme and make all the necessary arrangements. We obtained permission to use a Fascist gymnasium in Foggia which could seat over a thousand people. Our workshops decorated the walls with traditional Jewish motifs in colour. Pertinent excerpts from the service were pasted in large Hebrew inscriptions round the hall. Behind the head table the wall was covered with a map of Eretz Israel flanked by figures of steel-helmeted soldiers and chalutzim spade in hand. The senior American officer in the area was invited with his aides, as were all the Jewish refugees who were with us at the time.

For hours before the Seder service our cooks had been preparing all the traditional dishes which they could mass produce on their portable kitchen equipment, and H.Q. personnel were mobilised to set up trestle tables and benches. Before sundown all the men who could be relieved of their duties began to assemble and we found that news of this Seder had spread far and wide. Representatives of the Free French Forces appeared, and Jews enrolled in the partisans wearing British battle dress with a red star (from Tito's forces in Yugoslavia) arrived to join us, hundreds of U.S. troops, Jews from British units and several parents or relations of our own men, discovered recently among the refugees – all were seated along the tables which stretched from one end to the other of the huge hall. The Brigadier and his staff joined me at the head table where the microphones were installed. Just as I was about to open the proceedings, there was a commotion at the entrance and in poured pilots of the U.S. Air Force, straight from the airfields, still dressed in their heavy leather, fur-lined jackets, having just returned from a bombing raid on Central Europe. We made room for them, and I asked the non-Jews present to don their caps and hats and our first Seder service in liberated Europe began.

The youngest refugee present asked the traditional questions as soon as the kiddush was completed. The Unit had mimeographed copies of the special Haggadah, illustrated by one or two of our artists, and the story of Israel's Feast of Freedom was told again in traditional Hebrew, with many contemporary references to the liberation of the oppressed from under the heel of the modern Nazi Pharoah. Each portion of the service was assigned to as many different communities as were represented round the hall. I translated the pertinent passages to the U.S. Brigadier and his aides, who were deeply impressed by what they witnessed. It was indeed an unusual occasion and the singing of the ancient and modern Hebrew

> songs led by the Palestinians seemed to carry the message of hope and determination to see us one day a people free and rooted in its own soil.

Wellesley's unit helped Jews in every place they came to – Foggia, Vasto, Ancona, Florence and Rome. But his was not the only unit engaged in helping Jewish survivors of Hitler's regime in Europe. It soon became clear that their efforts would be better coordinated if each knew what the other was doing. So a conference was called at which Wellesley presided.

> There were some officers who refused point blank to get themselves involved in what they regarded as illegal activity. Others were afraid we might be sent back to Palestine, or court martialled or otherwise disposed of. Some said this was not soldiering nor was it fit for combatant troops to indulge in such unmilitary activities. One officer left the conference as a demonstration, but the rest agreed to go along with the work, and expand it as far as our resources permitted.

Those officers who feared a hostile reaction from higher military authorities were correct that there would be one sooner or later. It was brought to Wellesley's attention several times that a file was being compiled of his Unit's unorthodox and unauthorised movements. Wellesley too knew that there would eventually be a reckoning and he was prepared for it. But nothing deterred him from doing what he judged to be imperative for the remnants of the destroyed Jewish communities of Europe. During the advance towards central and western Europe, it appears that Wellesley recognised that the Allies were not going to exempt Jews from the decision to return all refugees to their countries of origin, whatever their fate might be there. He realised too that British policy towards the Jewish independence movement in Palestine was not going to become more sympathetic even in the light of what was emerging about the murder of millions of Jews in Europe. It was during these months that Wellesley seems to have committed himself unconditionally to the Zionists' plan to bring refugee Jews to Palestine, even if that meant flouting British authority and law. Now halfway through his expected life span, he opted to be a wholehearted, wholly committed Palestinian Jew.

Eventually the confrontation with the military authorities took place.

I was dealing with routine matters in the Company office one afternoon when the Sergeant-Major opened the door and asked me if I was willing to receive two staff sergeants of the Field Security Service. He looked a little worried and I asked him what it was all about. He told me that the two sergeants had been talking to some of the men and had asked a number of questions about the movement of our vehicles during the preceding few days. As they had apparently not been able to get the information they were after they had come to Company H.Q. and asked for me.

I told the Sergeant-Major to show them in. One of them was carrying a bag. They saluted and introduced themselves and asked if they might put some quesions to me. The bag was then opened and a substantial file of documents extracted which was handed to me. The file carried the title '178 G.T. Coy. (Palestine) R.A.S.C.'. The documents went back nearly twelve months and I could see at a glance that they were concerned with supplies drawn at various points and the movement of vehicles through check posts all over Italy. Having briefly examined the file I asked the staff sergeants if they were prepared to take down a statement which I was ready to dictate and sign. They said they would do so, and I proceeded to make a clean breast of the whole story in a few paragraphs. I began by explaining that on landing in Italy the plight of our fellow-Jews in Europe was a perfectly natural source of concern to us. Since liberation had proceeded so rapidly in certain areas, in the absence of official action we had done whatever we could to alleviate suffering and provide urgently needed supplies of food and clothing. Frequently we had moved families and individuals to points where they could be more effectively assisted.

I described the methods we had used, emphasising that at no time had we failed to fulfil our military responsibilities in respect to transportation and other calls made on the Unit and that this would be substantiated by the evidence of our vehicle availability, discipline and general performance. I added that I personally was solely responsible for what had been done, as it had been planned and carried out with my full knowledge and consent.

While the statement was being typed in the company office

the Sergeant-Major came in and asked to see me alone. He was appalled at the frank admission I had just made, which not only he but others had overheard as I dictated it. He felt that the consequences would have widespread repercussions and would probably result in my being relieved of my command. I told him not to worry, and duly signed the statement. The staff sergeants then took their leave and that was the last I saw of them. But it was not the end of the matter which was only finally disposed of shortly afterwards.

A few days after we joined the Jewish Brigade in Fiuggi I was informed that Brigadier Benjamin wanted to see me at once. I went over and was greeted in a manner that clearly portended trouble ahead. Brigade-Major Jackson handed me a thick file of documents bearing on its cover the insignia of Allied Forces H.Q. and asked me to take it in to the Brigadier who was expecting me, and wished me luck. Having saluted the Brigadier I handed him the file and waited for some indication of what was in the wind. The Brigadier adjusted his monocle, opened the file and said he had been instructed by A.F.H.Q. Caserta to read me a memorandum. It contained a request for satisfactory explanations regarding a series of alleged offences against King's Regulations by 178 Coy., R.A.S.C. over an extended period. Failing this, the Brigadier was ordered to hold an official inquiry and subsequently, if so indicated, to set up a court martial to deal with those implicated in the matters referred to.

So this was obviously the inevitable moment I had been anticipating for quite a time. After Brigadier Benjamin had finished reading neither of us stirred. He then looked up at me and asked if I had any knowledge of the matters referred to. I said I knew all about them and was personally responsible for everything. He asked me if I realised the serious implication of what I was saying. I admitted I did, and added, that I was, if necessary, fully prepared to face a court martial and take the consequences; in fact, it would always be a source of satisfaction to have been in a position to do what I had done in a cause, to which I believed every fair-minded man would subscribe. He then said he had heard vaguely that my company had done a lot to help civilians and refugees during the Western Desert campaign and realised that, except in the technical sense, no

> offence had been committed. Furthermore, he said he had seen reports of all Commands to which we had been attached and these had all been highly complimentary.
>
> Turning to the memorandum again he said there was only one offence that he thought was of serious importance and that was the first one mentioned, i.e. the use of War Department transport for purposes other than those authorised. Could I possibly provide an explanation which would satisfy A.F.H.Q. and if so we could forget the whole thing and get on with winning the war. Whereupon I made and signed a formal statement. This apparently answered the question to everybody's satisfaction. The Brigadier said he felt 'the least said the soonest mended', shook me by the hand and invited me over to the mess for dinner that evening.[1]

Wellesley continued to be involved at the highest level with refugee work. Before the Jewish Brigade left to take up position in the front line, a conference was called to reconsider this policy in the light of the move northwards. Wellesley, emphasising the welfare aspects of their deliberations, sought and got permission from Brigadier Benjamin to hold the conference in Fiuggi. Wellesley was chairman and the Brigadier attended the opening session to wish the participants well in their deliberations. Uppermost in the mind of many a soldier was the natural desire to trace relatives as they moved into Europe. The conference dealt with the redistribution of responsibilities in the light of the impending move forward. A Brigade Refugee Committee was set up. It undertook to draw on 178 Company for food, clothes and cash as and when required. Soon the Brigade found itself north of Faenza along a ridge of rolling hills overlooking the southern bank of the river Senio.

> The German Parachute Division with its armoured units held the northern bank and the hills above, which overlooked many of our outposts. We were based on the little village of Brisighella which was surrounded by vineyards and fruit trees typical of what, in peace time, was prosperous farming country.
>
> We moved into our positions two days before Passover on March 25th and began relieving the units who had manned the

[1]Nowhere has Wellesley disclosed what he put in the statement which satisfied the Allied Forces Head Quarters.

front before us. We had already had some casualties in, killed and wounded, mostly due to the minefields which covered the German positions. Although the Brigade was now in the line, arrangements for the Seder were well in hand and on Passover eve three Seders were held and attended by as many men as possible. The Seder at 178 Coy. took place in a large barn and about 200 officers, N.C.O.s as well as a handful of guests participated. Ted Lurie, war correspondent representing the *Palestine Post*, was again with us and brought a number of other war correspondents for the occasion. Within sound and range of the enemy artillery and on the eve of battle the Seder service was particularly significant, and once again a special Haggadah had been prepared for the occasion stressing the historic importance of the traditional service and equating the past and the present and underlining the relative role of the Yishuv with the Brigade and its mission. ...

On April 3rd Mr Moshe Shertok (Sharett), head of the political department of the Jewish Agency in Palestine, arrived at Brigade H.Q. to be present on the occasion of the official ceremony of the raising of the Jewish Brigade Colours. An area in a field in front of Brigade H.Q. was roped off and a flag-pole erected. About 200 officers and men who could be spared from their duties were on hand and heard Sharett's speech and the Brigadier's reply, after which we all stood to attention as the colours were unfurled from the flagpole. A short prayer was prepared by Rabbi Bernard Casper, the senior chaplain to the Brigade, and all present realised that history had just been made by this simple ceremony.

The Passover week was one during which the Brigade suffered its heaviest casualties. An area was set aside for a small Jewish military cemetery. Under the Brigade symbol and the Shield of David two dozen graves lie side by side amidst the vineyards of this fertile Italian farm country. These, as so many other soldiers' graves scattered throughout the battlefields of the Mediterranean, are symbols of the price of victory.

D-Day for the Brigade meant the crossing of the river Senio which was in no-man's-land. ... The R.A.F. provided air support. There was a story circulating that, prior to the first sortie, air H.Q. had phoned Brigade H.Q. saying that the squadron leader commanding the operation was an English

> Jew who had specially requested the privilege of leading the air strike and please note that the squadrons were flying in a special formation – that of a six-pointed star – the Shield of David. However, they were over and gone so fast that in the welter of battle this courteous salute was never verified. Nevertheless it was an unusually friendly gesture.
>
> The Brigade rapidly obtained its objective and the road to Bologna was soon clear of the enemy. Taking my staff car, I proceeded to the city standing in the plain, its tall central buildings visible in the distance. Rabbi Casper had managed to argue his way into Bologna and we set about locating Jewish survivors, if any. Although the synagogue was badly bombed and empty, it was decided to hold a Friday Eve Service there and steps were taken to broadcast that fact in the city. There had been a Jewish community in Bologna numbering over a thousand before the war. Three hundred attended the service of reconsecration that first Friday night. The scrolls of the law were located, having been given for safe keeping to an Italian Catholic who must have risked his freedom in accepting them. . . . On 3 May 1945 Hitler's suicide was announced to the world, and the end of the war was now merely a matter of formality. Although no excuse was really required, a party to end all parties took place after dinner that night in the officers' mess. It was only memorable in so far as it was, to my knowledge, the only time when all present completely shed the reservations which generally restrained us from indulging in the sheer enjoyment of the occasion. The war was over and the war was won. A few days later I was told by the Brigadier that I was to proceed home at once on extended leave of absence.

Awards were made to only four Jewish Palestinian officers of field rank. Wellesley was one of the four. He received the M.B.E. On 20 September 1945 the *London Gazette* published the following citation:

M.B.E.

Major (temp) Wellesley ARON (1395201)

Royal Army Service Corps

Major Aron was an officer of the first Palestinian R.A.S.C. Company to see active service in the desert and is the senior Palestinian R.A.S.C. Company Commander. He has commanded 178 Coy (Pal) R.A.S.C. for the last 4 years and has been responsible for its conversion from a G.T. Coy to a Bde Group Company. He has succeeded in making it a highly efficient unit in its new role in a very short time. His administration, man management and arrangements for the care of his troops are excellent and he has also put in considerable work on post-war resettlement and welfare of Palestinian enlisted personnel.

Major Aron has proved himself to be an officer of outstanding merit who devotes himself wholeheartedly to the interests both of his own unit and of the formation he serves.

CHAPTER TEN

Palestine and the USA – Israel's Independence

His army career at a virtual end because of his unofficial efforts to help Jewish refugees in Europe, Wellesley returned from Italy to rejoin his wife and two daughters. They were living in a hotel in Haifa, although they had been given the opportunity, together with other civilian British passport-holders, to shelter in South Africa during the war. Rose, however, had chosen to remain in Palestine. Ylona, the younger daughter who was just a toddler when her father went off to war, had been sent to a kibbutz boarding school. His elder daughter Sharona was a pupil at the Reali school where her father had taught during his early months in Palestine twenty years earlier. Like many other men in his situation, Wellesley did not easily re-adapt to civilian life.

While he was away, the Aron advertising agency had had to move out of its spacious offices in Allenby Street and was just ticking over in two small rooms in a building directly opposite the Barclays Bank building where it had previously flourished. Once or twice a week Wellesley went to Tel Aviv to oversee the business; but his heart was not in it any more and he spent much of his time hanging around Haifa waiting to be demobbed. He had many visitors; some came to offer him employment once he was released from His Majesty's Forces. Some were just curious to meet the celebrated Palestinian Jewish major and to hear of his exploits at first hand. Others came to explain and apologise for the fact that he had not become the commander of the Jewish Brigade when it was finally established in 1944.

He turned down a number of jobs, including one at the nascent Jewish Ministry of Information, another as head of the Hadassah hospital in Jerusalem, a third as headmaster of the recently established military school at Beit Sefer Reali in Haifa, where the Teutonic Dr Biram was still in power. He was also approached by the head of an orange exporting company who asked him to become responsible for transporting the export crops worldwide, on the assumption that his army experience must have equipped him perfectly to do that. Wellesley acknowledged that any one of these jobs sounded all right, but none fired his imagination. He experienced a brief respite from the frustrations of looking for employment when he was asked by Moshe Sharett to give evidence before the Anglo-American Commission of Inquiry in Jerusalem,[1] but before he did that he was more or less ordered by Jewish Agency officials in Jerusalem to go to London to brief Weizmann and other Zionist Executive officials on certain aspects of the situation in Palestine.

He was able to get a seat on a military plane to England because he was still a uniformed officer. No doubt Dr Bernard Joseph, a former Canadian lawyer who headed one of the Zionist Organisation's departments in Jerusalem, counted on this 'privilege' when he gave Wellesley a number of highly secret and sensitive documents dealing with the military situation in the Middle East, to hand over to the Zionist Executive in London. Much of the information had been obtained illicitly from British General Headquarters in Cairo, but Wellesley agreed to take the risk of delivering it to London. This had unfortunate and completely unexpected repercussions for him. He woke one morning while staying with friends in Cheltenham to read a startling headline in the *Daily Express*

> 'WHO IS W-------Y A--N FROM PALESTINE? WHAT IS HE DOING HERE?' The story was the result of a question in the House of Commons put by an MP who spoke for the Arab lobby. He asked the Colonial Minister why I had been allowed into the country, that I was regarded as a subversive character, that the army had forbidden me to go to Europe and that I could only do harm here. I was very shocked especially as he asked for my expulsion. I didn't know why I had appeared in the headlines and in the House of Parliament debate. I went into the matter and the fact was that after I had left Jerusalem

[1] Rt. Hon. Richard Crossman (1907–74), Labour MP 1945–74; editor *New Statesman* 1970–72; Minister of Housing and Local Government 1964–66; Leader of the House and Lord President of the Council 1966–68; was a member of this commission and gave a personal account in his book *Palestine Mission*, published by Hamish Hamilton, London 1947. He became and remained a consistent supporter of Israel as a result of the Commission's visits to Displaced Persons Camps in Europe where they met Jews who had survived the Holocaust.

> Dr Joseph had cabled, by open cable, not even in code, to Dr Weizmann in London saying 'Please expect Wellesley Aron who is coming to see you and he carries with him some information of importance.' This was quite enough to get MI5 going, or whoever was dealing with intelligence, and they tried to find out what I was up to.

Moshe Sharett and his wife were at Victoria Station to greet Wellesley on his arrival in London for his first visit since before the war. They told him that he was to address the Zionist Executive in his old office at 77 Great Russell Street the following morning. His report, which he chose to deliver wearing his British Army Jewish Brigade major's uniform, was more optimistic than Dr Weizmann had anticipated. Wellesley expressed his conviction that the experience gained by Jewish Palestinians during the war would enable them, if properly directed, to fend off Arab violence in Palestine. He was complimented by Weizmann and others for his war-time achievements and his report. Soon afterwards Professor Brodetsky took him aside and offered him a job as director of information at the Jewish Agency. Wellesley takes up the story.

> Now I had had some previous experience in working with Dr Brodetsky. In fact he had sacked me from the Jewish Agency many years before after I had established Habonim and I didn't want to repeat the experience. I told him so in no uncertain terms. He said, 'I don't believe you and come into my office.' I followed him, and there were assembled Sir Wyndham Deedes,[1] Victor Gollancz,[2] Tosca Feivel all of whom I knew, and a few other literary, journalistic and other gentlemen who were, in fact, the people who assisted in disseminating Zionist information to the public and he introduced me as the new director of the department. I said 'I am very sorry Brod, I cannot and will not accept it. 'Well,' he said

[1]Sir Wyndham Deedes (1883–1956), a British Christian Zionist who served as chief secretary to Palestine's High Commissioner Sir Herbert Samuel from 1920 to 1923. In 1943 he founded the British Association for the Jewish National Home and in 1948 the Anglo-Israel Friendship Association, which is still active today.

[2]Sir Victor Gollancz (1893–1967), born in England to Orthodox Jewish parents, became a publisher and author. In 1936 he founded the Left Book Club to publish books which would expose Nazism. He publicly opposed the British Labour Party's post-war anti-Zionist foreign policy and insisted that Jews who had survived the holocaust must be allowed into Palestine. He consistently worked for Jewish–German and Jewish–Arab reconciliation and co-existence.

'you'll come to spend the weekend with me in Leeds and talk it over.' I went to Leeds and he did his very best to persuade me, but was unable to. I came back to London and was promptly asked whether I would take over the business management and administration of the Jewish Agency world office. I said 'No, I couldn't.' They asked why not. 'Well,' I said, 'you can ask Mr Locker[1] who is in the building at the moment to come and see us in this office.' They did so. I asked him to empty his jacket pockets. He asked why. I said, 'It is a question of an investigation we are making here.' He asked, 'Any reason?' I replied, 'You'll see the reason in a moment, and put anything you have in your pockets on the desk in front of you.' He emptied his pockets and there he had two cables unopened, both from David Ben-Gurion[2] and they had been in his pocket for a week or so. He had never referred to them, he didn't even know he had them. He just took them from the mail man at the desk and then put them away. I spoke: 'That's the reason I will not and cannot reorganise this office, because there is no order here, there is just chaos and you can't get people like Locker, who has been brought up in a sort of revolutionary underground activity to obey any instructions and I will not be associated with it. You will have to go on as you have done up to now.'

It was obvious that I had nothing more to do in London. I went to Manchester to talk to Sir Lewis Namier's[3] students about the situation in Palestine. He was very complimentary and very friendly and I made another few speeches up and down the country to try and combat the anti-Zionist activities of the British Foreign Office and the Arab propagandists. Sharett and I both spoke to a group of people at Barney Janner's[4] house. I spoke about my experiences in Palestine and

[1]Berl Locker (1887–1971), Labour Zionist leader, member of Jewish Agency Executive in London 1931–48; joint chairman Jewish Agency Executive 1948–56.
[2]David Ben-Gurion (Gruen) (1886–1973). In 1935 he was elected chairman of the Jewish Agency Executive, in 1946 he became the de facto leader of the World Zionist Organisation. He declared the establishment of the independent Jewish state called Israel in 1948 and was its first prime minister and defence minister until 1953, when he retired to lie in the Negev desert. In 1955 he returned to politics as defence minister under Sharett, becoming prime minister again in 1956. In 1963 he retired completely.
[3]Professor Sir Lewis B. Namier (1888–1960), distinguished British historian, member of the World Zionist Organisation and Jewish Agency political department in London 1919–31.
[4]Sir Barnett (later Lord) Janner (1892–1982); Liberal MP who, in the House of Commons and elsewhere, consistently supported Jewry and the Zionist cause.

> the army and when I had finished I saw an elderly gentleman wending his way through the crowd to the foot of the stage where I was standing. He put his hand out and said 'Wellesley, you don't remember me do you?' I said, 'No sir I don't.' He continued, 'I'm Dr Lefkovich who attended the family in the good old days when you lived in Hampstead and I knew your parents very well and I've known you since you were a child. I want to tell you that if your father, may his soul rest in peace, had heard your speech tonight he would have turned in his grave in horror.' I just looked at him. He went on, 'But I, on the other hand, congratulate you. I think it was a wonderful speech and I am delighted to find that you know what you are doing. I am very proud of you. Goodbye, I don't suppose we'll ever meet again,' and he disappeared.

* * *

Wellesley suffered a terrible personal loss during this time. The two accounts in his memoirs are both characteristically matter of fact and what follows is an amalgamation of them both. Whether this severe shock influenced his decision to reject all offers of employment in London remains a mystery, but he was certainly wrestling with a lot of painful emotions and memories during his time in England. On his arrival in London he had installed himself in a room in Kensington and tried immediately to contact his mother whom he had not seen since before the war. He traced her to Eastbourne and she arranged to go at once to see him. Their reunion was at Victoria Station.

> I went to the station and it was packed with soldiers coming and going, some on leave, some going back to their units and there was a tremendous amount of khaki and air force blue and so on around and the train that she came on was very full. I noticed her at once when she got out, she hadn't changed very much. She was a tall, distinguished-looking woman with high white hair, very elegant and very well turned out. She stood there until she spotted me and then I turned towards her. As I approached I saw her look at my uniform very carefully and then she suddenly put her hand on my shoulder and said, 'What is that?' I replied, 'That's a brigade flash,' and there sure enough was a golden Shield of David on a blue and white

background and above and below in Hebrew and English the words Jewish Infantry Brigade Group. She was absolutely staggered. She said 'Why a Shield of David? I've never seen anybody except a Jewish chaplain wear a Shield of David. What are you? Are you a chaplain? Why do you have to advertise the fact that you're Jewish, nobody else does, I've never seen that before, why do you do it?' She was plainly embarrassed and I said, 'I'm a commander in the Jewish Brigade.' 'What's the Jewish Brigade? What have you got to do with that?' So I tried to explain but she said, 'I still don't understand,' and she never did understand.

We went home and she said that she'd had a very nice letter from a member of parliament, congratulating her on some decoration I had received and that it was very pleasant. She repeated that she did not understand what I was up to and that she had never understood. I only saw her once or twice before unfortunately on the 5th November she was run down in the streets of London, on a dark night, after all the blackout was more or less still in existence, she was wearing black, and she was killed by a car in the middle of the street as my father always predicted she would be, by virtue of the fact that she never had the patience to wait for the traffic to go by.

I happened to be at the Jewish Agency when the news was telephoned to me by the police and I had to go and identify her body in Cricklewood where she was lying. She was buried in the Willesden Jewish cemetery. Strangely enough Lily Montagu, a violent anti-Zionist, performed the ceremony and came and picked me up with her Rolls Royce at 77 Great Russell Street on the way to the funeral. I said to her, 'This is probably the first time this car has ever stood outside the World Zionist Organisation.' 'Yes', she replied. She did a very quiet and dignified job in burying my mother in London. Thus ended a chapter in my life. She had never understood why I went to Palestine.

* * *

It was November 1945 before Wellesley was returned fully to civilian life, but he still did not know how he was going to support himself and his family. His appearance before the Anglo-American Commission of Inquiry in Jerusalem was evidently a highlight of his public life in post-war Palestine. Wellesley was asked by the Jewish Agency to concentrate on the military contribution made by Palestinian Jews to the British war effort. The hearings took place in the YMCA building in Jerusalem. Golda Meir,[1] Ben-Gurion and Dr Weizmann had already given their evidence on the political situation. Wellesley takes up his story.

> I was wearing my Hawks tie deliberately because I knew that Judge Singleton, the 'hanging judge' as they called him in England, was the chairman and being a Cambridge man would probably recognize me. He did, and I think I disappointed him very substantially by my evidence. Manningham-Buller, who was said to be something in the War Office was the Commission's expert on military affairs so that he and I were obviously going to cross swords. I explained that I had personally participated in the war effort and said why I had done so. I told them that I had been responsible to some extent for the formation of the Jewish Brigade, was the first Jewish commanding officer in the field and recounted some of my experiences. I went on to indicate what the Jews had done and what they hoped to do in the future. I was asked what the Palestinian Jews had been paid and I had the opportunity to remind him that they were paid Maltese rates. This, I pointed out, was deeply resented. I explained that some Jews in Palestine had formed a committee attached to the Jewish Agency which raised funds to pay subsidies to the families of Palestinian Jews who had volunteered to serve in the British forces. I was asked what I thought of the Mandatary government's attitude to the war effort and there of course I let my hair down and related how instead of getting support, my recruiting efforts had been sabotaged by the Palestine government, who offered neither cooperation nor assistance. The Commission's members were uneasy. Judge Singleton looked at me very severely and asked what was my solution to the Palestine problem. I replied, 'I've always said that if the Arabs love and are attached to the land as much as the Jews are then they wouldn't be selling land to the Jews and there would be no need for regulations and laws preventing them from doing so. I personally would allow the

[1]Golda Meir (Myerson) (1898–1978), Israel's First Minister in Moscow 1948–49; Minister of Labour 1949–56; Prime Minister 1969–74.

> forces of history and a free market, such as it is, to play themselves out and let the best man win.' This was received as absolute heresy and I was asked to leave the session. Hardly had I got down from the stand when I got a note from Richard Crossman, whom I didn't know personally but only by sight as a member of the Commission. He asked me to lunch with him and I agreed. We met outside the YMCA and while walking across the road to the King David hotel he said, 'You are probably oblivious of the fact that while you were giving evidence, a file was handed around, provided by the CID in Jerusalem, naming you as a criminal, with a record and indicating that your testimony was invalid. They were trying to damn you in the eyes of the committee. It just gives you an idea of the dirty tricks these people use in this game. I, on the contrary, think you came out of it very well and would like you to remain in Jerusalem for a few days and assist us with your advice.' He introduced me to one or two other Commission members including the Americans, one of whom, Bartley Crum, I met again later on when we shared a platform in New York to celebrate the UN's decision to partition Palestine.

Clearly at a loss as to what to do with his life after the demanding and very fulfilling war years, Wellesley was persuaded by one of his former advertising clients to become the director of one of his London companies. Leaving his wife and children in Haifa, he returned to England to work in an office at Oxford Circus. Before long Rose and the girls joined him to set up home in Lowndes Square. Ylona was sent away to school again, while Sharona was enrolled in a finishing school in London known as the Monkey Club. Wellesley has not recorded anything about his work, which suggests that it was not at all to his liking. However, he did not detach himself altogether from the Zionist world. He was a guest speaker at the English Zionist Federation conference in 1946. There he met a Mr Wigoder[1] from Manchester who suggested that Wellesley should go to lecture in the United States. This was not the first time that this had been proposed. Sharett had already unsuccessfully encouraged Wellesley to do so. Wigoder said that he could arrange a tour and Wellesley agreed in principle to go. Sharett

[1]Basil Thomas Wigoder, b. 1921; Life Peer; Q.C., M.A.; Recorder, Crown Court; Liberal Chief Whip, House of Lords.

promptly popped up to ask Wellesley to represent the Haganah while he was in America. Not knowing what would be involved, Wellesley agreed to take on both tasks. He expected to be there for three months, but remained for four years. In all his lengthy, detailed memoirs, this is the only occasion when he hints at the disruption his frequent movements caused to his family: 'Thus it is in this semi-public life, one cannot plan ahead and one's family is affected by the uncertainties.'

RECRUITING FOR THE HAGANAH

Wellesley arrived in New York, without Rose and the girls, to prepare the way. Lecturing did not occupy much of his time and to begin with he had no specific work for the Haganah. Quite soon he bumped into his former Hebrew teacher, who had originally introduced him to the Reali school in Haifa. Shlomo Bardin was in the throes of organising a residential camp for Jewish youngsters and asked Wellesley for help. With characteristic enthusiasm, Wellesley agreed and went out to Los Angeles for about a month. There he not only helped with the Brandeis camp, but was a very effective propagandist amongst Jews and Gentiles for the Zionist cause in Palestine. Wherever and whenever he could he cultivated wealthy and influential Americans who might help the cause financially or in any other way. After a month or two his wife and daughters arrived in New York. He was there to meet them and together they drove across the United States to set up home once more, this time in Los Angeles. Sharona went to university there to study sociology; Ylona was again sent away to boarding school. This was the period leading up to the United Nations General Assembly resolution proposing that Palestine be partitioned into two states, one for Jews, the other for Palestinian Arabs. The resolution was passed and a great rejoicing took place in the American Jewish communities. Wellesley was invited to New York to speak at the Salute to Israel celebrations. He then returned to the West Coast to continue the Zionist campaign.

Without warning his life took another dramatic turn when he took a telephone call from Emmanuel Newman, a member of the Jewish Agency executive.

'You are called for. You must come to New York at once.' I asked him what for and he said, 'I can't tell you on the phone, except that it's urgent and that there is a message from Palestine. I informed Jerusalem that you are to attend a meeting tomorrow at 1 o'clock.' I took leave of my family, who knew nothing about my plans of course and arrived in New York to find Rabbi Hillel Silver,[1] Dr Newman and Teddy Kollek[2] from Palestine and a few other dignitaries. We sat down and it became clear why I had been invited. They showed me a cable that had come in from Eliyahu Golomb,[3] head of the Haganah, requesting that I be invited to head the personnel section of a military mission and get to work at once to provide men with knowhow who could help in defending the newly established state, which was liable to be attacked. There was no alternative, here was a call of duty and so I agreed at once. I was thanked and informed that I would be getting money from certain sources and would have to operate out of New York. I said that I'd like to bring my family over and set up home as I'd been on the run for some years now. They agreed. When Sharona and Ylona had finished their terms at university and school they came with Rose to join me.

I then looked round for a place to live which was within my limited budget. Finally we took a suite in a quiet hotel off Park Avenue and I began the search for an office. I wanted a place where lots of people come and go, where there was a lot of traffic normally so that when, and if as I hoped, I got a lot of applications from young men ready to go and serve in the military forces in Palestine, they wouldn't be noticed. After a thorough search, I chose the Breslin Hotel which didn't have a very sweet reputation at the time. It was in the heart of the toy industry in Manhattan close to 13th Street. There I took a suite

[1]Rabbi Abba Hillel Silver (1893–1963), was an active Reform rabbi and Zionist leader in the United States of America; chairman of the United Palestine Appeal and co-chairman of the United Jewish Appeal; from 1943 he led the American Zionist Emergency Council to mobilise support for Zionist political aims. On 8 May 1947, as chairman of the USA's section of the Jewish Agency, he presented the case for an independent Jewish state before the United Nations General Assembly in New York.

[2]Theodor Kollek (1911–); Director-General of the Prime Minister's office 1952–64; Mayor of Jerusalem since 1965.

[3]Eliyahu Golomb (1893–1945), leader of Jewish defence in Palestine and main architect of the Haganah.

and proceeded to build up a staff to process the applications. The organisation was termed 'Land and Labour for Palestine' which of course was a euphemism for what it really was. It was a recruiting organisation which was illegal under American law, but there I was, head of it and ready for business. To drum up custom I had three or four meetings in Manhattan which took place on successive Sundays in relative secrecy. We used to take over an office big enough to seat two or three hundred people. We invited youngsters who might be interested in batches of two or three hundred to meet there. I told them what was required. As a result, business began to pick up and I soon had to expand my offices to take in three or four more suites. There was a constant stream of applicants of all sorts. I formed one or two committees of senior ex-military men, all Jews. They had experience in artillery, tanks, infantry and other formations. We vetted the applicants and soon discovered that quite a lot of young men were ready to go and do whatever was called for in Palestine. The seven Arab states surrounding the newborn state of Israel had attacked and our people were fighting for their lives. Our volunteers were willing to use the knowhow gained in the war in the United States Forces to help the besieged Jews in Palestine.

One of the problems we immediately encountered was that none of these youngsters had passports, much to our surprise because in Europe of course the moment you are of age you need a passport if you want to travel. Our volunteers had to apply to Washington for a passport and there seemed to be inexplicable delays in getting them. I soon discovered that there was a woman in the Washington office who knew what was going on. This Mrs Shipley did everything she could to prevaricate and delay the issuing of passports, so that our young men would apply and then wait around for weeks without an answer. Some went to Washington to see her and we ran a sort of war, I from New York and she from Washington trying to put the brakes on and to refuse as many applicants as she could. To force her hand I used whatever influence I could find – lawyers, well-to-do Jews, influential members of both the Democrat and Republican parties. I spoke to her once. She said, 'I know, Major Aron, what you are up to and I will see that you are frustrated to the best of my ability. What you are doing is contrary to the constitution and law of the United States.' I asked her how she knew that and explained, 'I am sending out young agriculturalists and specialists in horticulture and what have you, to help with the kibbutzim and other settlements.' She replied, 'It's all untrue and I know it.' Anyway, we did extract a number of passports from her.

There were some outstanding incidents during this campaign. I had an application from a young man who had been a fighter pilot in the American Air Force. He was nineteen or twenty, extremely able with the highest qualifications. He came to me bringing all his papers and I saw that he was someone extremely valuable. The next thing I heard was that his father was demanding to see me. Father and son arrived together. The father spoke first.

'I will not permit my son to go and fight in Palestine.' I responded, 'Aren't you the chairman of your Zionist organisation?'

'Yes, I am.'

'Aren't you supposed to be a dedicated Jew and a Zionist?'

'Yes, I am. Anything you like, but not my blood.'

I turned to his son, 'What do you feel about it?'

'I am absolutely outraged. My father is what he calls a Zionist. I'm prepared to go. How can he stop me?'

'You're under twenty-one, aren't you?' I reminded him.

'Yes.'

'In that case your father will have his way.' He went out very abashed and I never saw him again.

Another unpleasant experience involved a highly qualified senior officer from the United States Armoured Corps. He came to me and said he'd like to go out to Israel. We processed him quickly and he went off to Paris where Ruth Berman, who ran the office there, handed him on to Tel Aviv. Somehow or other he lost his papers and spent three months wandering around Tel Aviv looking for an address where someone would tell him what to do next. Finally he came back thoroughly disappointed. He complained because he'd 'lost' four months of his life and felt that he'd been led up the garden path. I apologised. He replied 'That's not good enough. I want money. I have written up the whole of my story and the *New*

York Times wishes to publish it.' I pointed out to him that that would be very hard for us and would probably ruin us, bring the organisation into disrepute and put us out of business. He answered that he didn't care, that it would cost us a couple of thousand dollars to get him not to publish. At that point I suspected that he had not really tried very hard to make contact in Tel Aviv. When I enquired, nobody had even heard of his arrival in Palestine. We paid him two thousand dollars nevertheless.

The problem of getting people we had accepted to Palestine was a tricky one. If we could find a way cheaper than flight we did so. Sometimes they went by sea either individually or in groups. I even had a camp up in Peakskill, which was a sort of staging post where people waited for the chance to go to Paris. From there they went to Marseilles, where they were in a camp until they could get a passage to Palestine. We had our failures. One ship, the *Marine Carp* docked in error at Beirut instead of Haifa. Everyone on board was arrested resulting in a short-lived international scandal. The Jews in America were sometimes very naive too, which caused us a lot of trouble once when the B'nai B'rith organisation in Chicago purchased a number of jeeps to send out to Palestine. A group of youngsters in specially designed uniforms were to drive the vehicles to New York for shipment. They were given a dramatic send-off in Chicago. Soon afterwards my office in Pittsburgh rang me up and said, 'We are in an awful jam here because a convoy of jeeps has arrived outside the town and has been stopped for speeding. The local sheriff wants to take them off to court which will be terrible publicity for us if it gets into the newspapers.' I said, 'You'd better make a deal with the sheriff,' which they did. I think two and a half thousand dollars was paid over to him. He let them go though, having first confiscated their 'foreign' uniforms.

Yet another unpleasant incident was provoked by a young man who burst into the office one day saying he'd just come in by bus from Los Angeles, California and wanted to join in fighting the Arabs. I asked him who he was. He gave me a completely un-Jewish name. I said 'What's the compelling interest?' He replied, 'I don't like them and I'm suspicious of them and I want to get into a battle. Anyway, I'm here.' I asked him to wait his turn downstairs. I made a few enquiries and my associates in the Los Angeles office told me that he was thoroughly unreliable and that they had rejected his application because they mistrusted him completely. While I was on the telephone, one of my people burst into my room. He had been hanging around downstairs watching what went on. 'Your friend has just been arrested,' he told me. 'What do you mean my friend?' I replied. 'Well the young blond boy from California drew a gun on the bartender, flashed it around shouting, "I'm going to shoot the Arabs with this thing, I'm on my way to Palestine. There's a Land and Labour organisation in this building. Major Aron is in command and he promised me . . ." ' He was held until the police came. I arranged some legal representation for him. When our lawyer had seen the boy he came back to me and said, 'You know we could be in a jam if this thing comes to court. If it gets any publicity you're out of business here.' So once again it was a question of how much. But we got him out and sent him back to California by bus. These were the sort of things that happened and it was not what I would call an easy assignment.

Once a Colonel Stone came to see me. He was a regular officer with field rank in the United States Army. He walked in unannounced and asked me to go to Palestine with him as his chief of staff. I didn't know who he was and the Jewish Agency had dealt with him without going through my office. When he had explained who he was, I told him that I couldn't accept his invitation unless I was relieved from my job by Golomb who had appointed me. His real name of course was Colonel Mickey Marcus.[1]

During the year I was running this organisation I was also lecturing, which was the work which entitled me to be in the United States. I had to speak to some group or another anywhere in the United States at least once a week which entailed a lot of organisation.

[1]Colonel Mickey Marcus (Marcus Stone) had served in the United States Army during the Second World War. He volunteered to help the Jews organise their defences in Palestine and did so to some effect. He was killed accidentally near Jerusalem by a Jewish sentry shortly before the ceasefire which ended the War of Independence in 1949. A somewhat theatrical account of his experiences in Palestine/Israel has been presented in the film *Cast a Giant Shadow*.

The Haganah's needs were not of course restricted to personnel. When the War of Independence broke out I began to get messages for all sorts of essential items. I realised I would have to communicate with the Haganah's headquarters outside Tel Aviv and needed a cheap system to do so. I called up a friend of mine, Peter Schweitzer, who had shown me his ham radio station in his basement when I had visited him once before giving a lecture to his local Jewish organisation. 'Look here', I said, 'this is thoroughly illegal of course but if I gave you a list of code words, could you transmit them for me?' He replied, 'Certainly. I am not even going to ask you what they are for.' 'That's jolly good', I told him, 'but I warn you that if somebody inspects your place and tries to shut you down, it is because you are involved with me, which is the Haganah of course.' He agreed to take the risk.

His brother too became a friend of mine. I met him at a meeting in a Park Avenue apartment where I spoke to a distinguished group of people including the deputy mayor of New York. Afterwards a man pushed his way through the crush to introduce himself as Mr Schweitzer. He was my radio ham's brother and had an astonishing story to relate. He told me that in the bank vaults, he had the original shares of the Jewish Colonial Trust which was the founding organisation for Bank Leumi, the national bank of Palestine. He said, 'I think they must be worth a lot of money. My father bought them at the time when Herzl[1] launched the idea and we've had them ever since. I would like to place them at your disposal on one condition, that you get a boat for illegal immigrants[2] with the money and name it after my mother.' I replied that I couldn't guarantee that, but I would look into it. I phoned Eliezer Caplan, the Jewish Agency's treasurer who happened to be staying at the Plaza Hotel at the time. He suggested that I took Louis Schweitzer to see him, which I did. I didn't realise then that one of the things the Jewish Agency most needed was

[1]Theodor Herzl (1860–1904), founder of the World Zionist Organisation and of modern political Zionism; author of *Der Judenstaat* (1896).

[2]Between 1934 and 1948 approximately 115,000 Jews were saved from the Holocaust and its aftermath by being smuggled into Palestine in defiance of British regulations; a further 51,500 were interned by the British in Cyprus. The British called this illegal immigration, the Jews *aliyah bet* ('ascent' B).

to have the founder shares of the national bank of Palestine. As far as I know they did a deal, but I never knew on what terms.

Louis Schweitzer also had a ham radio station which he used on our behalf when required. The third brother then invited me to visit the family business factory in New Jersey. The family fortune had been made from manufacturing cigarette papers. I went down there, and found a very charming man who was chairman of the United Jewish Appeal in that area. We had dinner together and we soon got to know each other pretty well. Now there was a third radio station available to me! Everything went well until Peter rang me up one day from Long Island and told me that the authorities were on his tail. 'They have come to inspect my equipment and they want to know why all these code numbers are being transmitted by me. I told them it was just an experiment and so on and managed to fob them off, but it is very fortunate that one of the inspectors happened to be a Jew. I took him aside and asked him to leave this matter in peace because we were engaged in vital matters.' I thanked him very much, because he had got himself into a lot of trouble and we would have been in trouble too if he had not been able to settle it.

When I was back in Tel Aviv a year later, very often I would get a message from Peter Schweitzer who would contact a radio ham in Beer Sheva. He could put me through to Peter by telephone. Later on Peter bought a yacht which he moored, I think, in Monte Carlo. He had a very powerful transmitter on board and used to phone me. You couldn't carry on a normal conversation, you always had to say 'over' and then reply. He came to Israel I think once, but didn't show any signs of wanting to live here. I think his whole family had been conditioned to make money and to be very successful in America and to treat Israel as a sort of charitable spot; although his father had bought, strangely enough, a stretch of land along the lakeside near Migdal, Tiberias. I once said to him, 'You know it would be wonderful to make a summer resort with a marina and so on and you could build a villa for the family.' He replied, 'We already have a villa in Connecticut and a lake much bigger than the Sea of Galilee and we are perfectly comfortable thank you.' That was all one could do with him.

Eventually two FBI men appeared in my New York office to

question me. I knew that I could remain silent unless my lawyer was present. I reminded them of this, but as one of my lawyers was in Venezuela and the other in Washington I was able to fend off their interest for several weeks. One of the two was an Irishman who soon decided to drop his investigation. The other persevered until I decided that the time had come to liquidate the whole organisation and to do it quickly. There was a meeting at the Jewish Agency and we decided to burn all our records and disappear. I sent instructions to all the local offices to do likewise. It was the end of my assignment and I was without anything to do.

CHAPTER ELEVEN

Pan Am's Representative in Israel

Immediately after Wellesley was released by the Jewish Agency he arranged a lecture tour for himself which gave him a good income for a few months. Amongst his hosts was the American Jewish War Veterans' Association which asked him to speak at its annual conference. He did so and received a standing ovation from an audience which included a senior United States politician and a number of high-ranking American military men. A General Klein[1] sent a note asking to meet him. During their conversation Klein invited Wellesley to lunch in New York at the Pan American World Airways suite in the Chrysler Building. There he was introduced to Mr Trippe, the head of Pan Am and a former aviation pioneer. Sam Pryor, Pan Am's head of public relations, also joined them for lunch. The purpose of the lunch was to invite him to join Pan Am as a consultant on Israeli matters. General Klein, who was Pan Am's representative in Chicago, had suggested that Wellesley would be an ideal person to do the job because of his many, varied contacts in Israel and the world-wide Zionist organisations. Without knowing what was involved Wellesley accepted the offer. He was paid a retainer which meant he could stay in New York with his family.

The airline was exploring the possibility of doing business with Israel. Wellesley was very concerned that such an involvement would not restrict the development of an Israeli airline and that Pan Am would not attempt to impose a monopoly in the country. Thus he was instrumental in introducing Klein and Trippe to Weizmann, who had become Israel's first president, when Weizmann was in New York. After this meeting Wellesley was asked to prepare a brief to accompany an application to the Federal Aeronautical Authority for landing rights in Israel. TWA already had those rights, but when it suspended all flights to and from Israel after the

[1] General Klein, National Commander of the Jewish War Veterans, former two-star general in the Quarter Masters Corps.

partition vote, just at a time when international communications were so vital, Israel's leaders began to look around for alternatives. If possible they wanted to dispense with TWA altogether. At a meeting with Pan Am officials and Lebanon's Ambassador to Washington, Wellesley argued in favour of Pan Am rerouting its around-the-world flight schedule through Tel Aviv instead of through Beirut. Not surprisingly Lebanon's government was not in favour and it never happened.

Wellesley soon realised that he was quite out of his depth when he discovered what had to be included in the brief and he engaged a sympathetic lawyer to do it. Shortly afterwards he was offered the presidency of the infant Israeli airline El Al, but he turned it down on the grounds that he could not break his commitment to Pan Am. He did use all his influence at Pan Am to obtain the planes and facilities El Al required, with little success though because Israel's resources were puny compared with its competitors.

Before long he began to feel that he wasn't earning his retainer and his longing to go back to Israel returned. He had made a minor contribution to Pan Am, but there was nothing he could really get his teeth into. Pan Am agreed to his departure and decided that he should set up a Pan Am office in Israel and that his retainer would continue to be paid. In 1950 he returned to Tel Aviv.

After a few months of settling down into the entirely novel experience of life in an independent Jewish state, Wellesley decided to have a house built for the family at Neve David.[1] Wellesley had been primarily responsible in obtaining this land for the officers and men who had served in the British Army during the Second World War. He was shocked and hurt when he was told that there was no plot left for him.

> When I was informed that there was no land left I said, 'It's quite impossible to leave me out of it since I obtained the land for you and you know perfectly well that I was behind the whole thing.' The one in charge retorted that as I had been abroad when the land was parcelled out, no one thought about reserving me a plot. I was appalled of course and went to see

[1]Neve David, named after Colonel Mickey Marcus. On his return from Italy Wellesley went to see Sir Harold MacMichael, who was then High Commissioner for Palestine, to ask that land be set aside for soldiers returning to Palestine as requested by his Unit's soldiers. The High Commissioner designated 1000 dunams (250 acres), part of which was for the exclusive use of Palestinian soldiers.

Mayor Rokach who received me rather differently now that I was out of uniform. He said, 'I'm awfully sorry but it's quite true. The municipality has taken over the remaining plots and there are none left.' I went forthwith to Moshe Sharett and told him the story. In fact I joined Amos Ben Gurion's name to mine because he had nowhere to live either and wanted the only other available plot. In my presence Sharett rang Rokach at the Tel Aviv municipality and told him what he thought of him. Rokach capitulated at once and agreed that the two plots earmarked for two municipal doctors would be reallocated to us. In the end Amos decided to live elsewhere and my eventual neighbour was the registrar from the Tel Aviv municipality who qualified for a plot because he had served in the British Army during the war.

He agreed to handle most of the technical problems as building a house in Israel at that time wasn't a simple matter. In fact we lived in three different houses for the year and a half in which the house was being built. We supervised it ourselves, but still had many problems. For instance I had a brick allocation from the appropriate government department because everything was rationed. Well I had this chit and was told to go down to a place in Holon where there was a man who would supply bricks. I took it to him. He was a great big fat tough guy. He looked at me and laughed and handed me back the chit. He said 'I'm not interested.' I asked him what he meant. 'Here are the instructions from the Ministry of Development ordering you to sell me 30,000 silicon bricks at a fixed price.' He replied, 'It's the fixed price that kills the whole thing because there isn't such a thing as a fixed price. We sell for what we can get and there is tremendous demand for everything, so you may have to pay two or three times what it says on this chit.' I was horrified and went straight back to the Ministry, where I was told to go back to my office and that someone would get in touch with me. A day or two later a man came in and said that he was a policeman dealing with my bricks problem. He asked for my chit. I gave it to him and he disappeared. I waited another two or three days. Meanwhile my contractor was complaining that he couldn't get on with the job without bricks. Suddenly the plain clothes policeman reappeared in my office. 'I think you could take this chit back to the gentleman who refused to supply the bricks. You'll find that he is only too willing to now.' So I went down again to Holon and found the fellow sitting there. He received me very differently. 'Oh yes, you want the bricks don't you?' 'I do', I replied, 'at the price stated.' 'That's alright, we'll send them up on a lorry to your address in the next twenty-four hours.' To my surprise that is what happened.

I contacted the people who had intervened for me to ask them what they had done. They told me that he was a well-known black-market brick supplier. They had been waiting for evidence to prove that he was breaching government regulations. 'You are the first person who did not capitulate to his demands for black market prices, you brought us the evidence, we followed it up and arrested him. We took him to prison, he sat there for twenty-four hours at the end of which time he asked if he could get out. We said, yes, on one condition, that you stop all this damn nonsense and supply Major Aron with his bricks.' That is how I got my bricks.

I had problems getting red roof tiles and water pipes too. Both were in short supply and the imported roof tiles used by my neighbours were of very poor quality. I wanted the type of red roof tile that had been used for the buildings in the early Rothschild settlements. They came from Marseilles and were very good. They were heavy and of excellent quality. The question was how to get some. I had a very helpful brother-in-law who was a member of kibbutz Degania, a father of four and a great fellow for getting things when nobody else could. He was also in partnership with an Arab who owned a flock of sheep; and had a job in the building industry. He did so well that he travelled once or twice to Australia to see his relatives there. He was a strange character and when he heard that I needed tiles and also some water pipes, he said not to worry, that he would bring them. And sure enough a day or two later he arrived with a lorry full of tiles, aged tiles, weathered tiles. I asked him where he'd got them. 'Oh in different parts of the Galilee. There are old farm buildings originally built by the Rothschilds which have been abandoned for years. I simply went around collecting them. I'm delighted to supply them and I picked up the water pipes en route too.' That made life a lot easier.

> I couldn't believe that our settlement, only a mile or two from Tel Aviv, would survive more than a year or two of independence. I was sure that it would eventually be absorbed as the city spread out. I was right. Within two or three years everything was built up around it and we were just a little island of red-roofed houses with a small garden in front and a larger garden behind; very charming; very quiet; very attractive and very suitable for our purpose. We lived there for twenty years, Rose and I, until she died of cancer.

Not surprisingly Wellesley was often asked what he did as Pan Am's Israel representative when Pan Am had no flights to the country and probably never would. He didn't really have an answer. On three occasions only did he really feel that his departure from New York benefited both Pan Am and Israel. Wellesley has not dated the first one but it coincided with the construction of the Intercontinental Hotel in what was then Jordanian-controlled East Jerusalem.

> One day I had a call from Golda Meir who was then Minister for Foreign Affairs. She asked me to go and see her at once. I dropped everything and went up to Jerusalem. She asked me to look closely at some photos and she showed me a large panoramic photo of the Mount of Olives and of Arab East Jerusalem. I looked and I saw that the Jewish cemetery which ran round the Mount of Olives was in a state of disarray. As far as I could see from the photos taken by the Israeli air force there had been a great deal of vandalism. Tombstones were broken and removed, the place looked to be a shambles. She asked me if I knew what this meant and then offered to tell me. 'You know there is a hotel being built called the Intercontinental Hotel on the Mount of Olives. It's under the auspices of Pan American Airways and I want to tell you that our religious people have seen this photograph and they are appalled by what is going on up there.' I said, 'What's that got to do with us?' She replied, 'You mustn't argue with me when I say that unless this business is stopped and put right, there will be a tremendous international outcry and probably a war, because our people will cross over and attack the Transjordanian frontier force or Jordanian army lines on the Mount of Olives and drive them out by force and we'll have a war on our

hands.' I asked what I could do. 'I only give you a week because that is all the time I've got. The Knesset[1] will debate this whole business in due course, but I've been able to hold off the Orthodox party to give you a week's leeway. I might say that if it hadn't been for you we would have already debated the subject before now.' I thanked her, returned at once to Tel Aviv and promptly called Sam Pryor and told him vaguely what was going on.

He asked me what I wanted to do. I told him I wanted to stop it and needed his help. He said that he was horrified and did not know that Pan Am was involved in such things. I told him that we were not, but that someone was taking advantage of the fact that Pan Am was in some way connected with the hotel and was turning the oldest Jewish cemetery in the world into a park. The tombstones were being used for buildings and pathways. He gave me carte blanche to deal with the situation because if it became known that Pan Am was associated with such a desecration it would severely damage its reputation, especially with American Jews who were, he thought, a significant proportion of their customers. I told him to contact Pan Am's representative in Jordan and to order him to meet me on the following day at the Israeli embassy in Rome. He asked me what I would do with their Jordanian man. 'I'm going to read him the riot act and I am going to give him 48 hours to stop the work, to see the Jordanian government and to get the whole thing under control.' He wished me luck.

I flew to Rome and waited at the Embassy. Sure enough the man who was in charge of the overall planning and construction of the Intercontinental Hotel turned up. He seemed very resentful of the fact that he had to leave his job in Amman to meet me. I told him that I had authority from the Pan American board and that he should listen very carefully to me because a lot of trouble was brewing. I went through the several points which I had discussed with Golda Meir earlier: all vandalism must stop at once, anything being done in the cemetery should cease; that the damage done was to be made good; that a wall be built between the property of the hotel and the cemeteries to prevent any further vandalism; that the

[1]Israel's parliament, which has only one house.

government of Jordan permit one or more rabbis to go to the site to reconsecrate it when it was restored and that all this should be done within five days. He looked at me and seemed to snigger as though I was talking nonsense. Whereupon I told him that I wouldn't wait for his reply in Rome as I was flying on at once to New York. He asked me why and I told him that I was going to the State Department on Monday morning and that he would be hearing from me. 'Meanwhile, I warn you that there won't be any Intercontinental Hotel built on the Mount of Olives unless all this is dealt with at once.' He looked very angry and I left him there.

I arrived in New York on the Sunday evening I think it was and Sam Pryor was waiting at the airport. 'We've got the executive plane waiting for you tomorrow morning at 8 o'clock and the president of Intercontinental Hotels will go with us to the State Department.' I explained the situation to the official who met us there. He couldn't understand what the excitement was all about. I told him, 'Mr Sanderson, my grandfathers and my great-grandfathers and all my ancestors' and predecessors' graves are or should be or may be on the Mount of Olives, this is the holiest burial ground of the Jewish people anywhere in the world. Anyone laying a finger on it is touching dynamite. There will be a conflagration such as you have never seen when the Jewish people hears what's going on under our auspices.' He retorted, 'Not under our auspices. Neither Pan American nor the State Department is responsible. The Jordanian government is doing it.' I added that 'I don't care who is doing it, but it has to stop forthwith or by this time next week we will be at war with Jordan.' He was surprised. 'Is it as serious as that?' I assured him that it was and that he should get through to the American ambassador in Amman and read him the riot act and tell him to get it stopped. 'You must also tell him that I am waiting for replies to the five or six questions that I have put to Pan Am's representative in Jordan. I want a letter on official Jordanian government paper signed by a minister in the hands of my Foreign Office by next Wednesday afternoon, the deadline given by Golda Meir, Israel's foreign minister.' Then I took my leave. Both my colleagues were very impressed as they had not appreciated the serious danger they were confronting.

> I returned to Tel Aviv, having arranged a meeting with Sam Pryor and the president of Intercontinental Hotels at the Mandelbaum Gate[1] at four o'clock on Wednesday afternoon. They were to bring me the letter I'd demanded from the Jordanian government. Well they were there, at the Mandelbaum Gate. I took them to the King David Hotel where the director-general of Israel's Foreign Ministry was waiting. I gave him the letter to take to Golda Meir. Then we had tea. They were going to leave by plane the next day and wanted to run down to Tel Aviv with me to see my home and to have a look around. I told them that one day I would be treating them to a cocktail in the Intercontinental Hotel on the Mount of Olives, but they didn't take this seriously.

Unlike the third incident, which arose out of the war in June 1967, the second incident did not involve Israel. Wellesley was called on to help Pan Am, perhaps as a quid pro quo for Pan Am's intervention with the Jordanian government during the Mount of Olives crisis. Sam Pryor phoned Wellesley from America asking him to fly to New York at once, which he duly did. On his arrival Sam Pryor explained 'the delicate and almost hopeless problem'.

> 'You see a Congress committee is starting an investigation into Pan American to look for breaches of the law of monopolies and mergers. As a last resort I suggested you should be brought over to try and stop it. You know a few people in Congress and the chairman of the Justice Committee is Emmanuel Celler. He is the oldest congressman in the house and represents Brooklyn and that's a Jewish community isn't it?' I took on the job without expecting any results. I phoned a Jewish congressman from New York who I knew well and who had been out to see me in Israel. He and his wife were friends with Rose and me. I had lunch with him and told him the problem. He was silent. Then he asked me to go to Washington DC as soon as possible, to be at a certain restaurant at 8 o'clock, to ask for a certain person. Then I would be seated at a largish table where I was to wait. I did what he asked. Soon I was seated at a table with 10 to 15 people, mostly, if not all, Jewish politicians. They asked

[1]The crossing point established after the ceasefire in 1949 in Jerusalem between the Jordanian- and Israeli-held parts of the city. The city has been united under Israeli control since June 1967.

me about conditions in Israel and this that and the other and I certainly didn't see the point in it all. After dinner one of them asked me to go with him. We walked to the back of the hotel where he told me to wait for a car to pick me up. I said that it was all very mysterious and what was it all about. He wouldn't tell me anything.

The car arrived and a woman introduced me to the man sitting in the back of the car. She said, 'This is Congressman Celler, Emmanuel Celler.' Then he spoke. 'Oh yes I know Wellesley Aron. We met at the Rotary Club in Tel Aviv. You proposed a vote of thanks to my speech years ago, don't you remember?' I replied, 'Good gracious I'd quite forgotten.' He went on, 'I remember very distinctly what you said and I liked it and I'm very pleased to meet you. How are you?' Meanwhile we were being driven through the night. ... I didn't know what was going to happen. We stopped at a new housing estate. He told me that we were going to celebrate the corner-stone laying of a house of one of his staff. There were about thirty or forty people, men and women gathered there with drinks in their hands and a lot of lighting in the trees and surroundings. It was quite a jolly cheery occasion. I was introduced all round. I didn't notice anyone that I knew. When we were all settled down I noticed that Emmanuel Celler was the centre of attention. He asked a few questions about different investigations and then he said, 'Well you know we have got this Pan American investigation coming up.' The moment I heard Pan American I listened very carefully and one of the younger men there said, 'We're turning up quite a lot of dirt you know. We've come to the conclusion that there is a very strong case.' Hearing that I suddenly thought this is my cue. I asked Emmanuel if I could have a few words. He said, 'Oh yes. I haven't introduced you properly. Major Aron represents Pan American World Airways in Tel Aviv Israel.' There was shocked silence. I began, 'Yes, I have the honour to represent one of the biggest airlines in the world and one of the largest American carriers. It doesn't fly to Israel but they appointed me to look after their interests out there and that I have been doing. Regarding your remarks as to Pan American's ethical and other activities, let me tell you of a conversation I had with Mr Trippe, the president of Pan

American World Airways.' There was utter silence. 'You know I listened to him very carefully before I joined the company which I had heard was not very interested in Jews or Palestine or Israel. They wanted me and I undertook the job and I suppose I'm the only Jewish member of staff on any senior level and I can tell you what the policy of Pan American is as it was told to me by Pan American's president, Mr Trippe.'

By the time I had finished there was silence, not a word and Emmanuel Celler spoke to me. 'Wellesley, I don't know whether you know what you've done now but whatever you came over here to do you've achieved.' I still didn't know what the score was. We had one last drink before I was taken back to my hotel. Sam Pryor had asked me to call him whatever time of night I got back, so as soon as I was back in my room I got through to him. He asked me where I'd been. I told him. He asked me who was there. I told him. He said, 'It's incredible. Do you know you've stopped this thing in its tracks? Don't you know who all those young people were? They are all the lawyers and investigating agents of the judicial committee of Congress and you had them all together. That was what Emmanuel Celler did for you. He took you down there, exposed you and you did the job. I want you to get in touch with Mr Trippe in the morning.' I reminded him that I was in Washington and wanted to go home, so he asked me to meet him in Washington the next day to pick up a letter which I was to take to Mr Trippe myself.

I picked up the letter and returned by plane to New York. I went at once to the Pan Am executive offices. I got out of the lift and there was nobody around, no guard and no sign of any security at all. I heard voices in the far corner and I walked across. The door was open and there was Mr Trippe talking to vice-president Leslie who was pacing up and down in his braces while smoking a cigar. I looked in. Mr Trippe spoke first. 'Oh, Aron I want to see you. I've been waiting for you. Sam Pryor has been on the phone telling me a few things.' I gave him the letter from Sam and he read it at once. He asked, 'What do you want?' I said, 'What do you mean, what do I want?' 'What would you like to have?' I replied, 'I have no idea. What are you suggesting?' He went on, 'Is there anything

I can give you, or do for you? Well, say something.' I said, 'I would like to talk to my wife long distance on the telephone. She is in Switzerland waiting for me. We are going to have our holiday.' He told me to use any phone I liked and talk to anybody in the world at their expense. I shook his hand and told him that the absence of any security made him very vulnerable to attack. He agreed that something should be done about it and that was that. I might add that Congressman Celler was as good as the word he didn't give me. The case was cancelled and never heard of again. Celler and I and our families became very close friends.

* * *

The Six Days War broke out in 1967 and finished very quickly. It was tremendously traumatic for everyone because Israel had tackled its neighbours from a position of great military inferiority from the point of view of numbers and armaments, yet had come out winning hands down. Jerusalem was captured and united; the whole of Sinai was taken and the position in Jordan was consolidated. One of the unexpected results was a telephone call to me from New York to tell me that the Intercontinental Hotel on the Mount of Olives was now in Israeli territory and I was asked to help to deal with it. I pointed out that I knew nothing about hotels or its status, or the condition it was in. I was asked to go up there and see what was going on. I got a military pass, because it was still out of bounds and there were still snipers about. Only the day before a journalist had been shot dead outside the hotel.

I arrived to find chaos there. The Israeli troops had driven out the Arab Legion and it was interesting for me as an ex-soldier to notice that none of the bottles of booze or wine in the bar had been touched. Yet the telephone exchange and other electrical equipment were missing and never found again. There were bullet holes in the doors and the whole building was affected by the shooting that had gone on. There was an overpowering smell of decaying flesh around. I asked what it was and was told that there were five tons of American meat lying in the hotel refrigerator and the electricity was cut off. The meat was rotting. So I had to get through to Teddy Kollek and ask him to get it removed as quickly as possible so that we could fumigate the place and make it bearable at least. There was nobody in charge at all. The manager and his wife, who were Austrians, had taken flight when the war began, quite rightly so because it was a very dangerous place to be in. The workers, waiters and other members of the staff, who were all Arabs, were standing around waiting for something to happen. I didn't know who they were and I didn't know how to begin so I asked who was in charge and was told that nobody was. I said that someone must have been senior, and was given the name Mr Halabi who had been in charge of accounts. He was at home somewhere in East Jerusalem. None of the houses had any numbers and the streets had no names. However I discovered him and dragged him up there. He was a very nice fellow. I asked him what he was doing and he told me that he was waiting for the danger to subside and for the shooting to stop. I assured him that it was all over bar the shouting and that he should come and give me a hand. The first thing I did was to open a bank account to pay the poor starving workers who could then go back to their villages in the surrounding areas and buy some food for their families.

I spoke to New York and told them what I had been doing and I was promptly put in charge. 'But I know nothing about hotels whatever,' I protested. 'Well you are in charge, you are our representative out there.' 'I don't even know what status this hotel has. It was apparently part of King Hussein's property, now it has been captured.' I was told to deal with the legal side and let them know what happened. So I got in touch with the relevant ministries and started sorting out the legal and financial aspects of this whole thing. I made contracts for the repairs to the building so that I could get it operating normally as soon as possible. We soon managed this and a few months later we were unofficially open again and doing business. This meant that I went up to Jerusalem at least once or twice a week to keep an eye on things and I forced the Austrian manager to come back until he was officially replaced. For the first year or two after the June war I was the person in charge. It gave me a certain amount of satisfaction to see that my prophecy of some years back was fulfilled and I was able to entertain certain vice-presidents of Pan American Airways and Intercontinental Hotels in the bar of the Mount of Olives Hotel as I had predicted.

CHAPTER TWELVE

Rotarian – Peace-seeker

In the 1950s and early 1960s Wellesley was mainly occupied with running his office, dealing with Pan American affairs as the occasion demanded, pursuing his interests with the Rotary Organisation in Israel and tackling a new sport – golf. In 1960, Israel's first and only golf course was laid out amongst the sand dunes at Caesarea. The project was promoted by James de Rothschild. Teddy Kollek asked Wellesley to serve on the planning committee, but he was somewhat reluctant to become involved. He was already very occupied with Rotary, Pan Am and Israel's Maritime League. He pointed out that he was 'sick of joining committees where the first order of business was raising funds and a very difficult job it was and I wasn't very suited for it'. He only accepted when he was assured that he would not be asked to raise funds, because the Rothschilds had agreed to fund the project. He soon became chairman of the golf club's board, which meant dealing with everyday problems, especially financial ones. This did not lessen his enjoyment of the game.

> The years went by and I concentrated on getting a low handicap. I was over sixty when I started to play and I got it down to single figures. I enjoyed the game very much but spent far too much time out at Caesarea.

Wellesley's other major interest at this time was Rotary. For two years he was president of the Tel Aviv–Jaffa Rotary Club, where he was able to take up again the kind of involvement with youngsters which had given him so much satisfaction thirty years earlier in London. His membership in Rotary brought him eventually to the activity which satisfyingly filled the last two decades of his life.

> I found a great deal of opportunity and satisfaction in doing certain social work, such as creating the means to establish a youth sports club in the most neglected area, Schunat Hatikva in Jaffa, which the police had told us was a breeding-ground for crime. The centre was established thanks very largely to the

fact that the Harlem Globetrotters basketball team was brought over through the Rotarians' efforts. They played three or four games to packed audiences of several thousands. The end result was that we had enough money to build the community sports centre.

In the course of my various activities, I became involved in the struggle for what in Rotary parlance is called establishing a Rotary District. Rotary had first arrived in Palestine in about 1929 when the Cairo Club established one in Jerusalem. In 1934 or thereabouts clubs were opened in Haifa and Jaffa–Tel Aviv, as it was then called. I was one of the first members and it was an interesting experience for me to sit for a meal every week with Arab and British Rotarians, I being one of the few Jews who was interested in being a member of the club. By the end of the Second World War there were some twenty clubs throughout the country, many with a mixed Arab–Jewish membership, and so far as socialising was concerned it was a definite catalyst. It brought the communities together side by side even in the midst of political rioting and what not. In fact in 1937 or thereabouts when the Arab riots broke out and there was unrest throughout the country, the Rotarians met in the Lorenz café in Jaffa on Thursday every week, even if a British armoured car had to remain outside to protect the members while they were eating.

After the war I was nominated to become what they called an administrative adviser. My job was to look after all the clubs and to do what I could to encourage them, but I was not what is called a district governor. We didn't have a district. So, together with Wolf Cegla, I started a campaign to try to get Rotary International, whose headquarters are in Chicago Illinois, to appoint or enable us to organise our district so that we could have a governor who would be trained, like all district governors, by Rotary International when they are called together in America once a year. Rotary was not interested and there was a lot of opposition, particularly from our Arab neighbours in Egypt, Lebanon, Syria and so on where there was a small handful of Rotary clubs. They said quite frankly that if Rotary in Israel was given the status of a self-governing district, then the Arabs would all resign from Rotary International. This was the challenge. Cegla and I went to Delhi to the Asian Conference of Rotary clubs. There I met Cliff Randall, a past president of Rotary, and told him our problem. I said that I could not understand why Rotary International did not stand up to this form of blackmail and show some courage by doing what was obviously required, since we were twenty-odd clubs already and the whole of the Middle East didn't have more than five or six outside Israel. There was a lot of correspondence and one year I actually went to Lake Placid where the district governors were being trained. I couldn't take part in their programme, but I could participate in what we call the Institute. There I got up and voiced our resentment at this discrimination and was asked to present the case to the Districting Committee of Rotary International.

I did just that, but the chairman was unfriendly and seemed to be actively hostile to my proposal. When I put the case I said that I couldn't understand why he would not district us. We had the requisite number of clubs and we could pay our way. He told me that he could see no reason to make Israel a Rotary District. I disagreed, but I got nowhere in that meeting. However, when Cliff Randall had listened to us and read the correspondence, he said that he would come to Israel on his way back to the United States and have a look at us. He liked what he saw, because on his return to America he recommended that we be given District status. This happened in 1960. I was elected Israel's first Rotary District Governor at the annual conference held in Herzliya. The friends and contacts I made during my term of office became an invaluable source of support later on.

In 1967, after the Six Days War, I attended the annual District Rotary conference in Jerusalem, largely as an observer. My days of activity were over and now other people had taken my place. I was sitting amongst five or six hundred people from all over the world, including our own Israeli Rotarians, feeling rather bored listening to some of the speeches. The District Governor for the year came up to me and said, 'Wellesley, I need you.' I asked him what for. He replied, 'You've got to chair a panel meeting in about twenty minutes.' I protested. 'I'm not prepared for anything.' He insisted. 'You are going to have to do this because there has been a breakdown in the programme and all these people are expecting this discussion which I want you to lead.' 'What's the subject?' I asked him. 'International understanding, goodwill and peace.' 'Really', I objected, 'This is the sort of subject one has to study and the presentation has to be thought about. I am not an expert on this and you ought to find somebody else.' 'No.' He was adamant. 'You're going to do it, and here's an Indian Rotarian from Bombay, who is the Governor of his District and a visitor here. He will be one of your assistants and here is a gentleman from Germany, a Lutheran and the first Gentile German to attend one of our conferences.' He left the three of us to our own devices. I asked them what they proposed to do. They replied that they had no idea, they would follow my lead. 'Well', I said, 'I haven't got the faintest idea. I might wander off to the Negev and that is where you may find me if you care to follow me. But I don't know how I am going to start this thing and what we are going to talk about.'

The doors were opened and we were ushered into the crowded hall. We sat down on the podium and we were introduced. I still hadn't a clue as to how to open the proceedings. There was a terrible silence, a very embarrassing silence as you can imagine. I knew I was the only person who could and should break the tension. I don't know what possessed me, but I got up and spoke:

'Fellow Rotarians, ladies and gentlemen, I'm looking for an address.' Everyone sat up. I went on:

'I want to find the address of a place in this world, anywhere where my grandson and other young people, men and women, boys and girls, pupils and students, may go for training in the field of peace. I know quite a lot of institutions where my grandson will be taught about war and we have seen the result of all these generations, but surely there must be some places or a place where Peace is the subject of instruction.'

My question had an explosive impact and a great deal of excitement, enthusiasm, and even hysteria followed it. Someone got up and proposed that an ad hoc committee should be established and that I should be asked to become chairman. The committee's task was to investigate where and if and how this whole idea could materialise.

* * *

I don't know to this day what possessed me to say this, but undoubtedly this question changed my life. Some fourteen years after that conference, I was still struggling with the problem which left me no peace. I must say quite frankly that I became an awful bore to all my friends and family. I could no longer play golf without discussing the problem. I could no longer enter a conversation without raising the matter of peace in education somewhere down the line. I noticed that people were beginning to avoid me. Although they were very polite to me they took my words with a grain of salt and were obviously saying to themselves 'This man is obsessed', which indeed I was. I couldn't relax and couldn't rid myself of this obsession until I made progress in my researches. I must admit that it seemed incomprehensible that in this world which was waiting for an answer to the dangers confronting it from atom bombs and nuclear fission, which implied imminent destruction, that there had been no serious attempt to grapple with the whole question of trying to educate or train experts and professionals by teaching youngsters about survival through first-class education in schools. I realised that this was where my heart really belonged. The more I went around the world, the more I felt the urgency of the matter. I went to the United States and to Europe, always looking for an answer to the question. I found that there was no real attempt being made to deal with the whole problem and I was appalled.

I was looking for a place where young people could go and take a course of study which would lead to a bachelor's or master's degree or doctorate eventually. These people would be highly qualified and have a reputation for their knowledge of the subject. They could be called in as experts whenever there was confrontation and disturbance and conflict and I found that there was no body anywhere in the world where this work was actually taking place in a serious and effective way. It is true that one or two institutions were just established. For example the Oslo institute for conflict resolution was just getting under way with Professor Galtung. But it was all very inadequate and I was more and more concerned and more and more horrified by the imminence of the disaster ahead of us and the lack of preparation to try and avoid it.

In my search for an answer to the question as to whether

peace could be taught as a professional subject in a secular atmosphere, I was surprised to read in the *New York Times* that the Manhattan College was offering for the first time a BA degree course in peace. I telephoned for a copy of the curriculum which I read with great interest while on a fund-raising tour of the United States for the Jewish Agency. I soon discovered that this was not a degree in peace, but a degree in 'Christian' peace. It was not what I had expected to find. When I returned to New York I phoned the Dean again to thank him for sending me the curriculum. 'I see that you are teaching "Christian" peace', I said. 'Yes, isn't that obvious?' was his reply. 'No, it is not obvious to me, I'm a Jew and "Christian" peace does not appeal to me as a secular subject for study. I know many others who would be disappointed to see that there is a "Christian" peace, a "Moslem" peace and a "Jewish" peace and all sorts of other peaces connected with religious affirmation.' He asked me who I was and I told him 'an Israeli'. Further questioning revealed that we were both from Cambridge University as were most of his colleagues. He told me that they were a Jesuit College. 'Having said that,' he went on, 'would you be prepared to come and address our student body and describe what you have in mind.' I had to refuse because I was off to the West Coast for the next part of my tour.

On my return to Israel, I found an invitation from Germany asking me to be Israel's representative at the first international conference to be held on the subject of 'Peace Education and Social Justice' in Bad Nauheim in November 1972. I immediately contacted the Foreign Office for their opinion. As I had anticipated they were negative. 'Don't go there,' was the advice. 'It is full of Arabs and Ugandans and Africans and other hostile characters who will use the opportunity to make anti-Israel propaganda and you will be snowed under by the whole thing and it may even be dangerous for you.' 'Well, if it's dangerous perhaps you could let the Ambassador know and he could provide a bodyguard as required,' I replied, but I had decided to go whether I got a bodyguard or not.

As I was checking into the hotel arranged for me by the conference organisers a young man walked up and welcomed me. He said he was there to see that I was all right. I told him that I thought his presence would be unnecessary but that I was delighted to see him. I went to the conference opening session and listened to speeches by some eminent professors, American, German, English, Scandinavian etc., and wandered around wondering whether there was going to be anything here which I could absorb and use in my quest for peace education. The next day I was approached by Professor Galtung from Oslo who chaired the committee on 'Strategy and Peace Education' whatever that meant. 'We're very pleased that you're here from Israel. Would you be co-chairman with me?' I agreed although as I told him I knew nothing about the subject. During the day several people came up to me and said how surprised they were to see me there. When I asked them why, I was told: 'Well you know you come from the Zionist state.' 'Yes, I certainly do.' 'It's aggressive and anti-peace, isn't it?' I replied, 'No, not necessarily, and I've come to find out what you people are doing and what is known on the subject generally.' There were people from ten or more different countries there, including a Ugandan professor who was at Oxford University, an extremely able man, but although nice to me personally, he was obviously contaminated by the vicious anti-Israel propaganda put out by his government. He admitted that he was taking cover in Oxford until Amin was removed.

A Lebanese girl came up to me and said she was shocked to find an Israeli participating, as it seemed absolutely contrary to the ideas on which Israel was being governed and so on and so forth. When it came to the meeting which I was to co-chair, Professor Galtung simply told the thirty or forty students of different nationalities that he was leaving the meeting in my capable hands and walked out. I soon found myself in the centre of a polemical argument concerning the horrors of modern German education. The most vociferous and violent participants were young German students who simply monopolised the discussion. When they had finished and saw that there was no more time to elaborate their views, I intervened and said, 'Now I am going to introduce myself and don't get a shock. I'm a Jew, I come from Israel and I'm a Zionist and I have something to tell you which may be of interest if you will listen quietly and settle down.' Then I told them that their idea of anarchy, which is what they were after, destruction, complete destruction of the German education system, would lead nowhere. I said I'd been listening for a couple of hours hoping that something positive would emerge. I went on, 'As nothing positive has emerged I can only tell you, as a representative of a people who have had two thousand years of education, that we are very careful not to destroy anything until we've got something better to put in its place, and we've survived as you see.' They took it from me and that was that.

That's about the only thing I got out of it. In fact I put more in than I got out. I was asked to contribute an article to be published in a collection of papers given at this first conference. I wrote one called 'Critical monitoring of the mass media, an aspect of education for peace'. I never heard if it was published or not.

The idea to hold a symposium in Jerusalem was taken up by Rotary in Israel. I set about forming a committee to plan and finance the project. I found a treasurer in my old friend Percy Manham of the Tel Aviv Rotary club. I began to look for partners because I knew that it was quite impossible for me to organise the thing alone.

At about this time it was announced that the Hebrew University of Jerusalem was establishing the Harry S. Truman Centre for the Advancement of Peace, to be built on Mount Scopus, Har Hatzofim. I immediately contacted the University and was told that a Professor Julius Stone from Melbourne University, Australia, was in charge of academic planning and that my old friend Harry Zinder was in charge of the construction of the new institute. I arranged to have lunch with them both and asked what was planned for the centre. Their answer was very vague and unsatisfactory as far as I was concerned. They didn't really know what was going to be done there. They asked me if I had a proposal and I told them about our Jerusalem programme, which was already printed, to organise a symposium on the problems of peace. Julius Stone read it and enthusiastically endorsed it. 'Could we open the Truman Centre with this programme? I think that's what we ought to do because the things that we have lined up are completely different. We thought of doing only research work at the

> centre on subjects like the economic problems of developing countries.' I said, 'That sort of subject can be dealt with at Heidelberg or Oxford or Cambridge or Yale or Harvard – anywhere – but what we are trying to do here is to use Jerusalem for something more important and significant.
>
> They agreed with me and we formed a joint committee of the University and Rotary. I was to be responsible for the non-academic side of things. I sent out notices to all sorts of institutions and almost by return got positive replies from well-known Nobel prize-winners, particularly from Germany, who asked if they could take part. We had got a tentative date, but hadn't raised the funds at this stage. Rotary contributed a sum sufficient to launch us with the understanding that the University and the Truman Centre would equal the amount (which they never did).

Wellesley was occupied with the peace project almost exclusively for months on end. Gradually he distilled his own thoughts as he gathered material and discussed the project with more and more people in Israel and from abroad. Wellesley settled on three themes for Rotary's opening peace programme: education and peace; mass communication and peace (including the creative arts); and youth's contribution to peace. He hoped passionately that the symposium would differ from the run-of-the-mill academic gatherings where expert would speak to expert and nothing new would surface. Israel's Rotary had agreed to endow a chair of peace studies at the Hebrew University. Wellesley hoped that it would inspire other universities throughout the world to follow the example in Jerusalem. He expressed his personal hopes for the symposium to his fellow Rotarians in a series of meetings he addressed to raise funds for the project.

> This in a sense will be a symposium which will leave a deep and abiding mark on all those who follow the proceedings ... surely peace must rank side by side with every priority that we can conceive and certainly, in my opinion, above scientific advance, and it is because peace has been relegated in our time, and in full view of all the generations, that the Youth are rebelling, because peace has been relegated to a secondary rank in the priorities of man – material progress, scientific advance, interstellar exploration, the expansion of power

> exercised by one group or another by any means available to man, with scarcely any reference to the ethical conditions without which this planet will revert either to a jungle or to a mere piece of dust floating in the empyrean.

The urgent need to disseminate peace studies directed Wellesley's mind to the role of the mass media as a means to reach out to people world-wide. Drawing on an unimplemented code of ethics for journalists drawn up by a UNESCO committee, Wellesley urged professionals to act more responsibly, to become more aware of the emotional effects of their work on their audiences, especially on young people, who he considered were being poisoned by the distorted information offered them by adults. He promoted a television peace festival to coincide with the symposium planned for 1970. He circulated invitations to film-makers and producers, but nothing came of it. He recognised bitterly that 'Bad news, unfortunately, is more exciting than Peace'.

His challenge was not limited to media professionals. He called upon musicians, dramatists, painters, sculptors, writers of fiction, all those engaged in the creative arts,

> that they should endeavour – however difficult – to dramatise and to fill with passion and with colour and with motion the concept of Peace which hitherto has been a slogan generally found etched and engraved on memorials to the dead, rather than on the banners of the living. If Peace is what you find in a cemetery, then that is one angle of peace with which we are all too familiar. There seems to be a symbolic element in that statement which I hope will be uprooted and transformed from something passive into something active by the time we have done our job in regard to the symposium to take place in Jerusalem ... therefore the challenge is to the creative arts to get into line and to associate themselves with the urgent necessities and to get away from the theory of art to its practical application for a purpose and a cause which surely is central to man's salvation.

The third theme attracted him most, but was the one which unnerved the academics from the Hebrew University and Truman Institute. Wellesley did not conceal his admiration for the young, especially for teenagers to whom he dedicated several talks and a paper entitled 'In praise of teenagers'. What follow are some extracts from a talk he gave in March 1970.

> Most of us have some contact or other with the young . . . some of us still have enough vitality to be able to cope with the teenage group, with the disturbed and unhappy young men and women on the threshold of life who find the world an entirely unsatisfactory place in which to build their future. And they look around as all dissatisfied human beings do, and all those who are enmeshed in frustrations of one form or another – they look around for someone to blame – and in this instance, they have every right to blame us; you and me, the generation which is here and will not be here to see the results of all the things which are happening around us today. But the youth will have to live through a period which many of them believe may end in death, destruction and devastation, and possibly eternal oblivion as far as man as we know him today is concerned on this earth.
>
> Those of us who have enough imagination, commiserate with the young. We know the horror of living with the sword of Damocles. Most of us have been confronted with it in one form or the other ever since we became cognisant of the world in which we live. It may not always be a bad thing to have some sort of spur to incentive and to progress, but holocaust and doom and destruction is surely not the thing to confront young people with, and this is the legacy we have given them and they know it and they see it and they resent it . . . These youngsters have to respond to this challenge and it is all they can do to fulfil their obligations to maintain adequate protection for what has been created here in Israel in the face of such tremendous difficulties and in such unlikely and unpromising circumstances. But there may be a limit to what we can expect from them, for there must be at least some hope, some feeling that what we are involved with here is not an eternal situation, but one that could be repaired, and shall be repaired and must be repaired by actions that are not only political, but by things that are spiritual and by things that have been thought out according to some specific plan which began in the silence of one's early life. Only this can lead even the most unpromising human beings towards an understanding of their obligations to their fellow man.

These young people who have rebelled from one end of the world to the other, and in the most unexpected areas, wherever they have had an opportunity to express dissatisfaction with the powers that be, with the type of education that they are getting, with their lack of participation in the design of training which has been prepared for them by forefathers and their predecessors, who wrapped in sanctity and tradition and emotionally and sentimentally propagandised by every institution which reveres its past and clings to it as something familiar, unlike the future which is of course always a question-mark – these youngsters are prepared to kick over the traces and to strike out and destroy the sanctimonious, holier-than-thou attitude which they find so often in the teachers at whose feet they are supposed to sit as a disciplined and obedient group, accepting with perhaps too little challenge a lot of things that are propounded to them as being sacrosanct because they have been taught that way for so long.

I say quite frankly that I am on the side of the young – the young have not only the responsibility to bear the difficulties of living in the world such as they are born into, and apparently without their previous consent – for we are all here by virtue of things happening that we never planned to participate in and are only the result of – we therefore have no responsibility except to do the best we know in each generation. Well, the best that the youngsters know is to say that they are thoroughly appalled by this world which however much advanced, is still so far from being at rest, so far from being a place where justice, harmony, understanding and egalitarianism in one form or another has been created; a world where so much emphasis is placed on the financially speculative elements, and so great are the prizes offered and so far and so often out of proportion are they to the effort involved, that they find far too much irrationality in the world that surrounds them . . . and our generation will always be the recipient of the criticism of the next in line. This may be to the good as long as we provide the means for intelligent and comprehensible discussion; and as we believe in freedom – to try one's own powers rather than be led by somebody who assumes they can do the job better than we can – so we must encourage the young to set out on the adventure and make whatever mistakes lie ahead,

> but give them the HEART and the COURAGE, the opportunity and above all, to say and do what they think is right.
>
> Thus it is that the symposium has catered for youth. But it has done so in what may be regarded as a typical Rotary spirit. It has done so on the practical level, on the positive approach, rather than on the critical one, and it says to the young – who may be anywhere between the ages of eighteen and twenty-five, married or unmarried, of any sex, race, colour or creed – all those who want to participate in the symposium and to make their views felt and justify their presence as participants will be listened to with interest and included wherever the opportunity arises ... we hope that those who come to the symposium in Jerusalem will be able to get a first-hand impression of what young people demand, not only of the world, but also of themselves.
>
> May tolerance be taught from the nursery to the grave. May all the things that man needs to survive on this earth as sensient, intelligent and reasonable human beings, be included in the institution we shall call the Institution of Peace and may the symposium move, however small a step, towards that goal, Amen.

There were joint meetings of the University and Rotary committees in Wellesley's house two or three times and progress was slowly made towards their goal. Then, quite suddenly, at one of these meetings someone from the Hebrew University said, 'We've decided not to proceed with this programme.' Wellesley takes up his story again:

> It came as a stunning blow to all present. I asked him why. 'Your emphasis on the importance of youth reduces the significance and the importance of this whole symposium. We don't want to be a sort of amateur group of people catering for the young, we want to be an academic body examining the whole area and the whole question on a very high level.' I reacted, 'It is going to be a lot of work and will probably involve a lot of money to organise this symposium. If it's to give a platform for professors, however well known they are, and they are to be paid; and Nobel prize-winners are going to come and make propaganda speeches in Jerusalem; I personally am not going to be a party to it, although I have no objections to their doing

it. But if that's going to be the limit of our activities, the whole plan falls to the ground. I believe in the future and if it's a question of the future, then we must have the youth involved here. The young people are going to be the leaders of the world in a few years' time, and if we can attract them to the symposium and give them something that they are looking for, and they can come in their hundreds and thousands if necessary and be present here, then we shall have succeeded as far as I am concerned.' Then the University people objected, 'That's exactly what we don't want, you are going to turn this whole thing into a Woodstock and we don't want to have that in Jerusalem.' I replied that if I organised it, it would not be anything like that. There would be a certain moral background to it and some sort of moral discipline.

The meeting broke up and I was back to square one with a very highly developed programme for the symposium which was destined never to take place. I had concentrated particularly on subjects which I knew would interest young people such as the various methods of communication – television, radio, newspapers – as well as on other activities which very urgently needed to be examined from the point of view of peace. The whole plan collapsed and I had nothing more to do. I wandered around, in America and elsewhere, talking to foundations and various other bodies trying to interest people, but they all seemed to make difficulties. I made no progress. Around this time my wife Rose passed away. Before her death she asked me to promise to go on with my project whatever happened and I promised her to do that. When the shock of her departure waned and I began to come back to normal, I thought to myself: what can I do to get off this dead spot?

CHAPTER THIRTEEN

Salvation – Peace Education

Wellesley returned again and again to wrestle with the problem of how to turn people away from conflict and towards co-existence. He struggled to define what he meant by that term.

> Now co-existence is the condition which results from knowledge based on mutual understanding. This develops from acquaintance and familiarity with the respective dreams, prayers, hopes and problems of all parties involved. These are the fabric of life which guides, directs and impels the human being towards the things deemed necessary for survival. These elements cannot be guessed at or understood and appreciated except on the basis of experience. To play a musical instrument one must first be familiar with it. To play it satisfactorily one must practise until many of the actions acquire the reliability of reflexes. Surely it is asking too much to expect that individuals who have never enjoyed the benefit of a training in co-existence can ever attain and develop the requirements called for in the search for peace. Therefore all educational curricula in the primary and secondary stage of schooling should include training in co-existence as a fundamental and essential element in their programmes. If the assumption is true that Peace in its widest, deepest and most meaningful sense can only be achieved on the foundations of co-existence then such a foundation must be created.

He saw education in peace and conflict resolution for the young as the only way forward towards this goal. He never wavered in his conviction that change would only follow a radically different attitude towards children and young people. Although his own experiences with the Boy Scout movement in England had partially inspired his Habonim programme, the real source of all his educational projects was his recognition that children, especially teenagers, respond creatively and respectfully to other people and the world around them if they themselves are treated respectfully and justly and above all without hypocrisy. In 1983 he recorded some of his ideas for the Institute of Contemporary Jewry.[1] In reply to many questions about the founding of Habonim he presented his beliefs about education.

> Now I happened to believe in the youth, as I do here now in Neve Shalom. We're dealing only with young Arabs and young Jews. The youth is the key to the lock of the community. I knew the right key would open the door. My Habonim programme was outstanding. I say it myself in modesty. I happen to have a gift for this sort of thing; I'm inventive and creative and I had the opportunity to use these gifts and I did it. And I wasn't overwhelmed by it. The child's future I deliberately left to the decision of the individual child . . . our job is to expose the children to a complete wealth of information. I'm not imposing anything on anybody. I was not interested in ideological and organisational conflicts. I have a very strong opinion about the difference between propaganda and education; and here already you've got propaganda. Let's make them into Labour Jews and Labour Zionists and chalutzim. Others said let's make them into rabbis and religious leaders. All this, I said, is for the future to decide. I will not do what Ignatius Loyola did for the Jesuits who said, 'Give me a child until he is 7 (I think it was), and he's mine for the rest of his life. I captured him; I brainwashed him. He'll never get clear of it.'
>
> I was very frightened of doing harm. Doing harm and going beyond the bounds of what I call education. Possibly all these questions (ideological etc.) were inherent in the movement. But I refrained from going beyond what I thought was normal for children up to 15 or 16 years of age. Teddy Kollek came over from Ein Gev. He was in charge of the youth, I suppose, for the labour people. He immediately put the whole thing into hachshara and dotted the i's and crossed the t's. Suddenly I see there's hachshara going ; and suddenly I see there's going to be a kibbutz. That was propaganda for the left and the socialists. I don't think it was a bad thing, because I know a lot of these youngsters did very well in the kibbutzim and they contributed

[1] Hebrew University of Jerusalem, Institute of Contemporary Jewry, Oral History Division; interviewer Naomi Bar-Joseph, 9 March 1983.

to the development when they came here. But I didn't think that was my purpose. I wanted to save them from assimilation, basically. Collect them and bring them back and then what they would become would not be my problem.

I launched the ship and it was sailing adequately if not completely and satisfactorily and that is that. But Habonim was never properly and completely applied, like most ideas. They never got around to using it all. They only used the superficial and obvious things. And it worked on that level. If I'd been in the movement I'd have made it deeper and deeper, so that it would have become a cultural youth movement, instead of being superficial and propagandistic. I know what I put into it and how little of it came out. It wasn't enough to satisfy me as an educationalist. It was something like sending someone up to the fourth class of a secondary school and saying you're not going any further than that.

The Jewish people, per se, being a very able people – as you know – with a respect for tradition and keen for things that work in Jewish life, have been ineffectual largely in the educational field, except for certain things. When it came to training kids at school they remained in the medieval condition of a cheder, which was abysmal in the twentieth century. So that there was not a Jewish school in England that inspired. What Jewish education ought to have provided in the emancipated world of the West it failed to do as it was archaic, antedeluvian. And to sit these children down and make them learn by rote (and obviously they didn't) was deadly. That's what Habonim broke. Habonim broke that vicious circle and displayed the fact that children, given something interesting and exciting to do, will respond accordingly. Professional Jewish educators fall down on this isssue. First of all I didn't want propaganda as an easy way out. You see, when people have no ideas they begin to be propagandists. They have one idea and they force this on the child, and all the rest goes by the board.

He agonised at what was on offer in the guise of education.

And what are the teenagers offered? A world they soon discover, which while not of their making requires them to conform to ways which are often unreasonable and generally dishonest, to which they must subscribe – if not sincerely, then

> theoretically – if they are to be accepted as members of society and are to find a valid place for themselves. Often such a place does not in fact exist and they soon find themselves caught in the toils of ongoing conflict. Caught is the word . . . is it fair, or even useful, to launch teenagers into a world which they have begun to distrust, to query as to its moral values? The truth is that they are already in a condition of pollution so far as their personal attitudes have been generally diverted, subverted and contaminated by their surroundings, the media and their seniors – whether in the family circle or by the environment. Thus, full of misinformation, prejudices and the basic anxiety of the world which surrounds them, they are expected to behave in a so-called relaxed manner and to take their places among their peers and to contribute to progress and positive values. How grossly and patently unfair and unreasonable!
>
> The teenagers, stumbling on an unfamiliar path in a jungle of untruths, misconceptions and often unrepentant lies, search for a way out and after finding none, engage in activities which while absorbing their frustrations, are often anti-social and worse. No questions are ever asked of the young . . . on whom the very future of our society, perhaps even of the whole world may well rest. Why not, for once, examine the problem with compassion and devise a solution which serves the needs of the young and not the convenience of adults? Anyone observing teenagers will soon discover their basic honesty, courage, commitment and endurance. They are in fact equipped by nature to serve the very values which the world so freely adumbrates and so casually discards when in difficulties.

It was his faith in youngsters as the hope for the future and his unwavering impulse to be involved in education as his way to express his faith which got him off the dead spot he experienced after the near simultaneous death of his first wife and his peace symposium. The turmoil into which these events plunged him and his fury at the failure of all educational systems to offer children some knowledge about how to coexist with the people amongst whom they lived drove him to action.

> Suddenly I decided to contact headmasters of certain schools about teaching peace. None was interested. They said that I was not talking practical politics. Then I decided to contact the

Ministry of Education in Jerusalem and ask for a meeting of the relevant personnel on the subject of peace education. To my surprise about twenty senior officials were there and I outlined my plan. They were startled of course. I told them that I would like to hold an experiment in Tel Aviv and the only facilities I needed were pupils and a room. They looked at me with some degree of scepticism but in the end agreed, much to my surprise. Now I was confronted with what I would do and where I would do it. I didn't think that the officials would really follow through, but in due course I was informed that there were three schools and would I contact the directors and let them know if I was going to use the facilities. The first director I called to see was out, but the second greeted me warmly and I liked him at once. I felt that this was the school where I could try out my idea. He welcomed me, but told me that he didn't understand my idea and that no one in Jerusalem had understood it either. I told him vaguely what I had in mind, but he insisted on a written curriculum because 'I couldn't let you into this school without knowing exactly what you are going to do'. 'The trouble is', I replied, 'I don't know what I am going to do because I've never done it before and to my knowledge nobody else has done it and it's all a question of trial and error.' I wrote a curriculum to show him and he said it was all right. I asked him what he had been looking for. He answered, 'I wanted to know whether there is any communism or anarchism or any other destructive subject you were including.' I said, 'The other subjects may be destructive but we've still got to get them listened to.' He told me that he had sixty teenagers aged between thirteen and fifteen who were anxiously waiting to meet me and to find out what all this was about. They had volunteered for the course.

I had at no time any difficulties of a disciplinary nature with the pupils of any age – but then I enjoyed their company and apparently they enjoyed mine. Experience had shown me that I had an ability to convey my ideas and to express them in a manner which is easily assimilable, understandable and acceptable to young people of all ages. This furthermore confirmed me in a basic fact that all young people – whoever they are, are human beings – boys and girls, are basically unspoilt and equally teachable, approachable and attachable from the point of view of human relationships. I was trained in England that one of the worst mistakes that a teacher could make would be to single out any individual for favouritism or special treatment. I was as fair as I could be and invariably firm.

We met. They looked at me and I looked at them and I said to them quite frankly that this was an experiment, which might succeed or fail. 'A lot of it depends on you and your enthusiasm or sustained interest in this subject which you know nothing about and which I know very little about, but you get ready and we'll start.' We met once a week after school between two and four. The headmaster joined in the first two meetings and took part in the discussions. There was a lot of participation and I collected quite a lot of work from them. Later on I asked if we could meet in the gymnasium hall rather than in a classroom. This was agreed and I didn't mind them sprawling around and taking it easy as long as they were interested. This changed the whole atmosphere of the lessons of course. Everybody relaxed including the headmaster who came in and also had to lie down or sit on the floor as I was doing. We went through a number of games and programmes such as we had developed from our experiment. This was the time of Anwar Sadat's famous visit to Jerusalem, so peace was very much on the agenda and in everybody's mind. In order to connect to that great moment, I suggested that all the pupils should begin to collect and make an album of the leading photographs, speeches, cartoons and what have you. This they did and we used it to good effect whenever we wanted to show people what we were doing. People were really impressed as they are when they see something that is really well done. So the course proceeded. I was very much put upon because I had to keep up with the kids who were extremely intelligent, very interested and they forced me to learn and to study and prepare for each session and exploited me mercilessly. I really hadn't intended that I should work hard on this whole thing, I wanted to find out whether one could use the word 'PEACE' for educational purposes and I was finding rapidly that it not only could be used, but that there was a tremendous need for it to be used. The young people were grabbing at it and developing it quite beyond my expectations.

Towards the end of his teaching in Tel Aviv he noticed a young woman observing his classes. He asked her why and she replied that she and her husband had just gone to live in a small community called Neve Shalom/Wahat al-Salam,[1] where they wanted to start dialogue between Jews and Arabs. She offered to introduce him to the people on the hill.

> Meeting with the Dominican Father Bruno Hussar was a milestone in my work. I had heard that he was somehow involved in a plan to set up some sort of centre which he described as a religious centre of Arabs, Christians and Moslems, and Jews to live together as a community. I liked him at once and I trusted him. I went to see what was taking place on this hillside at Latrun above the valley of Ayalon, one hundred acres of empty hillside, without trees, without houses, without anything except a few shacks. There I met a small community of ten or twenty people with a whole group of youngsters coming down from Jerusalem and some from Tel Aviv to participate at weekends in a sort of get-together. The atmosphere was quite unique, very free and very inspiring for me at any rate. There was a lot of singing, a lot of praying and a certain amount of instruction and learning and discussion all on a very high level. I felt exhilarated by it. We were approaching February by that time and Tu B'shvat, Judaism's new year for trees, was approaching. I went to the headmaster of my school and asked him what they did for the festival. He said, 'We've given up planting trees. There are enough trees planted and there is no point in making a whole business out of it.' I explained, 'On the contrary I think it is a very good opportunity and I would like to exploit it if you give me permission.' He said that I could and asked what I wanted to do. I answered 'I'm going to take my kids out to Neve Shalom to the place I have been talking about, the hill beside Latrun, and I'm going to get an equal number of Arab schoolchildren of the same age-group and they are going to get together and plant trees

[1]Neve Shalom/Wahat al-Salam (Oasis of Peace – in Hebrew and Arabic) was founded to be an ecumenical settlement by Father Bruno Hussar and a few friends in 1970/71. They settled on a hilltop adjacent to the Latrun monastery. Father Bruno rented the land for ninety-nine years at a nominal rent. The original founders gradually dispersed, but in 1979 Father Bruno had attracted four couples, one Moslem, the others Jewish, to join him in an effort to start a mixed community.

together and the togetherness is the significance of the occasion rather than the actual planting.' Could he come along? Yes, he could come along and we went out with about forty of my kids and about thirty or forty Arabs, boys and girls. They looked at each other and met and we put them through the elementary stages of what was to become the classic curriculum of Neve Shalom, getting to know each other as a first step. The first half hour together we spent seriously getting acquainted. We sat in a circle and each one had to describe what they had been able to learn about their neighbour to the right.

They went off to plant trees together on the hillside and it was quite an interesting experience to watch these two groups getting to know each other, bending down digging, making holes and planting saplings. In fact the headmaster also took a young Arab boy and planted a tree together with him. He told me afterwards that he felt it was quite a significant experience. Later they played football and basketball, the girls got talking together and exchanging addresses and telephone numbers and what have you, and in due course they all got into their vehicles and set off homewards, the one group back to Tel Aviv, and the Arabs to Lod and Ramle.

I went into school the next day to see my pupils. I noticed the janitor, a Yemenite Jew, looking at me. Suddenly he stood upright and saluted me. I asked him what for. He replied that I must be doing something remarkable to the kids. I told him that I'd be very pleased to know what. 'They came in this morning', he said, 'absolutely full of their visit to Neve Shalom wherever that is and they seem to be changing. There is something happening to them.' I was delighted. I went into the teachers' room. All those who had been cynical and sceptical and derisive about what I was trying to do suddenly looked at me with new eyes. They said that I was really having an effect on the kids. I told them that I was delighted, that I hoped it was going to be a good effect and that it would last.

The following Thursday I went to a Rotary lunch in Tel Aviv and there the newly appointed American Ambassador to Israel, Samuel Lewis, came up to me and asked me what I was doing. I looked him over and said that I didn't think he'd be interested in my doings. He said, 'How do you know?' I replied that I had the feeling that he had other more important things to deal with, such as the political situation and so on. He insisted, 'No, on the contrary, come and sit down.' I sat down with him and told him. He said, 'I'm fascinated and I believe that what you're doing is most important and I would like to know more about it.' Here was again a chance to find a friend. I invited him to come out to Neve Shalom one afternoon and see a course of instruction along with Arab and Jewish kids, all teenagers. He came out. He saw it. He said a few words of greeting and wished us well. He took me aside afterwards and said 'I think your work is most important, most important.' 'Well', I said to him, 'Mr Ambassador' 'You call me Sam' 'What I am doing is rather basic. While you went to Camp David with the President signing the peace treaty between Egypt and Israel, I was in your consulate in Tel Aviv. You don't know that, do you?' 'No, I didn't.' I went on, 'While you were signing the formal peace treaty, I had a meeting in your library down below of twenty to thirty Arab and Jewish children, who were looking at video tapes that you have down there and are never used to help Jewish–Arab understanding. We had tea together, talked together and made friends down there. That, I think was the beginning of the infrastructure for the peace treaty and I think that's important too.' He agreed and offered his assistance. I said I didn't know what he could do at the moment but that I was sure a day would come when he could be of considerable assistance.

I had been trying for years to interest the Rotary Organisation and clubs in Israel in this concept of mine of peace education almost to no effect. Year after year at the District conference, I got up and asked for the floor when it came to international understanding as a subject for debate, and propounded my ideas and there was a tap on my shoulder and I was told to sit down. They said they liked me very much and I had every right to say what I wanted of course but I shouldn't waste their time. Well this year at the annual conference in Netanya, when I finished my usual twenty-minute exposition, the chairman said that he wanted to say a few words. 'I want to thank Wellesley Aron for persistently getting up despite the discouragement which he's had from us and insisting that we should listen to him. I think the time has come to do something about it and I propose that we establish a Rotary committee to deal with this subject and investigate what can be done.'

Well, I knew then that I had at last broken through. It had taken me fourteen years but it had happened. They formed a committee and Sam Lewis became a member of this ad hoc committee of the Neve Shalom Rotary project. They became a very valuable aid, because now we could reach out and find people who could help us to do something with the things we had in mind. One of the things Sam did was to talk with the Director-General of the Ministry of Education, asking him to be good enough to listen to me. Then he spoke to me and suggested that I prepare a written report of my work, which I did. I met the Director-General and gave him my report and thought that well, that will be about the end of it. It actually could have been except that Sam Lewis had some influence with the man and persuaded this man to go to Neve Shalom. I wouldn't have him in my school because my course was so experimental that it could break down at any moment and I didn't want him to see it. To my astonishment Sam Lewis came with the Director-General Eliezer Shmueli. Those living at Neve Shalom involved in education were equally astounded. I had to find an important man to get someone from the Ministry of Education there. We had been trying to attract the Ministry's attention for months and had got nowhere, now here was the Director-General asking what the Ministry could do to help. After a thorough review, it was decided that with the small amount of financial aid available, we would be subjected to so many controls as to possibly endanger the development of the curriculum. So we didn't get very far with him.

My project in Tel Aviv lasted a year and a half and there was no question about it, my programme worked and I was very relieved and delighted with the results because I saw that my supposition that peace could be incorporated through the curriculum of secondary schools, or earlier for that matter, was a practical possibility and that it should be promoted and injected into the ordinary curricula of the secondary schooling. As an example, it was quite clear that what had been achieved at Neve Shalom by that day out on Tu B'shvat should be consolidated and therefore when the headmaster of the

Arab Lod secondary school talked to the headmaster of my school, it was suggested that a visit should take place. When the headmaster put it to me I agreed. 'I would love my kids to go and in fact I want to accompany them and let them see what an Arab school is like and what an Arab town is like.' I soon discovered that my kids had never had any contact with Arabs whatsoever and knew nothing about any of them except what they had learnt in Neve Shalom. We went to Lod, to the secondary school, and were received there with a warmth and knowhow in hospitality which the Arabs have a natural bent for. It was a delight – music, song and a presentation of cakes and goodies and so forth. Then there was a visit round the town with the families. We lunched together and afterwards there was a programme of joint activities and games. By the time evening came everyone was delighted with the day and had formed, I thought, fairly substantial contacts and friendships. We thanked our hosts and went back to Tel Aviv.

I said to the headmaster that we would have to reciprocate. Months went by and he did nothing about it. Finally I said that I was going to do something and a date was fixed and a programme arranged. The headmaster and I waited with our pupils for the visitors. The bus brought them and a disastrous day took place. I can only say that this exemplified to a great extent the sort of deficiencies in hospitality shown by the Jewish population. The Arab is a natural host and the Jew is not. The first time we meet Abraham in the Bible, he is receiving guests. It was a very special ceremony and a momentous occasion when guests graced the tents of nomadic ancestors. We seem to have lost this facility and this intuitive hospitality over the centuries, among other things no doubt. As an illustration of the mistakes we make, I shall recount the day of the return visit. First there was something which was absolutely wrong and contrary to all the ideas which had prompted this visit. There was a basketball match between Jewish and Arab girls. It was witnessed by the whole of the school who surrounded the court. It was a disaster for the Arab girls, because they had nothing like the training or experience of their Jewish hosts and hostesses. It was a disaster and a massacre. In the middle of this game a young Jewish pupil shouted, 'Come on Israel' in Hebrew. I asked him 'Who is Israel here?' He said 'Our people.' I said 'Don't be ridiculous. Here you've got two peoples. Which one is Israel? Aren't they both Israel?' He blushed and said, 'Oh yes, I never thought of that.' I told him that this was the sort of thing that we do which divides people and ruins relations between them.

Later on they had a folk-dancing session in the gymnasium. All the music and dances were Western and the Arabs knew nothing about them. They stood around the hall while their Jewish hosts enjoyed themselves dancing all sorts of Western and Jewish dances. I stopped it in the middle and said 'Don't you see what you're doing here?' The man playing the accordion said that he didn't know any Arab tunes. So I said that we would sing them without accompaniment, but we couldn't go on doing this to our guests. Anyway, it came to an end and it had clearly been a flop. When the time for departure came, the leader of the Arab group came up to me and said that he was a little embarrassed. I asked him why and he explained that they had brought presents for their hosts but had been given no opportunity to offer them. I apologised and told him that the programme had not been discussed with me and added that the presentation of gifts was not a normal part of our hospitality routine. I suggested that he keep them for another occasion. Then someone said that it was time to leave and asked where they should go. One of the Jewish kids cursed and said, 'You have to go back to the bus station and start from there.' Nobody offered to accompany them, nobody offered to see them off and hardly anybody said goodbye to them. That I think was a disaster.

The interesting thing was that the next day when I saw the headmaster he said what a wonderful day it had been. I told him that it could not have been a worse day. 'You did immense harm to the work I'm doing.' He couldn't understand it. He couldn't grasp it. I tried explaining to him but he never got it. This illustrates the sort of unnecessary difficulties and obstacles that arise in this world of peace and co-existence.

As the months went by I discovered that I had chosen the wrong school in Tel Aviv, because it was a comprehensive school which only took pupils for two or three years before they were sent off to other schools. My group was divided and got lost in the shuffle, although I tried very hard to keep them together. A few of them came to see me privately, but from my point of view it was the wrong thing to split them up. I should have had them for another couple of years. After I had stopped teaching at the school, Kol Israel, an Israeli radio station, asked to interview me. I said of course and immediately invited some of my pupils to my house to be there when the interviewer arrived. He immediately asked, 'What's all this?' and I explained that I wasn't going to be interviewed, but that he should talk to the children instead. Whereupon they interviewed each one of the kids present and I learnt a lot from this experience, because many of the facts of life emerged there that wouldn't have normally appeared in their relations with me. I found out that many of them had suffered a good deal of rejection and criticism in their own circle because of what they were doing with me. I heard them say, 'Well my father said it's a waste of time and nothing will come of it.' Another one said that his father had said that it was ridiculous, and that he should be doing electronics or something more practical for his future; that he shouldn't waste his time on some man's theory that peace can be taught. This youngster's mother on the other hand had disagreed with his father and said that it should have been done much earlier, long ago and that there was a tremendous need for it. I was very impressed with the fact that these youngsters had stood up to the criticism from their sisters and brothers and friends at school. They had maintained their interest in what we were doing in spite of being confronted by a good deal of derision, criticism and laughter.

CHAPTER FOURTEEN

Home – Neve Shalom/Wahat al-Salam

I was going out to Neve Shalom fairly regularly by this time. I liked it and the people there more and more. I got to know them and they got to know me. I heard them say how impressed they were with the fact that I'd gone to the government and got permission to run my experiment at the school in Tel Aviv. One day I approached the group in Neve Shalom and said, 'Frankly, I would like to join you physically.' They replied that I could be on the advisory council or could chair a committee. I agreed to start with that, but added that what I really had in mind was to live there. They were rather surprised and taken aback, but Father Bruno thought that it might be arranged. Meanwhile I would be chairman of the board and would help the community with my various contacts. I found the work quite interesting but not very constructive because we couldn't get access to the various authorities and institutions whose support we needed.

At about this time I had to go to England to deal with some personal matters. While I was there I was asked if I could arrange for a group of some ten to fifteen Israeli Arab and Jewish youngsters to spend four or five days in London. At the time they were in Germany staying at a centre which encouraged meetings between peoples who were in conflict, but who were willing to meet and listen to each other. It was very short notice, but with some help from Rabbi Hugo Gryn[1] and Habonim I was able to arrange accommodation and a series of interesting visits and meetings for the group. Their visit was a great success because it attracted the attention of a

[1]The senior minister at the West London Synagogue for British Jews and a leading activist in many organisations devoted to peaceful co-existence between people of different religions and nationalities.

number of people in England who subsequently became the founding members of the British Friends of Neve Shalom. In particular Marcus Sieff,[1] then head of Marks and Spencer, thought that our work was most valuable. I contacted many people and we had a few meetings and got the ball rolling. When I returned to Israel I was hopeful that we might be able to resolve our financial problems if the Sieffs and the Rothschilds really came forward with their promise to support us. I was very optimistic. But it was three years before the first small contributions arrived.

I returned to the attack and repeated my request to move up to Neve Shalom. I had already told Ylona, who had either been living with me or next door to me since Rose died, that I was going to give up my flat in Tel Aviv. It was at this point that my name was put up for membership and the formal procedures began. When I thought everything was more or less in the bag, one of the young women asked whether I would give her a few moments of my time. She talked to me like a Dutch uncle saying, 'You're an elderly man and you have to be looked after, you can't look after yourself, we haven't got time to look after you. We're all mothers and wives of the few members that are here. We're fully occupied and we can't take on the responsibility of being at your beck and call if and when you want us. Look if you come up here, the only condition in which you can be accepted is if you will bring a woman who will act as a companion and a help to you and live with you.'

I was a bit disappointed. I couldn't believe that they were serious because I thought with my experience and contacts in Israel, I should be so valuable and important to them that they would overlook my age and so on and that they would probably find a *modus vivendi* for me. No, they were quite adamant.

* * *

I wandered around Israel asking myself who would possibly be not only suitable, but willing to share my life in this rather bare

[1]Lord Sieff of Brimpton, Baron cr 1980 (life peer), Marcus Joseph Sieff b. 1913; Chairman Marks and Spencer plc 1972–84, Honorary President from 1985; President British–Israel Chamber of Commerce since 1975; B'nai B'rith International gold medallion for humanitarianism 1982.

and elementary place at Neve Shalom, which at that time presented basic practical problems for everyday living. Well, eventually, Providence, a word that Father Bruno likes to use, led me to see a friend I'd known for many years in the person of Coral Benjamin, who was running an art gallery in Caesarea. It suddenly occurred to me that perhaps she would be interested. I knew that she was a wonderful human being, that she was divorced, that she had a daughter with two children and that she might be lonely and unfulfilled. At any rate I went to see her and in the course of a meeting or two, I asked her point blank whether she would come to visit Neve Shalom, of which she had never heard. I was delighted and relieved when she said she'd like to and I took her up and showed her around. Well there wasn't much to show and I must say it took a great deal of faith, confidence and optimism for a woman to envisage making a home up there. I showed her the little house which I hoped would be allocated to us. It was a pre-cast square with three rooms and a shower room. It was perched amongst some large rocks and had of course a lovely view of the valley of Ayalon right over to the coast as far as Ashkelon in the south and Tel Aviv in the north; but it certainly wasn't what I would call an inviting prospect. To my surprise she said that she thought she could make a home up there. I asked her if she was serious and she replied that she was. 'Then would you be prepared to come and join me and live with me up here?' I asked her. She answered that she thought she could.

Within a few weeks we had come to an arrangement and I was able to go back to the committee whereupon they asked to meet the lady who had agreed to live with me. In due course I produced her at a meeting and she was asked to say a few words to explain why she was prepared to join me and why she wanted to come to Neve Shalom. It didn't take very long for them to see that she might be an ideal addition to the community and the vote was taken and we were accepted. That was really a basic milestone in my life. I didn't know then how significant it would prove to be and how much help Coral would be in whatever task she took on. It didn't take long to see that she was a woman of many parts. She had tremendous energy and a capacity for work and a great determination to do things, however difficult. She had a certain pioneering spirit, which I had rarely found in a woman, but which I admire tremendously. I think of the time when she started from scratch to make us a home. She was undaunted by the various difficulties such as the frequent electricity cuts, the shortage of water and other facilities which one normally takes for granted. In November 1980, just a week or two after the vote, my furniture was moved up very carefully from Tel Aviv. What wouldn't fit in I disposed of, and we were rapidly installed. In less than a month the house was running smoothly, attractively, invitingly and comfortably and that was the beginning of our relationship together at Neve Shalom.

Soon, Coral, with her usual hospitable and generous nature, was providing all sorts of cookies and cakes for the various social occasions which the community shared together. Within a year or so she was dealing with administrative matters for the community, doing the secretarial work, taking telephone calls and dealing with public relations. She produced admirable newsletters for our supporters in Israel and abroad. Coral always contributed a great deal in a generous, tactful and discreet manner. I was very grateful to see how the young people came round to ask our advice and to be with us in the evenings when we sat discussing problems of mutual interest. They seemed very much at home with us and I felt that we were an important asset to the community.

We lived together for a year before Coral asked if I would agree to marry again. She didn't like the deception of introducing each other to newcomers as husband and wife. I said, 'Why not?'

We could not marry in Israel because Orthodox Judaism prohibits a Cohen, which I am, from marrying a divorcee. This meant that we should either have to live in sin as we were doing, or go abroad to marry. In due course we went to England where we had a wedding which satisfied us both. Strangely enough it took place in the West London Reform Synagogue where my parents had been members in the early days. Now and again my father adorned himself in silk hat and dark grey striped trousers. He and my mother, bedecked in Sunday best so to speak, went off to a place they called Upper Berkeley Street in the West End of London. This was the same West London Reform Synagogue where an organ was played to accompany the mixed choir. When I was old enough my father took me with him on these rare occasions. I saw that he could follow the prayers, but he had taught me nothing and if it were not for the fact that parts of the Reformed service were in English I would not have understood anything. My mother sat upstairs in the ladies' gallery and I could just glimpse her through the ornate grille. A good deal of social importance was attached to these visits to this decorous House of Prayer and as far as I was concerned they were occasions which I really enjoyed.

Rabbi Hugo Gryn married us and spoke very charmingly about Coral. All our friends were present and members of her family too. A very nice day was had which I shall always remember with gratitude.

* * *

It occurred to me to begin to create some sort of network which would bring Neve Shalom into the Rotary orbit. This was not an easy thing to do because 'the people on the hill', as we call ourselves, had scarcely heard of Rotary and what they did know of it was hardly conducive to enthusiasm on their part, since they thought it was probably a middle-class, reactionary, conservative group of middle-aged men, very set in their ideas and quite out of step with the thinking of the rather left-wing, radical young people up on the hill. They were right of course in principle, but I was determined that they should meet some Rotarians and find out for themselves whether there was anything in common. After all the advancement of international understanding, goodwill and peace was part of Neve Shalom's programme too. This relationship was strongly encouraged by Sam Lewis. He agreed to serve on a committee if I wanted it and from that moment the whole status and standing of Neve Shalom and the idea that I was promoting changed for the better.

We were very fortunate because for the first time in its history Rotary International had decided to hold an Institute meeting in Jerusalem. My old friend Wolf Cegla had by this time become a member of the Board of Directors of Rotary International and it was largely due to him that the meeting was to be held in Israel. I asked him if he could try to include a visit to Neve Shalom in the Rotary's President's programme. He was not enthusiastic, perhaps because he thought us idealistic and unrealistic and that our community would do nothing to solve political and other difficulties. Our policy of course stood for compromise with our Arab neighbours, so far as co-existence is concerned, and this is something which he found difficult to contemplate. Nevertheless, somewhat reluctantly, he agreed to produce the Rotary President Stanley McCaffery if I produced the American Ambassador Samuel Lewis.

The meeting took place on a very cold rainy day in January 1981. Bruno had his head wrapped up against the bitter wind. Israel's District Governor Samuel Kahan came too, but I didn't expect anybody to be enthusiastic about Neve Shalom in those conditions. Sam Lewis and the Rotary President came to our house where one of our members gave them coffee and explained what we were trying to do. To my surprise and delight and relief McCaffery spoke immediately: 'I think this is a wonderful project. It is absolutely in line with the Rotary ideals and Rotary concepts and anything I can do to help I will do.' We wondered what that would be. 'First I would like you to prepare an article with pictures. Send it off at once to the editor of *The Rotarian* because it will take two or three months before the article appears.' Samuel Kahan added that what was needed was more accommodation and particularly more classrooms, since we had only one, and another hostel of some sort with enough beds to house more youngsters and older people too who might want to participate in courses.

It was decided there and then to work out a project and apply to the Rotary World Community Service Committee to have it included in the Committee's Library of projects looking for support. These things were done. But it was eighteen months before the article, emasculated by a well-intentioned editor, appeared in *The Rotarian* magazine. Meanwhile a plan for a hostel with fifty beds and a classroom which could take up to fifty students was worked out. Thanks to Samuel Kahan's persistence and ability he was able to take this plan to a meeting of the World Community Service Committee where it was adopted. No one knew how long it would take to raise the seventy to eighty thousand dollars required from Rotarians worldwide, but especially from Europe. The young people at Neve Shalom were not enthusiastic about becoming involved with Rotary, but I persevered because Neve Shalom suffered peculiarly so far as institutions and communal support was concerned. It didn't belong anywhere, didn't fit into any framework or niche which suited the bureaucratic government departments. Some members of the government didn't even want it to exist. In other words it needed roots and, thanks to Rotary, roots began to grow.

One or two or three or four Rotary clubs arrived to visit us. They brought picnic lunches with them and sat outside in the spring sunshine on the carpet of flowers looking out at the fantastic view from the top of the hill. They wanted to help in Neve Shalom's development. Gradually, slowly, we began to get some recognition, which our teaching work with youngsters didn't attract because they had no influence at all, except that their own participation was a proof positive that they believed in what was going on up here. Very slowly, as my contacts and those of other Rotarians bore fruit with local council and government offices in Jerusalem, and the electricity and water authorities, the rather unusual young people who formed the community of Neve Shalom granted Rotary a certain recognition. These various authorities would help us if properly approached, which hadn't happened before. When I first arrived at Neve Shalom I was appalled by the lack of contact between the community and these secular bodies.

As far as religious bodies were concerned, Father Bruno had already done a great deal of work in getting together influential friends in the different religious communities of Jerusalem and elsewhere in the country, some of whom served on a sponsoring committee for Neve Shalom. Mayor of Jerusalem Teddy Kollek was one of those concerned, but no real action was undertaken by these people. Our plans for a School for Peace, as Bruno and I were inclined to call it, were put into practice in the limited accommodation we already had. Before long courses, seminars, workshops and summer camps were taking place.

As far as the status of Neve Shalom was concerned, it worried me very much because it was quite clear that we belonged to nobody, got no support from anywhere except by fortuitous circumstances. I noticed that our balance sheet contained relatively large contributions from Germany, mostly from Catholic charities. I was told that German groups came to visit Neve Shalom from time to time and were very impressed. They had returned to their communities and set up an organisation in Frankfurt headed by Dr Lotte Schiffler of Frankfurt. The money she raised from her co-religionists as well as from the larger Catholic foundations was used to buy basic necessities such as an electric generator, garage equipment and a communal car. Some money came from France, where Father Bruno and Anne LeMeignen, one of Neve Shalom's founders, had family and contacts.

What shocked and surprised me was the lack of involvement in the United States. I knew that the only way to remedy this was to use my friendship with Ambassador Lewis. In 1981 I broached the matter to him and he said, 'I'll see what we can do with some of the foundations.' I knew that it would not be easy because of the amount of work required in preparing reports on the proposed projects. For example, we sent letters to ten foundations describing our work and inviting support. Eight didn't even reply, one wrote to say that the project was too small for them, and the tenth had no money available. This came as quite a disappointment to the Embassy people but not really to me. There are thousands of charitable foundations in America and the money locked up in them must amount to billions of dollars. Many of them have peace and understanding and ethnic inter-faith activities included in their objectives, but when it comes to getting money every difficulty is raised, mostly by the lawyers and others who are entrusted with handling the funds.

We decided that it might be more effective if we sent two of our members to the United States to talk about our work at meetings which our Embassy friends would arrange. With perfect timing a certain Mr David Tulin from Pennsylvania came to spend a week or two with us at Neve Shalom. He was in charge of an organisation called Fellowship Farm in America and we liked each other very much. He knew exactly what we wanted because we were clearly on the same wavelength. He agreed to administer and promote anything we

8. With General Moshe Dayan

9. With Pandit Nehru in Tokyo for an international Rotary Club conference, 1965

10. Putting over the peace message: The American Ambassador to Israel, Samuel Lewis, was in the audience (seated, second left) along with a group of people already participating in the embryonic School for Peace

11. Children and members of Neve Shalom/ Wahat al-Salam being addressed by Wellesley on the occasion of a visit to the community by the Israeli President, Chaim Herzog, in September 1985. The messages on the notice boards symbolically spell out a welcome in both Hebrew and Arabic

12. Wellesley with his second wife, Coral, on their wedding day, 5 April 1982

13. The growing family: Wellesley and Coral with his two daughters and her daughter and some of their grandchildren

14. Bridging the generation gap: Wellesley with some of the children of Neve Shalom/Wahat al-Salam, 1985

could arrange for the States. We said that we would put him in touch with wealthy and influential people who might be interested in supporting us and he agreed to follow up these contacts.

In due course arrangements were made thanks once more to Ambassador Lewis, who obtained some Fulbright funds which paid the travel expenses for our two representatives, Abed Elsalam Najjar, our Arab neighbour, and Kobi Sonnenshein. In 1982 they went to the United States, taking their wives and children with them at their own expense. They were away for two months and were received by Tulin, who had contacted communities throughout the country. They went to New York, Miami, Chicago, Detroit, Los Angeles, San Francisco, Philadelphia and even had the opportunity to visit the Rockies and the National Parks and to make contact with some people in Canada. As far as public relations went our representatives did very well; they appeared on television and radio; they gave many press interviews and had photos in many newspapers. They were on a coast-to-coast network at midnight from Florida to Seattle and quite a lot of excitement was engendered, but not much money unfortunately was forthcoming; although they did cover their expenses. When they returned we realised that the follow-up process was going to be even more important than their original endeavours and that even so it might be some time before any substantial sums of money would be forthcoming from the sort of people who are interested in what we are doing.

I have to say here that the Neve Shalom idea of understanding, peace and co-existence between ethnic groups and particularly between Arabs and Jews in Israel is not a particularly popular concept. The Jewish communities are deeply involved with the Zionist endeavour, which means collecting funds for the United Jewish Appeal and other bodies to underpin and build Jewish hospitals, schools, universities and what have you. They help to build up industries to enable the State of Israel to survive and strengthen itself in accordance with the Zionist concept. This is the great purpose of American Jewry officially and it is a little bit difficult to inject into that programme a policy to understand the Arabs in Israel too.

This was almost entirely ignored by the Zionists who were so anxious to establish a foothold and to put down roots; to establish a community and to create a state in the land of Israel, that they didn't have the patience or perhaps the wisdom or even the possibility to have a continuous relationship with the Arab inhabitants. As everybody knows there was a good deal of argument and struggling to obtain land from absentee Arab landlords. I would not like to put too much blame on my colleagues and my co-religionists and co-nationalists whose endeavours to establish a state have been so successful, because it is beginning to be ever clearer that there is a deep dividing line of mutual suspicion between Jews and Arabs. Although Arabs and Jews lived for generations together in different parts of the Arab world, the Jewish communities were in a minority and treated as inferiors, tolerated but dependent on the goodwill of the Moslem conquerors. Compared with the Jewish communities in Europe they were much better off, for they were allowed to remain where they were, to practise their religion, to engage in commercial and other activities provided that they did not threaten the Moslem environment.

The Arabs were accustomed to seeing Jews in this way, so that when the State of Israel was established and Jews were a majority with political independence for the first time for two thousand years the Arabs had to confront Jews in a completely different light. Here was the Jew, an equal amongst equals in the Holy Land, in Palestine, in Israel with of all things an Arab minority in the midst, to which he had to adapt and accommodate his policies. The resentment engendered amongst the Arabs was basic and considerable. It is the source of a lot of the strains and misunderstandings and resentment, envy and prejudice and hatred which can be seen in the Arab world. This situation will change in time, but meanwhile this is the problem, which is why when it came to getting support from other parts of the world, it was so difficult to find anybody that one could go to with any hope of success.

More Christians than Jews supported us. In a few cases Jews and Christians banded together and contributed generously to our funds. But we really needed an organisation in America, ideally of Jews, Moslems and Christians, who believe that

Neve Shalom is an essential ingredient for the future of the Middle East, which as a matter of principle must be supported. When I say adequately supported, I know and I think it is probably generally recognised that we are not in this business to build an empire with large sums of money. What we need is some underpinning to establish the community on a solid basis, to pay the salaries of the teachers and to create an acceptable centre where people of different religions can come and see our work taking place.

In 1981, just before Christmas time, a television crew came here and decided that Neve Shalom was a wonderful theme for a Christmas documentary. A few of us were interviewed and some of our activities were filmed on videotape and a twenty-minute documentary emerged. The network released it in Detroit on Christmas Eve and it gave us very good publicity for our ideas and educational programme. Not long afterwards the English BBC made a forty-minute programme for Radio Four, which also gave us the chance to explain what we are doing here. Gradually our message is getting through.

We had felt for a long time that we should try and let the public know more about us and so it was decided to hold an 'Open House'. We invited all our friends and associates and anybody else who might be interested in spending a day in our company. It could only be arranged during the winter and the bad weather forced us to postpone it to a later day. It was nevertheless a bitterly cold day but we decided to go ahead irrespective. Two to three hundred people came, including the American and German Ambassadors to Israel. Both spoke to the guests reiterating their support for our community and peace education programmes. While these speeches were going on, I noticed the Abbot from the neighbouring Latrun monastery listening carefully. Although we had met, he did not come and speak to me, probably because the monastery, which had leased the land for Neve Shalom to Father Bruno some years before, had embarked on a course to change the terms of the lease, which they now argued was not in accordance with canon law. Discussions were going on between our lawyers and the atmosphere was not very friendly. Finally he said a curt 'How do you do?' and disappeared. The attempt to change our lease continues. By November 1982 we were eight

> families – about 30 souls altogether – and there were other people waiting to join us as soon as we had more accommodation.

Wellesley continued his account of Neve Shalom/Wahat al-Salam in January 1985. In the intervening years he had worked tirelessly to persuade people to help the community and its peace-school work. Marcus Sieff and his wife continued to support the community. They were largely instrumental in having the buildings constructed for the community's kindergarten – the first in Israel to educate Arab and Jewish children together using Arabic and Hebrew to teach all the children. The opening ceremony was on a cold, blustery spring day. Wellesley was extremely ill and in obvious pain. There appeared to be no chance of his attending the ceremony. Incredibly, after a pain-killing injection, he summoned up the resources to see him through the afternoon. He could not walk. Several young men and women from the community came to his home and carried him, in his chair, up the steep slope to the courtyard where the guests and members had assembled. He wore his favourite red jersey and a jacket and had a warm rug around him. He was so obviously loved by the adults and children with whom he was sharing the last few years of his life. He was so joyful, because his dream of a school where Israeli Jews and Arabs would learn together was coming true.

> When I look back, I can see the amount of effort that went into persuading adults – I can only talk about Jews because I had no contact with Arabs – of the validity of what we were trying to do and how difficult it was and how critical they were and how destructive their comments and how discouraging the conversations were with most of these men who were so successful in business and in their professions, and intelligent and dedicated in many cases, dedicated Zionists and Jews and when it came to talking about understanding the Arabs they shied off. I always asked them, 'What is your idea of a solution to the obvious on-going problem of the fact that there are two peoples of different ethnic and religious background living in the same country like it or not?'
>
> There was generally silence and it was clear that they hoped the problem would be swept under the carpet or would somehow miraculously be solved. But what we were trying to

> do with the youngsters they considered a waste of time. Well, anyway we struggled along.

Wellesley's efforts for the community were concentrated on attracting support, dealing with adverse publicity and solving practical problems through his large network of Rotarians and ex-Army comrades. Two reunions were held at Neve Shalom/Wahat al-Salam: one of pupils Wellesley had taught at the Herzliya Gymnasium in 1926 and 1927; the other of soldiers who had served with him in the Second World War. Many of his favourite stories, some thought to be apocryphal, were confirmed by these people who greeted Wellesley after so many years with abundant affection and respect.

The educational work with ever-increasing numbers of Arab and Jewish children was carried out by younger members of the settlement. The curriculum was developed slowly and responsively to what the teachers and children experienced. The Neve Shalom/Wahat al-Salam leaders taught a number of their students to assist them in running the workshops and encounter groups. Gradually, with voluntary help from students and educationists from outside the community a variety of programmes evolved.[1] Here is Wellesley's account of the teaching activities in the early years.

> Starting with Father Bruno right through all the different types of people that we were, when it came to agreeing to some sort of matter of principle, there was an immediate relaxed consensus when the right formula was found. We laid down that there should be no politics or religion in our teaching, that what took place in the workshops and meetings with teachers was nothing more than the application of a technique which we were developing, whereby they were able to clean their minds of the poisons that they had picked up from their environments and from their families and from the media among which they lived. Normally Jews and Arabs did not meet, even though they may have been living side by side, in close proximity or as neighbours on a kibbutz and in an Arab village. The people in these groups never came face to face as human beings. It's true that they had on-going relationships in

[1]Since Wellesley's death in 1988 the educational programmes have continued to evolve. In the Appendix on pages 197–201 are reports prepared in 1990/91 about the Kindergarten and Primary School and the School for Peace. There is also a list of awards received by the community for its work.

matters of agriculture and practical concern to their farmers and so on but they never discussed their own problems nor did they know very much about each other's way of life.

This is why the first meeting between Arabs and Jews at Neve Shalom/Wahat al-Salam was so important. Here they were compelled to look at each other, listen to each other and try to understand each other, and certainly to respect each other. In three and a half days we achieved this. We learned how difficult it is to change a person's point of view, especially a person's prejudices. We observed that most of the children were deeply affected by the on-going political tensions in this area; by the media which disseminated a lot of inaccuracies, not to call them lies, and misinterpreted anything that was being done and threw out the most negative, destructive interpretations. These were spread around by word of mouth and by other means, films, books, journalism and so on to the point where the position was regarded as chronic.

The amazing thing is that here we were able to dispel most of this evil, or rather it can be said that the children did it themselves, to themselves, for themselves, because of being young human beings with a desire to live as peacefully and as happily together in as beautiful a country as possible. They decided that this was necessary. For the record, however, this was an unpleasant and sometimes rather painful experience since no holds were barred in the confrontations that took place. The children were encouraged to be absolutely frank with each other and they were to the point where there was a great deal of tension. In fact there was often a crisis when there were a great many tears and pain experienced by both the girls and boys in discovering that their views often had to change in order to bring them nearer to an acceptable point when they could understand and talk to each other.

A few words about the fact that politics were not introduced into the curriculum. Of course political problems were discussed by the youngsters in the process of their cleansing themselves of their prejudices and superstitions. However, the teachers and Neve Shalom members were never allowed to project on to the young people their own political views or those of the political parties to which they belonged. They kept their own ideas to themselves, acting as catalysts for the young people, to enable them to express what they were searching for and to rebuild their ideologies. The same applied to religious matters.

We became a focus of interest for young people because they knew that what we were doing up here was an honest attempt to deal with a problem and the problem was co-existence. Our politicians and educationalists, religious leaders and others all talked about co-existence and did nothing. We were teaching co-existence and we were doing it. They experienced our co-existence and were influenced by it.

In April 1987 we held an Open Day. There was a lot more to it than met the eye. Aspects of the occasion were so original as to be inexplicable. Certainly history was in the making and the long-term significance of this 'happening' was almost certain to spill over and to affect areas of the Israel scene. Twenty thousand Jews and Arabs meeting together without benefit of any formal framework – either spiritual, social, political or academic – constituted an unprecedented occasion.

They were of all ages, with no particular common denominator. They came – young and old, children and parents – from all over Israel. They came by buses and by private cars, or on foot over the Judean Hills. Thousands of them. They were so similarly attired as to be indistinguishable. Who were Arabs, who were Jews? Generally one can know by the Arab kefiah and the Jewish yamulka; but here neither was visible. By design or by chance? Certainly the sum total effect was one of 'people'; people mingling freely and at ease. The atmosphere generated was, in itself, extraordinary and unprecedented at this time and in this area. Nobody stumbling upon this variegated scene of thousands of human beings sitting cheek by jowl to fill the large natural amphitheatre at Neve Shalom/Wahat al-Salam would have recognised what was in the process of being created. Why was everyone smiling? What was it that was producing an almost palpable aura of sheer pleasure?

It was only the second of such occasions, planned to happen every second year. The first had been a relative success, with over 5000 participants. But now a veritable multitude wended its way up the hill from the Ayalon Valley. The organising committee had done its work well. With the Israeli Arab and

Jewish artistes providing a continuous programme and other entertainment and activities arranged at many points around the area, there was ample room and interest for all. There were no speeches of any kind; neither political nor to propagandise. Nobody was being exhorted to 'do', to 'join', to 'support', to 'oppose', to build, to plant or to destroy – all of which in the normal course of events might have been anticipated.

The eight thousand teenagers who had been to courses at Neve Shalom/Wahat al-Salam returned to meet their youth leaders and fellow students with pleasure. Their anticipation on this occasion was well rewarded. Their expressions of pleasure bore witness for all to see. But there was more than this at work among the multitude. They had brought their parents to witness this ingathering of the convinced. It is no secret that the majority of Arab and Jewish parents view with little favour, and often with dislike, the prospect of their youngsters meeting and mingling with each other – for reasons which are not difficult to recognise. There is on-going conflict in the country and security is no theoretical element in any social activity where both parties may mix. Parents see nothing good resulting from the children's participation in Neve Shalom/Wahat al-Salam programmes (generally they are overruled by their teenage offspring).

But now the unexpected; unconvinced, but nevertheless impressed by the children's newly acquired attitude to their environment, the parents apparently agreed to join them for this Open Day. Arriving as cynics, they were taken in hand by their children who promptly insisted on introducing them to the parents of their friends – Arab to Jew; Jew to Arab. I observed this extraordinary process and watched the young people applying their understanding of the concept of co-existence by patiently inducing their parents to exchange courtesies with each other. And it worked! The two disparate parties now looked at each other and saw not an enemy but another human being; another father or mother with many interests in common – if alien in the context of their daily lives. They relaxed and smiled and gradually enjoyed the (for them) unusual experience of consorting with the hitherto unfamiliar. It was refreshing and basically quite natural. So, perhaps unrealised by them, the teenagers had triumphed over the

> normal cynicism and disbelief of their elders. A victory indeed. Something, perhaps, of another miracle in a place where biblical history has recorded strange happenings in biblical times.

Wellesley recorded many hours of his experiences, thoughts and hopes for the community on the hill. He spoke about each person who was living there when he joined them. His admiration for each one was unstinting. He loved being there with them. He loved them and the children who were born to the members during his years there. He had finally found loving co-existence in the home he had always longed for.

CHAPTER FIFTEEN

The Private Man

On 23 July 1968, Wellesley began to write his autobiography. His two grandchildren and their mother Sharona, who lived in Madrid at that time, were staying with him and Rose in Tel Aviv for the summer holidays. David was to be bar mitzvah in September; Talia was then eleven and a half years old. The opening paragraphs of his unfinished manuscript set out his motive for writing.

> The purpose for which I am putting the following facts together is really for the information of the young generation and those who follow.
>
> While there may be a certain vanity in recording one's own life story, there should be some interest and usefulness involved and it may be that the facts, as they unfurl, will have a bearing on those who follow in the generations to come, for in a way, the story that I am going to tell is that of a new beginning.
>
> Life on this earth is a continuous process and Man does his best to organise the time he spends here in a manner which makes sense to him and provides some reference points which can guide him and his associates in their path through life.

Wellesley's autobiographical notes relate what he knew of his parents' lives, his childhood, youth and early student years. He then set the project aside while he pursued his campaign to establish an institution for peace education. Some fourteen years later, Coral persuaded him to continue the project by tape-recording his spoken reminiscences. He did not change his original intentions, which, I conclude, is why he has not left us material about his closest relationships. Only during the last eight years of his life are his public and private lives inextricably linked by his marriage to Coral and their individual total commitment to Neve Shalom/Wahat al-Salam.

Wellesley's reticence about his deeper feelings is quite to be expected given his upbringing and education in pre-First World

War England. He has not concealed his lack of intimacy with his parents, nor his anger with them, his mother in particular, for treating him as an inanimate, unfeeling chattel. In his eighties he still recalled, bitterly and painfully, his mother's tie to his maternal grandmother who, he believed, had provoked their move to Germany at the onset of the First World War. 'I was dragged out of my school in 1914 and injected into Germany. The war broke out in September. I hadn't had a bar mitzvah. It didn't look as if I was ever going to have one and I didn't give a damn one way or the other.'

His memoirs trace his own gradual resolution of the conflicts he experienced as a child and teenager: a Jewish boy with English, Christian siblings; an upper-middle-class child whose only friend for a time was the working-class butcher's boy he met below stairs; an English boy with a German mother at a time of violent xenophobia in both countries, so that whether in Germany or England he, his father or mother, was each in turn the butt of viciously expressed prejudice; a semi-assimilated English Jew at an Orthodox Jewish boarding house in a conventional English, Christian boarding school; an assimilated, English, Cambridge undergraduate seen by some English Gentiles as an incomprehensible stranger in their midst.

He has expressed his feelings about these things indirectly in his writings, speeches and articles. My own view is that his adult life was devoted, sometimes consciously sometimes not, to reconciling the conflicts he had grown up with through his efforts to educate children out of the prejudices surrounding them. Coral, to whom he admitted he was more able to talk about his feelings than to anyone else, confirms that he did not speak directly about his own inner world; but she, like me, believes that at Neve Shalom/Wahat al-Salam he finally found an environment which fostered co-existence between people with different identities, a community whose members expressly worked to outlaw verbal as well as physical expressions of prejudice and hatred. As a somewhat patriarchal figure in his extended family on the hill he found what he longed for. His evident satisfaction and contentment at being there and at being able to contribute to what he most yearned for shone out in the last years of his life.

With minimal emotion Wellesley has depicted himself as a lonely child, a sensitive son who suffered deeply from the irrational hostilities he witnessed at home as he grew up. He was also an obedient son, who tried hard to honour his father's and mother's ambitions for him. Not that Wellesley lacked awareness of the likely consequences for children who did not receive their mother's or father's active interest and affection. He observed that his half-brothers and half-sister were emotionally affected by their mother's death. He acknowledged too that his father suffered directly because of his grandfather's frequent absences. I never heard him express sorrow or pity for his own strange childhood which presented him with so many intractable conflicts. It would not have been surprising if he had been overwhelmed by the emotional pressures he endured as a young child and later as a teenager when his half-brothers, nephew and father all died within a few months of each other. The stiff upper lip he had to develop when young, coupled with his sense of humour and his determination to make the best of every situation, masked the pain experienced in childhood; but his writings in praise of the young, especially of teenagers, suggest what he really felt during those years. The topics he chose to include in his peace education programmes reflect his abiding concerns and his deep reflection on them:

Words in the home – war in the world
Them and us
Generalisations are untrue – and dangerous
Verbal genocide – can be fatal
Teach tolerance – or else
Intolerance is vulgar and could be criminal
Genocide begins with words
Peace or the three R's – what is the priority?
Learn or Burn: The fuse of war is ignited by a small spark
Peace in the soul or war in the mind?
Peace, a word on everybody's lips
Peace, peace, but there is no peace
What are you waiting for? a big bang – then silence
The children's voices ceased
Peace is everybody's business.

His connections to his half-brothers, half-sister and nephew Berwick were based on their seniority and his own emotional need to experience a closeness not offered by his parents. Their influence over him led him to follow their pursuits and values. Although he always spoke of them in glowing terms, his writings do more than hint at a somewhat different reality in which he was bullied under the guise of fun and games by his older nephew, and became a target for his half-sister's mocking, derisory sense of humour. He remained devoted to their memories all his life, returning to England to see his half-sister Vio shortly before her death. He had no illusions about her snobbery and prejudices, but he appeared to bear no malice toward her for this.

His behaviour and feelings as a parent himself are not disclosed. He saw himself primarily as a man with a public duty to perform. He evidently left the raising of his two daughters to his wife Rose, who, he noted tersely, 'was always a wonderful home-maker and managed a home on very little, and was a very good mother into the bargain'. Following his own parents' example, he had little intimate contact with them when they were small. He was of course away from them for almost five years during the Second World War, after which he admitted it was very difficult to reestablish his previous relationships. In the briefest of comments Wellesley has expressed his admiration for his children's public achievements – Sharona as a singer and Ylona as a young ballet dancer and later as a painter.

He once told me how much he regretted that Ylona was sent away to boarding school so young and for most of her schooling, but offered no explanation for that decision. She boarded in London while she was a pupil at the Sadler's Wells Ballet School. Wellesley told me several times that she was too sensitive a person to withstand the fierce competition of such a life. He was strongly opposed to boarding-school education, which confirms my own view that his account of his life at the Perse was very selective in its emphasis on his enjoyment of sport and Scouts, and the omission of what he told me about the beatings that he, like all the boys, suffered; and about the extremely bleak, cold, meagre conditions in the boarding house.

Years later Wellesley was able to express what he thought of that type of education and what he remembered of his parents' expression as Jews.

> They were married in St Petersburg Place synagogue, a conventional Orthodox Anglo-Jewish establishment in Bayswater. Later on my parents left the Reform Synagogue and joined a new liberal community being formed by an American rabbi. I found it much less comfortable than either the West

London Synagogue at Upper Berkeley Street or the West Hampstead Synagogue which we had visited in the interim. But Judaism was not a living thing for me. It was never brought home to me in any positive manner.

The token acknowledgment of our Jewish existence at home contrasted starkly with what I was exposed to at school. I interpreted the novelty of having an Orthodox Jewish house in an English public boarding school as the Jews' attempt to have their cake and eat it. This was accomplished by segregating the Jewish boys into a separate house where Jewish prayers were said morning and evening; where chapel attendance on Sunday was replaced with a walk to synagogue on Saturday morning (while the Christian boys had lessons); while on Sunday morning we did our homework. On Saturday and Sunday afternoons we joined in with the Christian boys to play games and take walks. I thought that this arrangement was unhealthy and unsatisfactory and nothing has changed this opinion. It led to obvious disabilities and a feeling of being different which I and other youngsters found difficult to adjust to – we were separated, yet within the school bounds.

The school prided itself on being progressive and tolerant, yet friction inevitably developed between the Christian and Jewish boys. I sensed a lot of tension in the air as far as the Jewish boys were concerned. The other boys in my house had varying backgrounds – most of them were the sons of recent European immigrants and were consequently unacceptable in any normal sense to the rank-and-file English who typified the Christian Cambridge parents who sent their boys to Perse. I recognised the contradiction and clash between two ideologies which seemed to cancel each other out (leaving me with no identity at all – rootless). If the real motive of the Jewish parents was to ensure that their anglicised children remained within the Orthodox Jewish fold they were surely disappointed, because as far as I can judge few of the boys I knew, if any, remained conforming Jews.

Wellesley's experience convinced him that there was no prospect of Judaism being lovingly embraced by the boys in such physically bleak surroundings and when it was taught in a mechanical, unfeeling way. Doubtless this influenced his Habonim programme and all his subsequent teaching activities which he tried to make the opposite of his own early education. What he apparently couldn't overcome was his own emotional isolation, which was highlighted by his awareness after his mother's death that she had never accepted or understood those things which were most precious to him.

From his earliest years she had derided his athletic prowess which was the key to his relationships with his brothers and nephew, and his entrée to school society. His factual, and almost defiant records of his achievements at school and Cambridge, confirm what a tremendous solace his sporting abilities were to him. He admits later on that they were his passport to social acceptability at Cambridge and in his sister's social circle in Devon. But his parents, apparently, were never impressed and never came to see him compete at school. He remembered his parents' quarrels about where they should live and about his schooling. Their decision to send him to the Perse was probably an attempt at compromise between his mother, who insisted on sending him to an Orthodox Jewish or German school, while his father more likely favoured sending him to follow in his other sons' and nephew's footsteps to Rugby, where no suspicion of a Jewish education would arise and sports were greatly emphasised. Apart from his first visit to Perse, he never mentions that his parents went to the school again, neither does he mention that they wrote to him. How would he have felt if his parents had visited him at school? Most children fear being different from their peers, which all too often results in cruel mockery. Would he have welcomed a father who was well over sixty and who probably had a foreign accent, or a mother whose English was at best broken, who was stout and over forty? However, he must secretly have wanted them to witness his triumphs and to take pride in them as he so obviously did with his own children and grandchildren. These conflicting feelings may account for his silence on this aspect of life at boarding school.

Wellesley, Rose and their two daughters spent a number of years abroad while Wellesley was working in one capacity or another for the Zionist cause. Sharona and Ylona were both partly educated in Palestine, England and the United States. He has recorded with pride Sharona's refusal to comply with the rabbinate's pre-marital requirements when she applied to marry Arthur Broza, a fellow-soldier in Israel's embryonic defence forces. He notes with satisfaction that the rabbinate nevertheless carried out the ceremony.

Ylona married a fellow-artist, a German Gentile, while she was studying in New York. The marriage was not a success and Ylona returned to settle in Israel after a few years. Sharona too lived outside Israel for a time with her husband and two children. Whatever he may have thought of this, Wellesley has recorded his pleasure when they returned to settle in Israel. His own conviction that the only honest expression of Zionism was to live in Israel made him intolerant of Jews who chose a different path. He was most critical of those closest to him in this respect. This was my own experience with him when I left Israel in 1986 after five years. When I told him that my daughter Naomi would go to the English Jewish boarding school Carmel College to complete her sixth-form education, he was outspokenly horrifed. I was quite surprised at his intolerance and dogmatic insistence that I was destroying her life as well as my own. He tried earnestly to practise the tolerance and co-existence he taught, but he didn't always succeed, especially when he felt that the people he liked either didn't share his causes or, even worse, gave up on them. This fierce reaction stemmed perhaps from the shock of his own first encounter with Zionism.

> I came home one day to find a colossal uproar going on between my parents and Eustace and Berwick, both of whom were at Rugby School as fully participating Christian English boys. I hadn't a clue what was going on. The passions involved were unusual in our family. Since I was debarred by youth I only picked up fragments of this alarming fight. Apparently a Jewish neighbour had come for tea and had introduced something called Zionism into the conversation. Our visitor was prominent in the English Zionist movement and didn't temper his views for his audience. Whereas my father explained that his demoralising childhood had virtually eradicated any desire he might have had to be involved in Jewish matters, Eustace and Berwick were outraged (and no doubt threatened) at the appalling suggestion that Jews were indeed a separate people who might have a state of their own. They were violently rude to the guest who had soon left.
>
> I can recall no other occasion when the word 'Zionism' was uttered in our household. The echoes in my ears were of something unpleasant, distasteful and alien and totally out of keeping with our family's ways.

In a reversal of his family's reaction to Zionism, he reacted to non-Zionist and anti-Zionist Jews with the utmost vehemence.

He obviously thought a lot about the relationships between parents and children, particularly between fathers and sons. It requires little insight to recognise Wellesley's father as a man who had lost his way, who had to bear the death of two sons and his only grandson, all three of whom had fought in the British Army as Christians, while he, a German Jew, married to a German Jewish wife, whose German relatives made the weapons which were used by German soldiers to kill his English sons, sat out the war in neutral Switzerland. All his life Wellesley looked for fundamental and absolute answers to human existence as he experienced and observed it. That there may not be any he never admitted even if it occurred to him, but he thought very deeply about the motivations for people's behaviour and he wrote about the unsatisfactory relationships between several sons and fathers whom he came to know well.

The relationships in the Weizmann family puzzled him greatly. Weizmann's wholehearted commitment to Zionism was not shared by his son Benjamin whom Wellesley met at Cambridge. Wellesley was initially shocked when Benjy, who was studying agriculture at Cambridge, told him that he considered the whole Zionist enterprise unjustified and uninteresting and that he saw no future in it, largely because the country was too small and had no natural resources. Wellesley recognised Benjy's strong resentment against the Zionists, who, he speculated, had from Benjy's viewpoint been the most disturbing element in what might otherwise have been a most successful, secure, private, family life.

Wellesley's theory to explain his emotional rootlessness was the conflicting identities he grew up with. But it does not hold up if you take into account that his own father had been given an unequivocal Orthodox Jewish upbringing, yet had abandoned Judaism completely; and that Benjy who had been given an unequivocal Zionist education had no intention of following its precepts. Wellesley thought it important enough to write about it twice in his memoirs, perhaps because he wanted to illuminate his relationship with his parents as well as with his own children.

> Perhaps I should add a word here on the relations of the children of Zionists and other political leaders. There seems to be a chronic situation which develops between children of well known or highly publicised personalities, whose prominence is due very largely to the stories and articles and the pictures and the legends that spring up around them, either as leaders in their field or as personalities in their own right. The children always see them in a quite different light; as ordinary human beings bereft of all the glamour and charisma that is created by the media.
>
> This results in a tremendous strain between the generations and Dr Weizmann suffered particularly from Benjy, in a manner which embittered him and his wife. I often witnessed this tension go beyond endurance and it broke out in wild and passionate argument. I was terribly sorry for both parties because of what was implicit in the situation. On the one hand the Weizmanns were regarded as royalty by the Jewish people – it developed to a point where they only mixed basically with the jet set in the political field, whereas they had come from a rather simple Jewish background, adapting themselves with some effort to the standard of living and conditions in which they later found themselves. The same thing applied to the children of Dr Brodetsky, who also suffered from the same problems, not to mention Herzl of course. But it was a fact of life. The Weizmanns' London home was decorated in the latest style by a fashionable architect – they had a butler – and Benjy was embarrassed greatly in front of his college friends when the butler opened the door to them. The sitting room had illuminated alcoves containing Chinese porcelain ornaments, Benjy called it 'the hairdressing department'. His mother was appalled. She put great store on appearances and was in fact probably one of the biggest snobs that I ever came across.

Wellesley too was a snob about many things, especially about social graces and education. He placed much emphasis on keeping up certain appearances in his personal dress and life-style and liked to be with people who shared his tastes. When I first met him and Rose in Tel Aviv in spring 1972, they cultivated a very English style of house and garden, in the midst of a hot, dusty, somewhat arid neighbourhood. The autographed oar, a souvenir from his Cambridge days, was conspicuously displayed, his bearing was unmistakeably military and athletic. He was then seventy-one years old, handsome, charming, very amusing, but withdrawn in some way. He didn't seem to be a man who shared in domestic activities, but after Rose died he proved that he could do what was necessary when he had to. He certainly preferred to be taken care of.

It was my first visit to Israel with my then husband Julius Silman, who had been a good friend of Wellesley's for some fifty years already. I was sure I was being vetted by Wellesley, Rose and Ylona, who lived with them at that time. I only began to relax when it became clear to me that beneath his flippant social performance Wellesley was a person whose concerns mirrored my own in many ways. I was then just discovering Zionism, and was overwhelmed by a desire to learn more about Israel's history. I could not have found a more lively or dedicated teacher than Wellesley, whose own reminiscences and current passionate involvement with his peace project captured my heart and mind.

I knew his wife Rose less well and saw her only a few times before her death in 1978. She was evidently a fine home-maker and outstanding gardener, for which I admired her. Like Wellesley, she too was snobbish and emotionally reserved, but a fine hostess. Wellesley has written and spoken admiringly of her devoted work for certain charities, her linguistic abilities and her adaptability to the somewhat difficult financial conditions they often faced. He spoke most warmly of their first year together in Palestine, of their shared social interests in pre-Second World War Palestine and later of their enjoyment on the golf course. They were married for fifty-two years. Her great love was gardening and a rose garden has been planted in her memory at Neve Shalom/Wahat al-Salam.

From other people's memories as well as his own, I know that when he was younger Wellesley had an irrepressible sense of fun and adventure. He was tremendously good company and enjoyed being the centre of attention. He was a fine pianist and he loved improvising. He was still doing this in his seventies, but complained of his rustiness. Unfortunately he has left no stories about his wild adventures with his closest friend Francis Gaster, perhaps because he judged them to be unfavourable guidelines for the younger generation. But they certainly did him no harm.

Wellesley wrote about two close relationships only: his first with Allison which ended tragically, but opened the way to his 'new beginning'; his last with Coral which opened the door to their lives together at Neve Shalom/Wahat al-Salam. I stayed with them there several times and would easily recognise Coral from Wellesley's description. Her open-hearted welcome to me cheered me many times, the obvious love between them warmed my heart and I cherish the times I was in their home.

> I am told that it is very difficult for the elderly to change their habits, their environments or their daily routine. When it came to moving out of Tel Aviv, as I did, to come up into the hills of Judea and engage in what was for me a most urgent and important undertaking, I think that I don't know many other people who would have done it and, if so, that it would have been a success. Coral was brave enough to listen to me when I told her about it. For her, I imagine, the whole idea of moving away from her daughter, son-in-law and grandchildren must have been just as difficult or more so than what I was going to undergo. ...
>
> I don't want to be fulsome, but I do want to give credit to Coral. She is extremely competent in everything she does, she is extremely hardworking. She is a first-class cook and housekeeper and baker and manageress. She is a very good hostess, she's got a sense of humour, almost a girlie sense of humour which I find extremely attractive. She has an earnestness and a quickness of brain which I find outstanding. She sees the point quite a few seconds before I reach it and her judgement on the whole is so sound and valuable to me because I increasingly find I am dependent on her for her judgement of things that at first I don't quite see. I can only say that my cup has been filled to overflowing with an experience which I doubt any man can deserve and that is to say to marry a woman who is loyal and devoted to his welfare.

In the last year of his life Wellesley was ill. He was tormented by his declining physical abilities, abilities which had been so fine throughout his life. Julius and I and our daughter Naomi visited him at Passover two months before his death. He had a brief, unexpected remission. He seemed like his old self, very frail, but light-hearted, optimistic and so inspiring. Coral nursed him at home until June, then they went together to a hospice in Jerusalem where he died very peacefully on 7 June 1988, his hand in hers. He left his body to science. When the remains were returned to Neve Shalom/ Wahat al-Salam in November, his funeral was the first to take place in the community. His grave overlooks the Ayalon Valley. An Arab builder who works at Neve Shalom/Wahat al-Salam has planted trees nearby for shade. The rough-hewn rock headstone has engraved upon it these words from the first book of Chronicles, chapter 29, verse 3:

> As for me – in the uprightness of my heart I have willingly offered all these things.

I recognised in Wellesley a rare integrity. He was one of the very few people I have known or know of who mostly lived in accordance with their beliefs. A number of newspaper articles testify to the impact he had on people who are not usually impressionable. I have chosen two. One is from the *Jerusalem Post* of 17 April 1959 by Sraya Shapiro in her article called 'Record of a Rotarian' Personality Profile – Wellesley Aron:

> The curious thing about Wellesley – nobody, except total strangers, calls him by his last name, but there are not a few who call him Pinchas – the unusual thing about him is that he says exactly what he means and acts exactly according to what he says.

The second is from an obituary by Philip Gillon published in the same paper on 14 June 1988:

> Wellesley Aron, who died a week ago, a few days before his 87th birthday, could have been typecast for one of those BBC films about idealistic English upper-class officers and gentlemen who espouse what appear to be hopeless causes and convert them into practical successes, in defiance of prejudices and huge obstacles. Physically, he looked the part, with his ramrod-straight back and his major's moustache: educated at Cambridge, he also talked Nancy Mitford's U-language. And Wellesley could be summed up in one word – integrity.

The final word about Wellesley is, I think, best spoken by one of his beloved teenagers, Susan Musinsky, an American girl from Boston, Massachusetts, who met him on a visit to Neve Shalom/ Wahat al-Salam during a youth group tour of Israel.

WELLESLEY ARON

Pinchas

Overlooking the dusty valleys below
we spoke with the man from London.

You know it?
He spoke, dreamed and searched for peace,
and at the ripe age of 84 he'd certainly found it.
With his pipe in his hand, he spoke of his jolly old English friends
back home.
There was the stock market, the rounded bellies and the weather.
What had he found in this Palestine?
He looked so odd, was he now a stranger?
Wasn't life different without the local pub?
It'd been since 1926 since he'd lived in the English tradition.
He said he was happy.
His eyes confirmed this statement.

We heard about life;
and not only life here at Neve Shalom,
but life with peace for humans,
and internal peace.
He spoke with energy
and he had a purpose.
A peace specialist, who knew that in his lifetime steps had been
made towards his dream.

The Arabs were his friends,
but he was older and
the teenagers were the important ones for the future.
He saw prejudice and poisons, day one.
Peace, sports, music, friends, day three.
The foundations of Neve Shalom
What all 6000 who have been here take a bit of when they leave.

He was relaxed and spoke from his heart.
There was his paternal grandad, a rabbi.
His sister, a Roman Catholic,
His wife, a garden grower –
And he – one of those strange simple people who followed his star.

APPENDIX

Activities at Neve Shalom /Wahat Al-Salam

NEVE SHALOM/WAHAT AL-SALAM PRIMARY SCHOOL AND KINDERGARTEN

This year (1991) is likely to be remembered as an important turning-point in the development of our kindergarten and primary school. With the integration of 12 children from Abu Ghosh, we are beginning to learn about what is involved when we apply our educational methods to children who come from an environment different from that of Neve Shalom/Wahat al-Salam (NS/WAS).

The work has been both difficult and fascinating. Until now, the support of the children's home environment has been expected and taken for granted. Today the staff must deal much more intensively with questions of national and cultural differences between the children. This, of course, comes together with the outbreak of war in the region and new crises in Jewish/Palestinian relations. The primary school teaching staff and the School for Peace have recently begun to work together to study some of the aspects of this work. We regard this as an essential, preparatory stage for the coming years as we construct a school-kindergarten building which will accommodate as many as 150 children.

With all of its difficulties, the progress has been encouraging. For the first time we had a group of children who were used to a very different way of working and had never before been together with Jewish children. For the first time in their lives they were exposed to another culture and an unfamiliar religion with strange traditions. At the same time, our own children were confronted by others who knew nothing about coexistence – and certainly did not take such a way of life for granted.

It did not take long for the children to get used to each other. The atmosphere in the classroom is that of a 'big' school and visitors can see no difference between our children and those who bus in every day. The older children, in the fifth class, complain that they have only one 'new boy' – the others being spread out in the lower classes.

Little is being done in the field of peace education in Israel that can compare with the day-to-day binational, bilingual education of these children. While much of the work that is conducted between Jews and Palestinians is being temporarily suspended and re-evaluated, it is significant that the present crisis has not for a moment threatened the continuation of this school project in NS/WAS.

Ety Edlund,
Director,
February, 1991

PRINCIPLES OF THE NEVE SHALOM/WAHAT AL-SALAM KINDERGARTEN AND PRIMARY SCHOOL

As the only village in Israel in which Jews and Palestinians with Israeli citizenship have chosen to build a community together, the members of Neve Shalom/Wahat al-Salam are forced to face many questions which have never before been addressed. As the community grew and became more established, one of the first of such questions concerned the education of its children.

The Israeli educational system maintains a division between Arab schools and Jewish schools. The curriculum of each serves different interests. In NS/WAS an integral part of living together is educating the children in the same way. More than that, it is to establish an educational framework in which the study of one's language, culture or national interests will not be followed at the expense of another's. On this basis were the kindergarten and primary schools brought into being.

From its inception, NS/WAS defined the goals of its kindergarten and primary school as follows:

1 To provide the children with an education which reflects the values for which the village stands.
2 To establish the foundation of a regional school which can absorb children from outside the village and instil principles of coexistence into elementary school education.

3 To present a working model of a bi-national and bi-lingual school which can be used as a precedent, or reference, for similar structures in other Israeli schools.

From the age of three months, when they enter the nursery school, until the age of six years, when they finish the kindergarten, the children of NS/WAS are brought up bi-lingually, under constant exposure to both Jewish and Arab culture. Formal education begins in the primary school.

Six qualified teachers are employed in the school, each speaking only their mother tongue – three of them Hebrew and three of them Arabic.

A guiding principle of the school, as in the community itself, is to advance understanding and respect for national and cultural differences and pride, while stressing individual and national identities. In consideration of this, teaching is done on the open school method which provides each pupil with a framework for maximum self-expression. This approach has been proven to encourage the child's natural drive to learn and to strengthen his/her ability to take an initiative in independent study.

The curriculum is based both on the mandatory requirements of the Israel Ministry of Education and the determination of the community to raise its children according to its own standards.

THE SCHOOL FOR PEACE (SFP)*

From the earliest stages of the formation of the community, contact was sought with people from outside and special efforts were made to arrange meetings between the youth of Jewish and Palestinian communities in Israel. The proportion of the two peoples in the State of Israel is in the ratio of 83 per cent Jewish and 17 per cent Palestinian. From its inception, the SFP was faced with the fact that the educational system in Israel is set up in different frameworks for the two peoples – with separate schools and diverse curricula to cater for the two populations which, apart from minor exceptions, live in their own environments. This, of course, is the root cause of

* This is an extract from an article written for, and printed in *CONTACT*, a publication of the United World College of the Adriatic.

part of the conflict which exists today, for the people do not get to know one another. This encourages an acceptance of stereotypes and the resulting dehumanisation of the populace.

Initiating meetings between the Jews and Palestinians with Israeli citizenship has not been an easy task. It was understood from the beginning that the meetings were not the goals in themselves, but the means to achieve the goals set. The goals – simply expressed – were to develop an awareness of the conflict and to realise that it exists and is complicated. The SFP set out to develop a feeling of self-confidence in the youngsters, to allow them to give free play to their thoughts, beliefs and ideology. At all times it was considered of paramount importance that the young people should be given the opportunity to deal with the conflict on their own level of educational ability.

In order to disperse its work as widely as possible with the limited number of personnel at its disposal, the SFP has to work with a small but select group of teenagers to participate in its on-going programs. To this end 16 and 17-year-old high-school students, from both Jewish and Palestinian schools, are invited to participate in workshops during which those with leadership qualities are chosen by their peers to represent the school. Another qualification demanded is that they should have not only the motivation and ability to change themselves, but also the potential to change and to influence others. The students finally selected then participate in initiating activities which aim to strengthen their skills and to fortify their awareness of their own identities – particularly that of their respective national identities.

An important aim of the SFP is to develop in these young people the skills to express their emotional feelings and their intellectual understanding. At all levels, the participants in the SFP courses are given the opportunity to experiment with their peers, to sound out their reactions and feelings and to recognise the legitimacy of pluralism within their own national groups.

Thus prepared, the youngsters are brought to NS/WAS to meet in bi-national workshops which last for three to four days at a time. Here, working in small groups (5 Jews, 5 Palestinians and a facilitator attached respectively to each group), they experience the social and cultural background of the two peoples existing side by side. They find themselves dealing with emotions such as fear and distrust. They come to compare their inbred stereotypes with the reality of people with whom they are sharing this experience. They begin to recognise something of the human side of 'the others'. They begin to deal more seriously with the conflict and to become more aware of the complexity of it. They understand that the solutions advocated by the extremists on both sides are the easy ones ... and the very worst. The solutions being sought here are based on human values, respect and understanding.

The aim of our work cannot aspire to be the solution to the Israel/Palestinian conflict; but it does endeavour to allow the youth of both peoples to see it from its different perspectives and to deal with it in a reasoned, humane and responsible way.

Abed Elsalam Najjar,
(resident at Neve Shalom/Wahat al Salam since 1978)
August 1990

AWARDS TO NEVE SHALOM/WAHAT AL-SALAM

1986 The Armstrong Prize for Leadership. Presented by the International Cultural Centre for Youth, Jerusalem, to a group of Israeli Arab and Jewish students who gave a year of voluntary service to the School for Peace.

1987 The Buber-Rosensweig Medal. Presented by Der Deutsche Koordinierungstrat der Gesellschaften für Christlich-Judische Zusammenarbeit.

1988 The Bruno Kreisky Foundation annual award.

1989 Ahavat Shalom Congregation of San Francisco. Social Action Fund in memory of Steve Berman. Annual award.

1989 The Beyond War Annual Award, USA. Jointly with Jimmy Carter and the Carter Centre, and with Koinconia, a South African organisation encouraging coexistence between black and white citizens.

1991 Artisan of Peace Prize. Awarded by Arsenale Della Pace, Casa Della Speranza 'Michele Pellegrino'

1991 The Marcus Sieff Foundation Annual Prize. Jointly with Shlomo Buhbut, Head of the Ma'alot-Tarshiha Council and Rafik Halabi, Journalist.

June, 1991

INDEX